THE VELIZH AFFAIR

THE VELIZH AFFAIR

Blood Libel in a Russian Town

EUGENE M. AVRUTIN

OXFORD
UNIVERSITY PRESS

OXFORD
UNIVERSITY PRESS

Oxford University Press is a department of the University of Oxford. It furthers
the University's objective of excellence in research, scholarship, and education
by publishing worldwide. Oxford is a registered trade mark of Oxford University
Press in the UK and certain other countries.

Published in the United States of America by Oxford University Press
198 Madison Avenue, New York, NY 10016, United States of America.

Library of Congress Cataloging-in-Publication Data
Names: Avrutin, Eugene M., author.
Title: The Velizh affair : blood libel in a Russian town / Eugene M. Avrutin.
Description: New York, NY : Oxford University Press, [2018] |
Includes bibliographical references and index.
Identifiers: LCCN 2017011535 (print) | LCCN 2017012749 (ebook) |
ISBN 9780190640538 (updf) | ISBN 9780190640545 (epub) |
ISBN 9780190640521 (hardback : alk. paper)
Subjects: LCSH: Blood accusation—Russia—Velizh—History—19th century. |
Antisemitism—Russia—Velizh—History—19th century. |
Jews—Persecutions—Russia—Velizh—History—19th century. |
Trials (Murder)—Russia—Velizh. | Russia—Ethnic relations. |
Velizh (Russia)—Ethnic relations.
Classification: LCC BM585.2 (ebook) | LCC BM585.2 .A97 2017 + (print) |
DDC 305.892/404727—dc23
LC record available at https://lccn.loc.gov/2017011535

1 3 5 7 9 8 6 4 2

Printed by Sheridan Books, Inc., United States of America

To Yingying and Abi
for being there

CONTENTS

———◦◦◦◦———

PREFACE

ON THE MORNING OF DECEMBER 5, 1919, in revolutionary Petrograd, the historian Simon Dubnov walked several miles along a maze of dark and empty streets to a meeting of the newly inaugurated Commission for Investigating Blood Libel Materials.[1] This was a desperate time in the city. The brutality and chaos of the Civil War wreaked havoc on the early Soviet state. In the nearly two years after the collapse of the tsarist regime in February 1917, the population of Petrograd decreased by 50 percent. The death toll skyrocketed, as did the unemployment rate. Shortages of fuel, electricity, clean water, and basic food staples such as flour, eggs, bread, and potatoes meant a drastic fall in the standard of living for those who remained. The sudden collapse of all institutions of law and order resulted in an unprecedented number of petty thefts, muggings, robberies, and rapes. Empty apartments and boarded-up buildings could be found on every street corner. Rubbish littered courtyards and alleyways. The closure of markets, shops, factories, and restaurants brought an eerie silence to one of Europe's most dazzling cities.[2]

In the early days of the revolution, Dubnov had led a modest but privileged existence as an academic. The beneficiary of a special scholar's ration—consisting mainly of bread, thin soup, cabbage, and salted fish—the distinguished historian immersed himself in work. Like so many politically engaged writers, Dubnov worked tirelessly to build a new Jewish cultural sphere that lay dormant under the shackles of tsarist oppression.[3] Dubnov converted the kitchen, the only room in the apartment that reached a tolerable five degrees Celsius, into a makeshift study. He divided the time between writing his magnum opus, *The World History of the Jewish People*; lecturing at the newly established Jewish University; composing editorials for leading periodicals; and participating in numerous political and scholarly initiatives made possible as a consequence of the events of 1917. For nearly three decades, Dubnov called on scholars and Jewish residents in the Pale of Settlement to collect historical materials. Ultimately, he believed, historical knowledge would help regenerate spiritual Jewish life in the tsarist empire.

At noon sharp, Dubnov joined seven other members of the commission in an unheated hall of the old Senate building. Centrally located on the embankment of the Neva River, this magnificent structure, painted in cadmium yellow, overlooked the Square of the Decembrists. For nearly ninety years, the building was home to the most extensive collection of the old regime's records ever assembled. The Russian State Historical Archive, as it is known today, was formally consolidated shortly after the Bolsheviks came to power. Among other things, its holdings include the records of the most powerful administrative, judicial, and ministerial institutions, as well as public organizations, philanthropic societies, and the personal papers of leading statesmen, men-of-letters, artists, and composers. Since the implosion of the Soviet Union, scholars have been granted unprecedented access to the historical treasures. Scores of monographs, articles, and dissertations have been written in recent years—all with copious archival references. But under the Soviet regime, only the most privileged were permitted to read the files, and almost no one who was working on Jewish themes. The Soviet state classified Jewish records as highly confidential. Some were removed from archival depositories and sealed in special vaults; the most compromising files were destroyed.

For a brief moment, however, after the fall of the old regime and before the centralization of the new Soviet state, the possibilities were endless. Before the revolution, a handful of scholars wrote books and articles on Jewish subjects grounded in archival sources. But these publications barely scratched the surface of the extraordinarily rich materials preserved in the archives. The revolution initiated an outpouring of new cultural, artistic, and academic projects. Taking advantage of the new political conditions, the Jewish Historical-Ethnographic

Society—an organization specializing in recovering important cultural and historical texts pertaining to Jewish life in Russia—came up with a bold initiative to collect and publish prerevolutionary archival documents. The society organized an archival commission to work on three particularly urgent topics: pogroms, the history of Jewish schools, and the blood libel. The goal was to publish all the materials in their entirety, without any editorial redactions, and in their proper chronological order.[4]

The Commission for Investigating Blood Libel Materials worked primarily with materials in the Senate archive. As the highest judicial body in the Russian Empire, the Senate presided over the most controversial criminal and civil cases, many of which generated massive paper trails. The members of the commission were carefully chosen, to ensure an impartial discussion of such an emotionally charged subject. Dubnov joined the social activist Henrikh Sliozberg, the anthropologist Lev Shternberg, and the lawyer Grigorii Krasnyi-Admoni as the Jewish experts, while the celebrated historian Sergei Platonov, the director of the Senate archive Ivan Blinov, and the scholars Lev Karsavin and Vasilii Druzhinin represented the Russian side. The group met for twelve months, usually on Tuesday afternoons, spending most of the time working on a sensational blood libel case that had taken place in Velizh, a small town located in Vitebsk province, on the northeastern edge of the Pale of Settlement.

Now erased from historical memory, the Velizh affair was the longest ritual murder case in the modern world, and most likely in world history. Lasting approximately twelve years, from 1823 to 1835, the investigation generated a truly astonishing number of archival documents—around fifty thousand pages in total. All the materials are impeccably preserved in twenty-five bound volumes at the Russian State Historical Archive in St. Petersburg; an additional thirty volumes, many of which are duplicates of the St. Petersburg files, are housed in the National Historical Archive of Belarus in Minsk. The Velizh archive includes hundreds of depositions and petitions; official government correspondence, reports, and memos; personal letters and notes; as well as a detailed summary of the case of more than four hundred pages prepared by the Senate—known simply as the Memorandum of a Criminal Case (*Zapiska iz ugolovnykh del*).[5]

The colossal size of the archive complicated the work, making it difficult, as Dubnov observed in one of the first meetings, "to answer the question—what should we copy?"[6] According to the historian's calculations, even if the nonessential items were omitted, they would be left with three-quarters of the materials, requiring at least ten thick volumes and years of hard labor. The group discussed many things: how much of the archive to publish, the problem of decoding and reading the handwriting, how to organize the introductory essay, and whether they should publish other blood libel cases as well. Dubnov hoped to edit only one volume for publication, preferably the Senate memorandum, but his suggestion fell on deaf ears. In the end, the commission agreed to publish an exhaustive account, beginning with the 1816 case in Grodno and then all twenty-five volumes of the Velizh case.

Dubnov first came across the Velizh materials in 1893, while living in Odessa. In April, he received a letter from an antiquarian by the name of L. N. Etingen, who wrote that "after much hard work and a great deal of expense" he had obtained the Senate memorandum from an undisclosed source. Etingen could not have been more thrilled by his find. The Senate made a small number of hectographed copies of the memorandum for internal government use only. The document had immense historical value, and Etingen set his sights on *Voskhod* (The Dawn), the most respected thick journal in the field of Russian Jewish affairs. *Voskhod* featured a new monthly column publicizing historical discoveries. The only problem was that Etingen did not have the time and, more important, the expertise to carry out the scholarly work himself. This is why he turned to Dubnov for help. "Would you be so kind," he asked, "as to whip this into shape under the following guidelines?" Etingen requested that Dubnov take no longer than two or three months to complete the work, with the understanding that he would receive full credit for the publication and retain the exclusive right to republish the materials as he saw fit. For all this work, Etingen offered Dubnov the royalties from the *Voskhod* sales, a meager sum even under the best of circumstances.[7]

Although we do not know how Dubnov responded to such an unrealistic proposal, we do know that he did not pass up the opportunity to take a close look. Etingen sent the memorandum by special post to Odessa with the understanding that it be returned to him in exactly three weeks. At the time, Dubnov was working on a general history of Jews in Russia and Poland, while writing monthly columns for *Voskhod*, and was not in any hurry to accommodate the request. In May and June, Etingen penned two impatient letters to Dubnov, insisting that the distinguished historian immediately return the document and complete the article "as soon as possible."[8] Why was Etingen in such a hurry? Apparently, he was not the only person intrigued by the case. Miron Ryvkin, an aspiring cultural critic with direct ties to Velizh, was busy gathering published and ethnographic sources, including oral interviews of survivors and their descendants, for a major publication on the topic. At one point, Etingen even agreed to share the memorandum with Ryvkin but changed his mind at the last minute, deciding to keep it a secret until Dubnov had completed the work.[9]

Dubnov never bothered to fulfill Etingen's request, but he did take advantage of the opportunity to take detailed notes. In 1894, Dubnov published his own essay on Velizh in the Hebrew-language almanac *Luah Ahi'asaf* (Ahiasiaf's Register). Putting his notes to good use, as well as other fresh documentary evidence, Dubnov explored a little-known episode of the Velizh case as it played out in the town of Bobovne.[10] In his memoirs, Dubnov recalled that the blood libel had come up in his research from time to time and that he had even published some of the more interesting findings in a review article about seventeenth-century Poland in *Voskhod*.[11] But for reasons that remain unclear, a mysterious silence looms over Velizh, with no mention of his correspondence with Etingen and Ryvkin or of the *Luah Ahi'asaf* essay.

Perhaps Dubnov wished to make a claim on the case by getting there first? History is full of lively tales of discovery. After all, the race to uncover a lost stash of highly prized manuscripts or to publish a significant piece of research results in a type of immortality that only scientists, humanists, and explorers can truly appreciate. Whatever the reason may have been, after the publication of the essay, Dubnov's name continued to be associated with Velizh, and every scholar who worked on the case turned to him for help.

In February 1901, seven years after they first corresponded, Ryvkin pleaded with Dubnov to help him locate the memorandum. Ryvkin was busy working on several different projects about the case, and he wanted to convey the spirit and social conditions of the age by describing as many realistic details as possible. To do this he desperately wanted to get his hands on the memorandum. So he rummaged through antiquarian bookshops, but he did not know the exact title of the book, the place and date of publication, or the number of copies in print. "The copy that was once in your possession, if only a short period of time," Ryvkin explained to Dubnov, "is currently in the most unpleasant hands." But try as he did, Ryvkin did not have any luck locating the memorandum. Eventually, he managed to collect enough materials to write a detailed essay about the case, based on firsthand recollections, ethnographic materials, and published primary sources. Ryvkin also published a successful historical novel that appeared in Russian in 1912 and was eventually reprinted in several editions in Yiddish and Hebrew.[12]

That same year, Dubnov exchanged several letters with a talented young historian who had just received permission from the Ministry of Justice to work in the Senate archive. In the prerevolutionary era, no other scholar of Russian Jewry had access to so many classified records as Iulii Gessen. "You have always been so generous with your time," Gessen wrote to his mentor on February 5. "If there are any archival documents you wish to see, please tell me, and I'll do everything in my power to copy them for you."[13] Not one to turn down a good offer, Dubnov asked for several files, including a handful pertaining to the Velizh case. Gessen had outlined an extensive research program for himself long before he set foot in the archive. But all the topics on the list, he quickly realized, paled in comparison with the blood libel case. In fact, after Ryvkin had asked him to look at some of the newly discovered archival papers, Gessen decided to focus all his energy on Velizh. "Perhaps I am wrong," Gessen confided to Dubnov, "but I don't trust [Ryvkin] and this is why I am being extraordinarily cautious." "If you have decided to put aside your work on the ritual murder case in Velizh," he continued, "I would be grateful if you passed it on to me."[14] Dubnov not only approved the request, but he also shared all his research notes with his protégé.

At the archive, Gessen located the prized memorandum, as well as eight additional "bundles of uncatalogued manuscripts." To transcribe the entire case record would take months, possibly even years. Eager to make a name for himself in the scholarly community, Gessen wanted to publish his research as quickly as possible. He requested help from the Jewish Historical-Ethnographic Society, but the organization was not in a position to support such an extensive project. Undeterred, the ambitious historian pressed ahead. By August 1902, Gessen had managed to complete a full draft of a manuscript. The result is a concise and extremely valuable historical reconstruction of the case, based on a close reading of the Senate memorandum, as well as Dubnov's notes and additional published sources.[15]

For years, every scholar who worked on the Velizh case recognized its extraordinary potential—not only for narrating a highly dramatic crime story, but also for illuminating an entire historical epoch. Yet no one was able to make good use of the archival materials. Ryvkin had no luck locating the memorandum. Gessen did not have the time and the financial resources to read all the uncatalogued documents. In the early years of the revolution, the Commission for Investigating Blood Libel Materials decided to publish the entire archive, but those lofty plans were never realized. In late December 1920, as part of a nationwide campaign to centralize cultural organizations and initiatives, the Commissariat of Education and the Evsektsiia (the Jewish section of the Communist Party) dissolved the commission. According to Dubnov's recollection of the events, the scholars spent more time debating the veracity of the ritual murder charge than editing the documents for publication.[16]

Thus, in spite of all the noble aspirations, the Velizh archive sat untouched for more than ninety years on the dusty shelves of the old Senate building. Although I spent much time in the reading room of the Russian State Historical Archive, I stumbled upon the case by accident, in the most unlikely place—Washington, DC. In the spring of 2008, I was on research leave at the Woodrow Wilson International Institute for Scholars. Among the many privileges of working at the institute is requesting items directly from the Library of Congress. One afternoon while I was browsing the library's online catalog, a book entitled the Memorandum of a Criminal Case piqued my curiosity. To my surprise, I received an oversized volume, bound in sturdy brown leather, without an official title page or place and date of publication. After glancing at the first page, I quickly realized that this was the official protocol of a sensational ritual murder case prepared by the highest court in the Russian Empire. In all probability, the Library of Congress acquired the memorandum in 1931, when the Soviet government sold off some two thousand volumes of the Winter Palace Library of Tsar Nicholas II. Some of the books in the collection are deluxe copies in sumptuous bindings made specifically for presentation to the tsar. Others, such as the memorandum, are extremely rare legal and administrative texts issued in minuscule print runs.[17]

This was an extraordinary find, and I immediately arranged for a photocopy in hopes of working on the case at a later date. Several years later, when I returned to St. Petersburg, the Russian State Historical Archive had relocated to a modern facility at the very edge of the city. It did not take me long to find the index card in the card catalog. Russian archives are full of immaculately preserved court cases, many of which are large in size and include a wealth of documents in the dossiers: formal indictments, summaries of evidence, descriptions of testimony, depositions, petitions, letters, illustrations, and maps. Russian bureaucrats were well known for their exceptional record keeping, but the Velizh case, I quickly realized, was larger and more complicated than any I had ever encountered. Here was a truly remarkable opportunity to explore a time, place, and community that seldom appeared in studies of the Russian Empire or East European Jewry.

ACKNOWLEDGMENTS

―――――――⟖⟐⟐⟐⟐⟐―――――――

THIS BOOK HAS BEEN IN the making for over seven years. It is a pleasure to thank the friends and colleagues who took an interest in my work and helped along the way. They include Todd Endelman, Robert Greene, Beth Holmgren, Val Kivelson, Diane Koenker, Mikhail Krutikov, Binyamin Lukin, Alexander Martin, Harriet Murav, Janet Rabinowitch, Ellie Schainker, David Shneer, Shaul Stampfer, Jeff Veidlinger, Bob Weinberg, and Paul Werth. Elissa Bemporad and Hillel Kieval read the manuscript in its entirety and offered numerous constructive comments. Jeffrey Shallit of the University of Waterloo helped organize the trip to Velizh and allowed me to use his photographs. Lina Kachulina, the director of the Velizh Museum, gave us a personal tour of the museum and the town. I would like to say a special thank you to Emanuel Rota, David Cooper, Lera Sobol, Eleonora Stoppino, and Harry Liebersohn for their friendship.

I had the opportunity to present parts of the book at workshops, conferences, and talks. I owe a debt of gratitude to the feedback on my work at the Association for Jewish Studies; the Association for Slavic, East European, and Eurasian Studies; Duke University; the University of Michigan; the University of Montana; Tel Aviv University; the YIVO Institute for Jewish Research; the European Social Science History Conference; the Max Planck Institute for Human Development; and the University of Illinois.

The University of Illinois provided generous research and administrative assistance. Tom Bedwell took care of all the paperwork. Grants from the Research Board enabled me to hire three remarkable research assistants: Nadja Berkovich, LeiAnna Hammel, and Emily Lipira. The staff at the Slavic Reference Service and the Interlibrary Loan tracked down obscure references. I am deeply grateful to the staff of the archives and libraries where I conducted the research. They include the Center for Jewish History in New York, the Central Archives for the History of the Jewish People in Jerusalem, the National Historical Archives of Belarus in Minsk, and the Russian State Historical Archive in St. Petersburg.

This project has received generous support from different sources. These include the Tobor Family Endowment, the National Council for Eurasian and East European Research, the American Philosophical Society, the Workmen's Circle/Dr. Emanuel Patt Visiting Professorship from the YIVO Institute for Jewish Research, and the Memorial Foundation for Jewish Culture. A National Endowment for the Humanities Fellowship, a Charles A. Ryskamp Research Fellowship from the American Council of Learned Societies, and a Center for Advanced Study Fellowship from the University of Illinois gave me extended leaves from teaching and supported the research and writing of the book.

My editor at Oxford University Press, Nancy Toff, responded to all my queries in record time, offered numerous helpful suggestions, and was a delight to work with. I would also like to thank the team at Oxford—Elda Granata, Julia Turner, Tim DeWerff, and Elizabeth Vaziri—for their attention to detail and shepherding the book through the publication process. It was a pleasure to work with Dina Dineva on the index.

I could not have written this book without the support from my family. My parents, Michael and Tanya Avrutin, went above and beyond the call of duty, helping with things large and small on my extended absences from home. My wife Yingying and daughter Abi constantly remind me of the things that matter most. I dedicate this book to them.

THE VELIZH AFFAIR

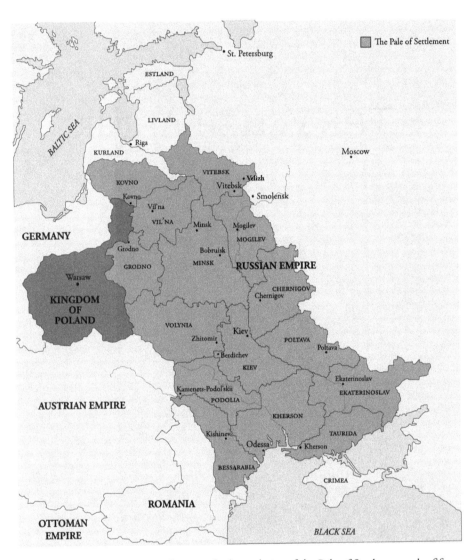

A map of the Russian Empire, showing the boundaries of the Pale of Settlement, the fifteen provinces in which Jews (with some exceptions) resided until 1917.

Introduction

AT FIRST, THERE DID NOT seem to be anything highly unusual about the murder. The idea that Jews killed Christian children to mix their blood with matzo for the Passover service had circulated in oral and written traditions since the Middle Ages. In its broad outline, the case resembled that of dozens of similar investigations from around the world. From the trial records, we learn that on April 22, 1823, in the town of Velizh, two small children finished their lunch and went to play outside. Fedor, a three-year-old boy with short blond hair, gray eyes, and a middling nose, and his four-year-old cousin, Avdotia, left their home and walked down a dusty path in an easterly direction. When the children reached the Konevtse Creek, Avdotia invited her cousin to cross a small bridge and continue on a walk to the forest. But Fedor refused and remained there alone, gazing at the construction site of a new home on the embankment.

It was Easter Sunday when the children went on their walk. Avdotia's mother, Kharitina Prokof'eva, did not supervise them and instead used the time to beg for alms. Kharitina lived at the very edge of town with her sister, Agafia Prokof'eva, and her brother-in-law, Emel'ian Ivanov. After receiving alms, Kharitina chatted with a neighbor for several hours until Avdotia came looking for her. To Kharitina's surprise, Avdotia was without her cousin. "Where is Fedor?" Kharitina inquired immediately. Avdotia replied that she had left Fedor standing alone on the bridge and had not seen him since. Wasting little time, Kharitina took Avdotia to look for the little boy, but try as they might, the search proved unsuccessful. Several days later, a town resident found the boy's body in the thick woods on the outskirts of town, stabbed to death in numerous places.

In small market towns, where houses were clustered together, residents knew each other on intimate terms, and people gossiped in taverns, courtyards, and streets, even the most trivial bits of news spread like wildfire. It did not take long before rumors began to spread that Jews murdered the little boy. Given the intimacy of small-town relations, it is tempting to make the argument, as so many scholars do, that ritual murder accusations were the product of deep-rooted anti-Semitic prejudice, motivated by ethnic hatred, spite, and resentment.[1] No doubt, these reasons help explain why certain individuals denounced Jews for engaging in blood sacrifice. Yet they do not offer a satisfactory explanation for the vitality of the tale in the popular psyche—for why almost all Christian neighbors in small towns like Velizh believed that Jews were capable of committing the crime. Was this some sort of conspiracy? Did the townspeople harbor resentment that was brought out in the open at the time of the investigation? Or were other, more powerful forces at work?

Thomas of Monmouth, a monk of the Norwich Cathedral Priory, crafted the definitive account of the first known accusation of Jewish child-murder. On the first day of Passover in March 1144, Jews allegedly seized and tortured a twelve-year-old boy named William. The murder took place in Norwich, a provincial Anglo-Norman city, during the High Middle Ages.[2] "Having shaved his head, they stabbed it with countless thorn-points, and made the blood come horribly from the wounds they made." Jews proceeded to carry the body in a sack into the woods and bury it in a shallow grave. Just as the streets of Norwich stirred with strange excitement, the town residents suspected that the Jews had wrought the evil deed. Shortly thereafter a fiery light "flashed down from heaven, the which, extending in a long train as far as the place where the aforesaid body was, blazed in the eyes of many people who were in various places thereabouts." Thirty-two days after the boy's death, the unmutilated and uncorrupted body was found whole and intact. Fresh blood gushed from the nostrils, astonishing the throng of bystanders. As the holy boy William, the blessed martyr of Norwich, performed miraculous cures and wonders, a deadly master narrative was born.[3]

In the centuries that followed, the accusations spread from medieval England to France and on to the Holy Roman Empire. The earliest known criminal investigation of Jewish consumption of blood took place in the Germanic town of Fulda in 1235. The precise details of a case could change according to the time and location of the accusation. But much of the basic storyline—that the killing took place during a ritually charged season of the calendar year, that it was done in imitation of Christ, and that Jews required Christian blood for a peculiar ritual custom at the time of the Passover holiday—stayed the same.[4] Just how frequently were Jews tried for ritual murder? The most reliable estimates cite no more than two dozen accusations, most of which occurred in the fifteenth and sixteenth centuries, although it seems likely that undocumented cases could be discovered in the archives.[5]

Growing Christian concerns with demonic activity and heresy, to say nothing of the religious fixation with blood, played an important role in highly elaborate investigations of ritualized infanticide and cannibalism. The vast majority of blood pilgrimages, host miracles, libels, and blood legends took place across the German-speaking lands of Central Europe. Ritual murder charges provided the judicial impetus for political persecution, riots, and the expulsion of entire German Jewish communities.[6] A great deal of the violence took place during the Paschal season, a time when ritual observances reenacted Christ's arrest, torture, and crucifixion. Holy Week, the most emotionally intense time of the Christian religious calendar, often coincided with Passover. The similarities between the two ritual systems could lead to intense misunderstandings between Jews and Christians, usually over the ceremonial consumption of unleavened bread, and even to violence.[7]

It is hard to deny that the blood libel was the product of a dark imagination. But much like fantasies about witchcraft, the emotionally charged tale of abuse possessed a rationality of its own, drawing its strength from a culturally specific way the universe operated. One of the most important reasons for the extraordinary popularity of the blood libel was the role that magic played in everyday life. Far from constituting ignorant superstition, or a false belief, magical practices influenced everyday events.[8] In a world where poverty and disease were common features of daily life, apprehensions about Jewish ritual murder provided convenient explanations of who was to blame for deaths and illnesses that defied explanation.[9] Spoken spells, potions, and charms not only protected against natural maladies but also caused personal misfortunes, and it was widely accepted that the Jew possessed the ability to heal and to harm. All these factors combined to make fears of Jewish ritual murder a very real occurrence in the popular mind, with deep cultural roots.

From the late Middle Ages to early modern times, religious and civic authorities began to discredit the intellectual and popular foundations of the blood libel. In 1247, in one of the earliest pronouncements, Pope Innocent IV pleaded for restraint "if the body of a dead man is by chance found anywhere. ... Duly redress all that has been wrought against the Jews in the aforesaid matter by the said prelates, nobles, and potentates, and do not allow them in the future to be unjustly molested by anybody on this or any other similar charge."[10] Discrediting the charge, it turned out, was easier said than done. This was a drawn-out process tied to the development of new theological and legal discourses and the dramatic social and intellectual dislocations in Reformation Europe. Somewhere at the end of the seventeenth century, official attitudes, especially in German-speaking lands, began to change to such an extent that it became extremely difficult to convict Jews of blood sacrifice in a court of law. The accusations waned for many of the same reasons that witchcraft prosecution saw a decline: the elimination of torture techniques in criminal investigations; the promulgation of laws restricting the prosecution of ritual murder to those accusations where conclusive evidence was found; and intellectual changes in science and philosophy that gradually repudiated belief in magic and the supernatural.[11]

In Western and Central Europe, new standards of documentation made it extremely difficult for judges and lawyers to prosecute the crime of ritual murder, even if judicial disenchantment did not signal an abrupt change in mentality. How can historians penetrate the complex worlds of belief? Scholars have shown that criminal trials reflect the preoccupations of the elites and that the frequency of legal cases is usually not the best barometer of judging the rise and fall of popular beliefs.[12] In any given time or place, many more ritual murder accusations were made than the number of cases prosecuted by authorities. Evidence from a wide range of sources—including print, music, painting, and theater—suggests that the tale continued to retain its power of persuasion long after authorities had successfully suppressed the trials. Thus, even after the number of documented trials declined, the blood libel tale continued to enjoy remarkable popularity in small market towns and villages. A rich folklore captures the symbolically related elements of blood, ritual practice, and magic in the imagination. Morality plays and woodcuts, chronicles and legends, folktales and songs, paintings and sculptures—all depict the Jew as a demonic figure, capable of the foulest crimes against their Christian neighbors.[13]

At roughly the time that the cases had declined in the West, the tale began to travel eastward. From the 1540s to the 1780s, Polish authorities investigated between eighty and one hundred cases, around 40 percent of which occurred in the eighteenth century.[14] How did the blood libel make its way to Eastern Europe? For years, scholars have argued that, as German Jewish communities migrated to the east in response to violence, persecution, and expulsions, so did the blood libel. According to this line of historical reasoning, a virulent print culture helped disseminate the tale to the public. In Poland-Lithuania, books and pamphlets on the theme went through numerous editions, achieving the dubious status of early modern bestsellers. Anti-Jewish writers, most of whom were Catholic preachers, accused Jews of using blood for religious ritual practice and of stealing or trading in church ritual objects. Renegade members of the Jewish community helped legitimize the accusations by describing Jewish theological rites involving the use of Christian blood.[15]

Notwithstanding the popularity of these arguments, recent research has shown that East European Jewry did not form as a result of large-scale mass migrations from Central Europe. Most likely, economic and demographic pressures, rather than violence and expulsions, forced individual Jews, and not entire communities, to travel the long distances to the east. Subsequently, the Jewish population in Eastern Europe grew naturally as a result of low child mortality and high fertility rates.[16]

Nor is it likely that the printed word was the only tool responsible for the cultural transmission of the blood libel tale. To be sure, the eighteenth century witnessed a rapid increase of publishing, while expert testimonies of Christian theologians and Jewish converts played no small role in the propaganda campaign. Yet however powerful the printed word might be, it seems highly unlikely that defamatory writings alone could disseminate the tale so widely. In small market towns of Eastern Europe, where there were no provincial newspapers and where the vast majority of people were illiterate, with limited access to published materials, the accusations circulated by word of mouth with striking speed and regularity. Fueled by sinister rumors and fears, the stories reflected a common reservoir of shared beliefs, fantasies, and everyday experiences. Fear may not have been a sign of weakness, but it was how people responded to danger and how panic was able to spread so quickly, often with fatal consequences.[17]

As a result of the three partitions of the Polish-Lithuanian Commonwealth (in 1772, 1793, and 1795), Russia not only acquired the largest Jewish population in the world but also inherited an established cultural tradition of ritual murder.[18] The blood libel did not enjoy a modern "revival," as some scholars have recently argued, but survived—and even flourished—in small market towns and villages since early modern times.[19] In the first half of the nineteenth century, almost all the documented cases occurred in the northwest region of the Russian Empire, in Minsk, Vil'na, Vitebsk, and Mogilev provinces (in present-day Lithuania and Belarus). Here, an unusually high proportion of the inhabitants—from the common folk to the well-educated members—believed that Jews were *capable* of committing the crime. For reasons that remain unclear, authorities in the southwest region, in Volynia, Podolia, and Kiev provinces (in present-day Ukraine), were reluctant to prosecute Jews for ritual murder save for two cases in Lutsk and Zaslav, although they had no qualms in charging Jews with sacrilegious behavior and the desecration of church property.[20] Significantly, this does not mean that the blood libel tale had lost its powers of persuasion in the southwest region, but only the fact that authorities in Vitebsk, Mogilev, and Minsk provinces had initiated the vast majority of the criminal investigations.

Much of our knowledge of the early cases comes from the highly controversial study of the blood libel commissioned by the minister of the internal affairs, Lev A. Perovskii.[21] Purportedly authored by the preeminent Russian-language lexicographer Vladimir I. Dal', the work drew on a wealth of foreign-language publications, as well as official archival papers of the Ministry of the Interior (many of which were destroyed as a result of a fire at the ministry's archive in 1862). Dal' cited dozens of alleged cases. But none played a larger role in helping to perpetuate the social memory of the tale than the murder of a six-year-old boy named Gavriil. The little boy lived with his devout Eastern Orthodox parents in Zwierki, a tiny village populated mostly by Uniates. In April 1680, a Jew named Shutko allegedly abducted Gavriil and took the boy to Bialystok, where he proceeded to torture and kill him. Although the ritual murder took place in Bialystok, Gavriil was laid to rest in Zwierki, where he lay undisturbed for many years. In 1720, a gravedigger discovered the body preserved in a state of divine incorruptibility. The church where Gavriil's body was transferred eventually burned down, but his relic fragments lived on, performing miraculous cures for children who suffered from ulcers and sores, hemorrhages and bleeding. In no time, word of Gavriil's miracles spread, and the little boy's cult became the object of popular veneration. In 1820, Gavriil was recognized by the Russian Orthodox Church as the patron saint of little children for his abilities to work miracle cures. Housed in a massive silver shrine, the relic fragments of the holy body—including the ritual stab wounds on his arms—were on public display for all believers to see and touch. In the nineteenth century, tens of thousands of pilgrims from all over the Russian Empire came to Gavriil's shrine in search of cures for their children, to pray and donate money, and to hear stories of martyrdom.[22]

Although no other body—dead at the hands of Jews—produced as many miracles or cures or was elevated to the status of a patron saint, the ritual murder tale lived on. The first documented investigation in the town of Velizh took place in 1805, at which time the body of a twelve-year-old boy was found along the Western Dvina, severely mutilated and punctured in multiple places. Three Jews (one of whom, it turned out, would be rearrested during the 1823–1835 criminal proceedings) were blamed for killing the boy. In 1816, several Jews in Grodno were blamed for the death of a young peasant girl whose arm had been cut off at the shoulder blade and whose body had several puncture wounds. Similar accusations surfaced from time to time in nearby provincial towns. In 1821, rumors circulated that Jews were responsible for another grisly death after the body of a young woman was found in the Western Dvina. That same year, in Mogilev province, yet another young boy was said to have been the victim of a ritual murder. In all these instances, the imperial government eventually dropped the charges after conducting exhaustive criminal investigations. Convicting Jews of blood sacrifice required empirical evidence of the highest order.

Beginning in the eighteenth century, the courtroom emerged as an important arena for debate, persuasion, and theater. Sensational court cases—on the themes of crime, sexual misconduct, personal betrayal, fraud, and transgression of authority—appeared on the pages of the French, British, and German mass circulation newspapers.[23] A large and growing reading public consumed stories of courtroom drama with great interest and apprehension. Systematically publicized for the benefit of the educated public, the stories followed tightly woven melodramatic narratives. Some of the most explosive cases turned into full-blown *affaires*, dividing entire communities and setting off intense polemics in newspapers and pamphlets all around the world.[24]

The Russian government did a masterly job in not permitting the investigation to attract much public attention or become a source of fascination in the popular imagination. Projecting an aura of command and confidence, Tsar Nicholas I did everything in his power to control the empire by his presence. The Third Section—the secret police and gendarmerie—controlled public opinion. No news, especially something that might poorly reflect on monarchical power, was allowed to appear in print. According to Article 165 of the 1826 censorship law, everything was forbidden "that in any way reveals in author, translator, or artist a person who violated the obligations incumbent on a loyal subject to the holy person of the Sovereign Emperor, or who transgresses against the worthy distinction of the most august royal house; and [such a person is liable] to immediate arrest and disposal to the laws."[25] During Nicholas's reign, only twenty-six periodical publications appeared in print, including scholarly journals, official government publications, literary journals, and children's magazines. The most popular newspapers of the time were concerned more with promoting the official sentimental voice of the government than with publicizing current events.[26] The English physician and traveler Edward Morton was keenly aware of how powerful a role the press played in sensationalizing crime: "English papers do certainly too often contain accounts of dreadful [crimes], it is because all that happen in the whole extent of the United Kingdom are at once published; and [Russian] journals never contain them, not because murders occur less frequently in Russia . . . but because the government never allows the details to be published; and eleven twelfths of the population never know or suspect that they have happened."[27]

Following official protocol, authorities in Velizh conducted the criminal investigation in strict secrecy, according to the guidelines established by the inquisitorial procedure code. First articulated in the twelfth century, inquisitorial procedure was a revolution in law and legal culture. By the sixteenth and seventeenth centuries, it was employed in many parts of Continental Europe, including the Polish-Lithuanian Commonwealth and Russia.[28] Premised on the interests of the public or state, the inquisitorial system called on the inhabitants of a community to denounce suspected criminals to the judicial authorities, and it made defendants vulnerable to coercive prosecutions.[29] Responding to public rumors, judges played a particularly active role in initiating legal proceedings. Oral testimonies were transcribed in special notebooks, ceaselessly recopied so as to prevent loss of vital information, and stored for posterity in government archives. The inquisitorial registers served as active instruments of knowledge. In early modern Europe, the system was used to prosecute an unprecedented number of witches and heretics, especially in places like southern France, Switzerland, and Germany.[30]

In the Russian Empire, authorities relied on inquisitorial procedure for crimes that threatened public interest or the security of the state. Before the judicial reforms of the 1860s and 1870s, the system was used widely to resolve criminal cases and to assert greater disciplinary control over the population. Borrowing from Swedish, Danish, and German military codes, the inquisitorial procedure, as set forth in the Military Process section of the Military Statute of 1716, required that every individual "must keep what happened in court secret and tell no one, whoever he may be, anything about it."[31] Authorities were required to pay particular attention to the collection of material evidence and eyewitness testimony. For the most serious crimes, such as murder, robbery, arson, high political, and religious crime, investigators, judges, and other experts involved in the case confronted the witnesses and litigants one by one in the privacy of the inquisitorial chamber. This technique helped accumulate an impressive mass of facts, opinions, testimonies, and interpretations. Ultimately, the inquisitorial mode helped establish the most faithful representation of the events in question so that the court, by a process of logical reasoning, could deduce the guilt of the suspect and pass sentence.[32]

The Velizh case unfolded in a town like any other town in the Russian Empire where people's lives were intimately connected, where rivalries and confrontations were part of day-to-day existence, and where the blood libel was part of a well-established belief system.[33] To come to grips with the pervasiveness of belief requires us not only to explore a time and place where ritual murder was accepted as a social fact. We also need to come to terms with one of the most fundamental contradictions of Jewish life in Eastern Europe: that, no matter how widespread ritual murder beliefs may have been and no matter the number of accusations, the largest Jewish community in the world continued to feel rooted and secure in its place of residence. At least until the second half of the nineteenth century, the extraordinary vitality of Jewish life, culture, and institutions expressed itself in the large demographic concentration of Jews in urban settlements, the indispensable role that they played in the regional economy, and the fact that the vast majority of the population felt self-confident in their cultural distinctiveness vis-à-vis their neighbors.[34]

In the East European borderlands, a large territory that extended from the Baltic regions to the Black Sea, diverse groups of people usually chose to live among their own types. Segregation did not mean that populations lived in isolation from everyone else. In the borderlands, ethnic boundaries were highly permeable. Since early modern times, residents routinely met and socialized in courtyards, streets, homes, and taverns. While ethnic groups did not always exhibit esteem or affection toward one another, people's lives intersected on a daily basis.[35] In this cultural landscape, neighbors—that is, those individuals from diverse religious and cultural backgrounds who lived side-by-side with one another in small-town settings—usually developed pragmatic relationships with one another based on distinct economic conditions and residential patterns in which they lived and operated. This does not mean that Jews had always lived in harmonious coexistence with their neighbors or that quarrels over the most trivial matters never got out of control. But the fact that Jews and their neighbors worked out their differences suggests that, at least in most instances, people continued to adopt practices that allowed them to live together in a state of relative tranquility.[36]

How do we explain this striking paradox? How is it possible for Jews to be simultaneously the victims of such vicious accusations and to be so integrated into the economy of the state and to feel so at home? For starters, ritual murder cases were always sporadic occurrences. Even if an exhaustive investigation of provincial archives unearths more cases, this would not change the empirical fact that the number was very small. It is important, therefore, not to exaggerate the significance of the trials or their contribution to Jews' sense of vulnerability and powerlessness. In the Russian Empire, the allegations never materialized into a full-blown panic along the lines of the early modern witch-hunts in France or Germany, or even Poland. Nevertheless, the fact that the blood libel popped up from time to time and that so many people continued to maintain that Jews were capable of committing the crime suggests that a well-established folk culture helped legitimize the narrative.

In the eighteenth and nineteenth centuries, the imperial Russian state attempted to eradicate superstition—the belief in the power of sorcery, miraculous cures, and spirit possession to shape daily existence—without much success.[37] Well into the twentieth century, these cultural beliefs and practices continued to offer convenient explanations for basic questions regarding life, death, and afterlife, while offering protection against numerous worldly dangers. The boundaries between religious and magical beliefs were difficult to distinguish with any certainty. That folk medicine and the supernatural played an important role in Jewish daily life only heightened the fantastical charge made during a ritually charged time of the year. Thus, at a time when spoken spells brought illnesses to enemies or warded off evil spirits, when gathering ceremonies enhanced the healing properties of herbs, and when churches, cemeteries, barns, and bathhouses were associated with popular magic and divination, there was nothing peculiar about the idea that Jews required Christian blood for religious ritual services. If, according to Belarusian folk traditions, witches preyed on unsuspecting children, why could not Jews kill little children for their blood?[38]

In the last years of the old regime, teams of ethnographers traveled to provincial towns and villages in hopes of unlocking the mysteries of indigenous civilizations. They conducted interviews, snapped photographs, and collected artifacts of daily life. Some worked on Russian Orthodox peasants, others on Jews, and various others on populations in the distant corners of the empire. Very few sources allow historians to penetrate the worlds these people inhabited. I am lucky in this respect. The Velizh archive offers a unique window into the multiple factors that did not only cause ruptures and conflicts in everyday life. These documents also allow us to observe the social and cultural worlds of a multiethnic population that had coexisted for hundreds of years. This extraordinary collection allows us to catch an unprecedented glimpse of small-town life in Eastern Europe: to overhear people mingling with one another on dusty streets and inside homes and taverns, to see snapshots of the clothes people wore and the food they consumed, and above all, to learn something of the dark fantasies, fears, and preoccupations of a community that rarely appear in the historical record.[39] A cache of intercepted letters reveals much of the pain, misery, and frustration of prison life. Many other documents help illuminate how ordinary men and women experienced the varieties of emotional life.[40] Coming to grips with these emotions—anger, despair, sadness, pain, frustration, and disgust—requires that we pay attention not only to words and voices but also to the facial expressions, gestures, and psychological states of ordinary people.[41] Every sound, gesture, and grimace the Jews made served as important clues to their guilt or innocence.

I

Fedor Goes for a Walk

LIKE MOST OTHER CHRISTIANS IN Velizh, Emel'ian Ivanov spent between sunset on Holy Saturday and the early hours of Easter Day at church, celebrating the resurrection of Jesus Christ. Having come home tired and hungry from the paschal vigil, Emel'ian proceeded to eat a modest lunch with his wife, Agafia Prokof'eva. After finishing the meal, the couple lay down for a nap—Emel'ian on the bed and Agafia on the stove. In no time, their son Fedor ran inside the cottage and asked his mother for a red Easter egg. Agafia begged her son to eat it, but Fedor replied that he was not hungry. Instead, he rolled the egg back and forth on the floor until it cracked into small pieces and then went to play outside with his cousin. Dressed in a black striped caftan, black leather shoes, and a faded light blue silk kerchief, Fedor went out around eleven o'clock in the morning, when all the other Christian residents were home resting after the long night.[1]

Legally classified as a state peasant, Emel'ian spent twenty-five years as a conscript in the Russian army. For eighteen years, he served as a musketeer, traveling to distant corners of the empire on assignment. After suffering an unspecified injury, he was transferred to a special regiment for invalids to complete his remaining years of service. The burdens of the work prevented most soldiers from starting a family, but Emel'ian was lucky in this regard. As soon as he arrived in Velizh, he met and married Agafia Prokof'eva, who came from the village of

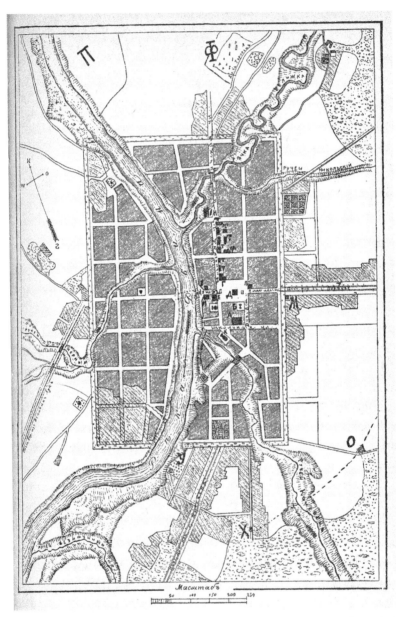

A hand-drawn map of Velizh, with the probable path of Fedor's walk marked in the bottom right-hand corner. Perezhitoe *3 (1911)*

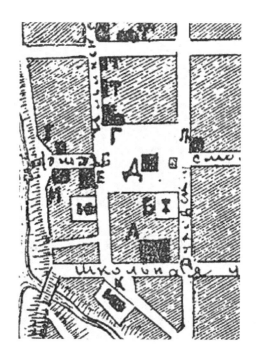

А	The Great Synagogue
Б	The Holy Spirit Uniate Church
Г	Mirka Aronson's house
Д	marketplace and town hall
Е	house where prisoners were confined, 1830–1835
И	Evzik and Khanna Tsetlin's house
К	Catholic church
М	town jail
Н	St. Il'insk Uniate Church
О	place where Fedor's body was found
У	St. Michael's Cemetery
Ф	Jewish cemetery
Х	Emel'ian Ivanov's house
Т	houses where prisoners were confined until 1830

Usviaty. The couple had four children, three sons—two of whom died prematurely at birth—and a daughter. After Emel'ian retired from active service, the entire family continued to live in the soldiers' barracks at the edge of town on Vitebsk Road. Although free from social control from their former masters, retired soldiers generally had a difficult time reintegrating themselves in civilian society. Most soldiers lived in poverty and wandered from place to place looking for work; the more fortunate like Emel'ian eked out a living by working as day laborers or petty artisans.[2]

On Easter Sunday, the parents waited for their son to return from his walk. Fedor never came home that day, and for two days and nights, a small group of friends and family members unsuccessfully searched the town and its environs for the boy. On the third day, while Emel'ian and Agafia were home resting after the midday meal, a stranger knocked on the door. From the testimony of several witnesses in the case, we know that the caller was a beggar woman named Maria Terenteeva. As soon as Agafia opened the door, Terenteeva declared that she would be able to locate the missing boy. She asked for a burning candle and, after placing the candle flame in a cold pot of water, revealed that Fedor was still alive, locked inside the cellar of Mirka Aronson's large brick house. Although there was lots of food and drink there, Fedor was not given anything to eat or drink. Terenteeva went on to say that she intended to rescue the boy that night, but was afraid that evil might already have struck and that he would die the moment she came to rescue him.[3]

Emel'ian dismissed the revelations as nonsense. "You're not fortune-telling but lying," Emel'ian told the stranger. "I've seen how sorcerers tell fortunes." Yet the more he thought about his son, the more anxious he had become. Emel'ian wanted to go see him himself, but Terenteeva insisted that his wife should go in his place. So he instructed Agafia, along with her sister Kharitina, to walk to the marketplace, the very center of town, where Aronson's house was located. If Agafia sensed the boy was inside, then she would go to the village of Sentiury to talk with Anna Eremeeva, a twelve-year-old girl with psychic powers. But the moment Agafia stepped inside the courtyard, she decided to leave, fearing that someone might mistake her for a thief. Later that evening, when the sisters reached Sentiury, Agafia begged the young girl to tell her about her son. After much prodding, Anna relented: "I've been inside the house where they're keeping your son. He's extremely weak. If you want to see him, then beware, he will die this very night."[4]

By the time Agafia had come home and shared this news with her husband, three police officers were busy conducting a criminal investigation. Earlier that day, Emel'ian had informed the Velizh police that his son had disappeared without a trace. Numerous witnesses were questioned in the case while the officers searched for Fedor. But long before they completed the investigation, rumors began to circulate all over town that the Jews had killed the little boy.

For four straight days, the police conducted an exhaustive search of the town and its environs. Finally, on April 28, 1823, unable to uncover a single lead, they suspended the investigation and declared the boy missing. The sudden loss of Fedor must have dealt a severe blow to his parents. Although the judicial records offer no hint of Agafia Prokof'eva's state of mind, emotions were running high when Maria Terenteeva appeared once again on the doorstep. "Why did [the officers] stop the search?" Terenteeva asked abruptly. Then, to Agafia's amazement, Terenteeva related just how the boy had disappeared. A Jewish woman by the name of Khanna Tsetlina had walked up to Fedor while he stood on the bridge. After giving the boy a piece of sugar, she escorted him directly to Evzik Tsetlin's courtyard, where he remained until someone transferred him to Mirka Aronson's home under cover of darkness. Terenteeva was confident that she would be able to locate the body and invited Agafia to accompany her to the cemetery. But as soon as she stated those words, Terenteeva ran out the door, not to be seen again that night. When her husband returned home, Agafia recounted the day's events, but Emel'ian refused to believe that Jews had abducted his son.[5]

Just as the rumors were gathering steam, a most unexpected discovery added fuel to the fire. On May 2, the day after Terenteeva invited Agafia to the cemetery, Vasilii Kokhanskii's horse broke free. Kokhanskii took his dog to search for the missing horse. They walked one third of a mile to the thick marsh at the edge of town when the dog suddenly ran ahead, barking loudly and uncontrollably. Initially Kokhanskii thought they had found the horse, but he quickly realized that the dog was barking at a dead boy who was lying on his back with his "body punctured in numerous places." Kokhanskii remembered that Emel'ian Ivanov's son had been missing for several days and went to share the unfortunate news with his neighbor.[6]

Early the next morning, a delegation of four officials inspected the scene of the crime and produced a detailed report. First, they observed, the body was found in overgrown shrubby grass in a swampy forest less than half a mile from the center of town and no more than half a mile from the parents' home. Second, the body lay around seventy-seven yards from Shchetinskaia Road, a dirt road that could be taken to the center of town by way of three cross streets. Finally, and most important, they detected fresh footprints on the right side of the dirt road leading inside the forest and directly to the boy's body. Based on this evidence, the officials hypothesized that as many as five people had transported the boy in a spring britzka, a horse-drawn carriage, with forged metal wheels. In fact, they were certain that the perpetrators had parked the carriage on the side of the road and then dumped the body in the shrubby grass. They were not able to determine the exact route the carriage had taken, for its tracks had been smeared by the traffic traveling back and forth on the dirt road over the course of several days. But since none of the people who lived nearby had witnessed suspicious persons (that is, Jews) leaving the forest in a spring britzka, they concluded that the perpetrators had returned to town. Unable to uncover any other evidence, they set themselves the tasks of questioning two of the most important witnesses in the case, Maria Terenteeva and Anna Eremeeva, and inspecting Mirka Aronson's home for clues that might help them solve the murder.[7]

The boy died a slow and painful death. When Inspector Lukashevich began the investigation, the autopsy report, prepared by the town doctor, Levin, had already revealed that little Fedor was stabbed numerous times with blunt nails. The entire body was punctured with little round holes that were no more than a third of an inch in depth: five on the right hand, positioned evenly from the elbow to the tip of the hand; three on the left hand; four on the top of the head and around the left ear; one directly above the right knee; and another on the back. The skin on Fedor's feet, arms, stomach, and head had hardened and turned a burned yellow or red color, as though someone had vigorously scrubbed the boy's body with a coarse cloth or brush. A piece of cloth was used to restrict the circulation of the blood to the feet and knees, both of which had turned dark blue, perhaps even black, from the trauma. The lips were pressed firmly against the teeth, while the nose appeared to have been smashed in violently. The dark crimson bruise on the back of the neck signified that cloth or rope was used to tie the boy's mouth. The internal organs, including the stomach and the intestines, were completely empty, filled only with air. Whoever punctured the boy fourteen times, the report concluded, did so to draw blood.[8]

On May 5, Inspector Lukashevich made a thorough search of Mirka Aronson's house, paying particular attention to the kitchen, tool shed, and stable, and was not able to uncover any evidence that linked Mirka or any other members of the household (her daughter Slava, son-in-law Shmerka Berlin, grandson Hirsh, and granddaughter-in-law Shifra) with the murder. He then asked to take a look at the cellar, but Berlin replied that the house had none. Lukashevich later learned that the house was equipped with two cellars—the first one located in the foyer, the other in the *lavka* (trade shop) where goods and spirits were sold. When asked why he had concealed the truth, Berlin replied that he did not see the point of showing them to the inspector: "Both cellars are in the most decrepit shape, and there is absolutely nothing in them." Clearly, Berlin felt that he had much to lose if the authorities uncovered anything remotely suspicious.[9]

Registered officially as a merchant of the third guild, Shmerka Berlin occupied a respected place in the social hierarchy of the town. Not only did he make quite a bit of money selling lumber and spirits and managing the only glass factory in the provincial district, but he also married into an affluent family that lived in the most magnificent house in Velizh. Mirka Aronson's two-story brick house was located in the center of the town. The southern side of the house overlooked the marketplace and town hall, while the western side faced Il'inskaia Street—one of the town's main thoroughfares, populated mostly by Jews. Considered large by any standard, the house had a grand total of twenty-four rooms, thirteen of which were located on the first floor. A tavern and grocery store, at least three trading stalls, two cellars (one of which was equipped with a secret staircase), and several additional chambers all could be found on the first level. Together with his wife Slava, Shmerka occupied one of the more spacious chambers on the ground floor, while their daughter and her husband slept in a slightly smaller one. Mirka Aronson spent

г. Велижъ.   Базарный день.

A postcard of the marketplace. Mirka Aronson's house is the fourth building from the right. *Velizh Museum*

much of her time in an adjoining wing of the house, comprising six additional rooms.

In Velizh, as in other market towns in the western borderlands, the boundaries between rural life and urban civilization were never rigid. This was also the case for the Aronson household.[10] Visitors would walk up to a sturdy iron gate on Il'inskaia Street, where they would be greeted by a domestic servant and escorted inside the courtyard. Here, they would find goats, roosters, and other domestic animals, a modest garden, and encounter all the sights and smells of small-town life. The courtyard was separated into two distinct sections by a long wooden fence. Several small wooden structures lined the eastern side of the property, including a guesthouse reserved for visitors, tool shed, stable, outhouse, and a wooden hut composed of three modest rooms built especially for the domestic servants.

Thanks to Miron Ryvkin's historical-ethnographic recollections (one of the earliest and most penetrating accounts of the case), it is possible to get a glimpse of details that are strikingly absent from the official judicial records.[11] On any weekday this imposing structure was the site of much activity and commotion. Customers from various parts of the town as well as the surrounding villages would come to drink beer or vodka at the tavern or purchase food from what was considered to be the town's best-stocked grocery store. Besides alcohol, they could acquire buns, cottage-cheese cakes, pickled herring, fruits, coffee, tea, tobacco, matches, candles, and so much more.[12] Visitors who came to town on business would walk up the wooden staircase to the *traktir* (inn), where they could get a bite to eat in the dining room and retire for the night in one of the guest rooms. From time to time the poor and needy showed up on the doorstep as well: Mirka Aronson, it seems, was well known for her exceptional generosity. Aronson's two sons lived quite comfortably only a few doors away on Il'inskaia Street, while Shmerka Berlin's brother lived right around the corner on Petersburg Street, next to two of Velizh's most prominent personalities, the town councilor Evzik Tsetlin and his wife Khanna. On Saturdays and on holidays, the entire extended family—around forty people in all—would gather for a meal on the second level of the house.

Without the support of their Christian neighbors, neither Shmerka Berlin nor Khanna Tsetlina would have been able to operate successful taverns. According to Ryvkin, all the respected residents of the town—from the wealthiest Polish landowners to the most powerful imperial bureaucrats—could be spotted, from time to time, at either Berlin's or Tsetlina's tavern.[13] We should, however, be careful not to paint life in Velizh as a multicultural idyll. The day-to-day exchange of goods and services not only brought people together but also produced many of the conflicts and quarrels between town residents. This was a world that was consumed by petty disagreements, disputes, jealousy, and gossip. And as in so many other small towns and villages around the world, communal unity in Velizh represented an ideal far removed from what was taking place in everyday life.[14]

If Mirka Aronson and Shmerka Berlin were regarded as upstanding members of the community, Anna Eremeeva and Maria Terenteeva were considered to be two of the town's most marginal characters. Anna had lived a hand-to-mouth existence in and around Velizh for more than twelve months when the boy's lifeless body was first discovered. On March 25, about a month before Fedor disappeared, Anna found herself in the village of Sentiury. While out on a walk, she suddenly felt weak and fell asleep on the side of the road. The townsman Larion Pestun noticed Anna curled up sleeping in the shrubby grass and decided to take her to his warm bathhouse. Fast asleep for two days and two nights, Anna dreamed of the archangel Mikhail, who took her by the arm and whispered in her ear that the Jews would murder a Christian soul on Easter Day. This was not the only time that Anna had dreamed of the archangel Mikhail: on Easter eve, he appeared to her one more time, revealing that Jews would seize a Christian soul and bring him to Mirka Aronson's home. When Agafia Prokof'eva came to Sentiury to inquire about little Fedor's whereabouts, Anna told her: "On the way here you walked into the very home where they're keeping your son. If you have the strength to rescue the boy, then do so. But if you don't make it on time, then stay vigilant and watch over [the house]."[15]

Like Anna, Maria Terenteeva had lived in Velizh for a year or two at the time of the investigation (it is impossible to determine for sure from the archival records), surviving on whatever food and money

A postcard of Smolensk Street. The marketplace and the town council are in the background. *Velizh Museum*

she could find. She married a man who spent most of his adult life serving in the army. Several residents testified that Terenteeva had led a "debauched" lifestyle ever since she came to town—giving birth to a son out of wedlock, stealing food every chance she could, and walking in the streets at all hours of the night screaming, "God help me, they're trying to suffocate me."[16] Abram Kisin remembered first encountering Terenteeva during broad daylight, when he caught her stealing carrots and beets from his yard. Once he confronted her, Terenteeva "hit him so hard that he barely made it back home that day." On other occasions, as well, Terenteeva would come by Kisin's house in a fit of rage to steal fresh vegetables from the garden or throw clean linens on the ground and stomp on them with her bare feet in a wild rage.[17]

Terenteeva testified that on Easter Day she begged for alms in front of a church and chatted briefly with a woman who was passing by. Afterward, she made her way to the outskirts of town, seeking charitable handouts along the way. It was already nightfall when she made her way to the Konevetse Creek, at which time she saw two small children standing on the bridge. One was a boy with white-blond hair, wearing a cap and dressed in a coat and boots. At that precise moment, Terenteeva recalled, Khanna Tsetlina walked up to the boy and took him away by the arm. Although Terenteeva did not say anything about the whereabouts of the other child, she claimed that Tsetlina took the boy back to her own home, where four Jewish women were waiting for her. Terenteeva was not certain if the women had come from Shmerka Berlin's home, but she was confident that she would be able to identify at least two of them. She then described her encounters with Emel'ian Ivanov and Agafia Prokof'eva and concluded the deposition by saying that Emel'ian had refused to believe a word she had said.[18]

Maria Terenteeva's testimony proved absolutely devastating for the Jews. Over the course of several weeks, authorities questioned dozens of town residents, both Jews and Christians, focusing their attention on four primary suspects—Evzik and Khanna Tsetlin, Mirka Aronson, and Shmerka Berlin—and on the missing spring britzka. Emel'ian Ivanov's sister-in-law, Kharitina Prokof'eva, was convinced by all the talk that the Jews had murdered her nephew. Another town resident, Efim'ia

Fedorova, heard from one of her neighbors that the Jews took the little boy inside their school, where they proceeded to torture and kill him. Avdot'ia Maksimova, who worked as a housekeeper for Khanna Tsetlina (and would later play an important role in the case), testified that she had not seen a Christian boy at the house and had not seen Tsetlina walk outside that day. Eleven other witnesses—representing a broad cross section of the population—declared that they, too, had not seen Jews with the young boy and had no knowledge of who had committed the crime. They acknowledged, however, that the Jews must have been involved in the murder. The investigators then proceeded to question twelve more people. Two testified that Shmerka Berlin's and Khanna Tsetlina's behavior had always been excellent; eight said they did not suspect either Berlin or Tsetlina of doing anything malicious; but all twelve were convinced beyond a shadow of a doubt that the Jews had killed the little boy.[19]

The court records demonstrate how influential tales of blood sacrifice had become in the mindset of the town residents. Witness after witness asserted that Jews had ritually murdered the boy, even though no one had actually seen them do this. The only person other than Maria Terenteeva who claimed to have observed Khanna Tsetlina with a Christian boy was Daria Kasachevskaia. On Easter Day, at either one or two o'clock in the afternoon, Kasachevskaia went to Shmerka Berlin's tavern to purchase beer. On the way, she saw Khanna Tsetlina with a blond-haired boy who was dressed in either a blue or green caftan. Kasachevskaia surmised that Tsetlina and the little boy were walking to town from either the embankment or the creek, but she had no idea where they were going. After purchasing the beer, Kasachevskaia returned home immediately and did not see either Tsetlina or the boy again that afternoon. It seems likely that Kasachevskaia based her narrative on the many tales that were circulating around town, for when authorities pressed her for additional testimony she could not remember anything else.[20]

Over the course of the investigation, tsarist officials attempted to obey the letter of the law by not casting blame on any suspects until they had interviewed all possible witnesses, exhausted all possible lines of inquiry, and reviewed all the forensic evidence. And as they questioned more and more people, and gathered more and more evidence, communal tensions began to rise. How could they not? The Jews, it seems, thought that it was just a matter of time before the most respected and wealthiest members of their community would be formally charged with ritual murder. On May 17, when Inspector Lukashevich interviewed Father Kazimir Serafinovich, who had come to town to visit his friend the land surveyor Kottov, more than one hundred Jews encircled Kottov's house, climbed on the fence, and began to shout to the inspector: "You don't have the right to treat the town councilor Tsetlin in this manner; he's our leader!" This unexpected turn of events put the authorities on high alert. Fearing that the heated emotions could easily escalate into unrestrained hostility, the magistrate issued an immediate injunction: none of the suspects or witnesses would be allowed to travel beyond the town's boundaries and everyone would be kept under strict surveillance until all the sordid details of the case were sorted out. The last thing the magistrate needed to deal with was a full-blown riot.[21]

The Jews, meanwhile, vehemently denied their role in the murder. Khanna Tsetlina testified that she was at home on Easter Day. Furthermore, she insisted that she never brought a Christian boy inside the house and had no knowledge of who had committed the crime. Several days after giving the deposition, Tsetlina submitted a formal appeal to the town council proclaiming her innocence, calling all the accusations "unfounded." "I never brought a Christian boy home, as [Terenteeva] has claimed, or left the house because I was home the entire day tending to my sick son." According to Jewish custom, a sick person could not be left alone, and for this reason several friends came by to help Tsetlina watch over her ailing son. Tsetlina invited the magistrate to interview Abram Kurin, Malka Baraduchi, and Genia Vezmenskaia, among other friends and neighbors, who would all testify on her behalf. She concluded the appeal by suggesting that, in all likelihood, Terenteeva had invented the "awful slander" to settle an old score. The beggar woman had a habit of walking around town asking for charity. On several occasions, after appearing on the doorstep, Tsetlina had "run her out of the house" without giving her any handouts. Each time such an incident had

Khanna Tsetlina's appeal to the Velizh town council proclaiming her innocence in Fedor's death. A professional scribe recopied the document in January 1829, when all the files in the dossier were being prepared for review by the Senate in St. Petersburg. *Natsional'nyi istoricheskii arkhiv Belarusi, f. 1297, op. 1, d. 190, ll. 217ob–218*

occurred, Terenteeva would tell everyone in town how unjustly she was treated.[22]

On Easter Sunday, Tsetlina's husband, Evzik, strolled around the marketplace browsing the items on display, and then went on several errands around town. For this reason, he could not say for certain if his wife went out anywhere that day, but he was convinced that a Christian boy had not set foot inside their house. At the age of seventy, Mirka Aronson tried to stay out of the day-to-day affairs of the family and avoided paying any attention to gossipy talk. While she had no idea who had killed the boy, there was no doubt in her mind that her son-in-law Shmerka and her grandson Hirsh were not involved in the murder because she knew for a fact that they stayed home the entire day. Showing signs of desperation, Shmerka Berlin made the outlandish conjecture that someone had "run over the boy accidentally and then proceeded to puncture the body" to mask the death as a ritual murder.[23]

As for the spring britzka, several witnesses had seen two mysterious Jews riding in such a carriage on Friday, April 27. One neighbor testified that around eight in the morning, amid heavy rain, she noticed two Jews riding around town. Early that morning, another neighbor was sitting by the window when she saw an open britzka pass by. No one in Velizh had ever seen the Jews before, but it turned out they were Shmerka Berlin's distant relatives. A middle-aged bearded man by the name of Iosel' Glikman and his fifteen-year-old son had come to Velizh for the very first time from the town Uly to purchase hay. Glikman and his son had parked the britzka in a neighboring courtyard and walked around the fence to Berlin's home, where they stayed until May 1. Authorities immediately suspected that Shmerka and Hirsh Berlin had used Glikman's spring britzka to transfer the boy's body to the forest, and so they proceeded to question Glikman, the Berlin family, and numerous other town residents. But Glikman refuted accusations that he was involved in the murder, testifying that his britzka did not have forged metal wheels and that he had borrowed the horses from the nobleman he was working for at the time. Shmerka and Hirsh Berlin provided solid testimony, as well, and none of the other witnesses said anything to cast doubt on Glikman's self-proclaimed innocence.[24]

The investigation of Fedor's death lasted nearly twelve months. The result was not an extraordinarily long judicial process or a particularly startling resolution to the case. The Velizh case followed the three basic stages of the inquisitorial process: a lengthy criminal investigation at the local level, the trial, and the review of the sentence by the highest court in the province. If convicted of blood sacrifice, the Russian government would not hesitate to impose the harshest penalties upon Jews for what it considered to be a most barbaric crime. Punishment could include eternal exile, knouting, beating by bastinadoes, and bodily mutilation.[25] Although the rumors circulating around town were vicious and cruel, the investigators did not rush to judgment. In the nineteenth century, the Russian government did not discredit the blood libel directly, as did many other European states, but it nevertheless maintained a policy of restraint.

On March 6, 1817, in response to a blood libel investigation in Grodno, Count Aleksandr Golitsyn had distributed a circular to provincial governors that called for more demanding standards of evidence and greater skepticism of the alleged crime. It declared:

> In view of the fact that in several provinces acquired from Poland, cases still occur in which the Jews are falsely accused of murdering Christian children for the alleged purpose of obtaining blood, his Imperial Majesty, taking into consideration that similar accusations have on previous numerous occasions been refuted by impartial investigations and royal charters, has been graciously pleased to convey to those at the head of the governments his Sovereign will: that henceforward the Jews shall not be charged with murdering Christian children, without any evidence and purely as a result of the superstitious belief that they are in need of Christian blood.[26]

In the event of a blood libel accusation, imperial law stipulated that Jews would have the same legal right to a fair trial as any other subject of the empire of his or her social standing accused of murder.

The authorities in Velizh worked systematically through the voluminous documentary evidence, attempting to carry out the investigation according to the strict standards of the law. Fourteen months to the day after Fedor disappeared, the appellate court handed down its verdicts. Although the court did not discount the possibility that Daria Kasachevskaia and especially Maria Terenteeva had invented their sensational tales to mask their own roles in the murder, it did not dismiss their testimony either. Based on a thorough review of all the material and moral evidence, Khanna Tsetlina was formally acquitted, but the police were nevertheless instructed to closely supervise her actions and behavior. Mirka Aronson and her household were cleared of any wrongdoing, as a thorough search of the home had failed to uncover anything remotely suspicious, although Aronson's son-in-law, Shmerka Berlin, was reprimanded for "spreading false rumors about the boy's death." In fact, the only person severely punished in the case was Maria Terenteeva: to atone for her licentious way of life, she was instructed to appear for admonition before an official representative of the Catholic-Uniate Council.[27]

The acquittal of the Jews did not mean that the judges, criminal investigators, and provincial bureaucrats presiding over the case were enlightened skeptics, but only the fact that a ritual murder case could not be proved at law. The Russian government may have elevated judicial standards, but it did not erase the crime of ritual murder from the law books. In the imperial Russian setting, the decisive turning point in acquitting Jews of blood sacrifice had more to do with the empirical demands of legal caution and documentary evidence than with enlightened skepticism. The doubt that plagued officials in Velizh, in other words, had less to do with systematic philosophical doubt than with the simple fact that there was not enough evidence to substantiate the crime with certainty.[28]

In the final analysis, we will never know what exactly happened to Fedor—whether he drowned accidently, was ruthlessly murdered, or died from some other cause—or who stabbed him fourteen times. On November 22, 1824, the most powerful court in Vitebsk province reviewed the case and wrote off Fedor's tragic death to the "will of God."[29] Whatever the reason may have been, the documentary evidence suggests that a small-town quarrel ultimately led to the ritual murder accusation. Most likely, the beggar woman Maria Terenteeva took advantage of the boy's death (or perhaps killed him herself) to get back at Khanna Tsetlina for her refusal of charity. The culture of giving—the teachings and beliefs about offering support to those in need—played an important role in both Jewish and Russian communal traditions.[30] In imperial Russia, as in the early modern world, where mutual aid provided a safety net for the misfortunate and needy, refusing charity signified a breach of neighborly duty. The act of denying food, drink, money, or other charity typically caused the individual who had been turned away to feel angry and resentful. When a personal misfortune subsequently happened to the person who had acted selfishly, the latter would often suspect that the beggar had cast a magic spell against them for their callous behavior.

Across most of Western and Central Europe, the overwhelming majority of witch cases conformed to the pattern that took place in Velizh—involving one neighbor's refusal to give a handout to another neighbor—although in our case the internal logic was reversed and the end result was a charge of ritual murder against a neighbor who refused to offer charity. To put it in slightly different terms, it was usually the very person who failed to perform a social duty who would accuse the person they had turned away of witchcraft. In contrast to the typical witch case scenario, then, Terenteeva represents the "victim" who took matters into her own hands to get back at her well-to-do neighbor Tsetlina for failing to fulfill a social obligation.[31]

If an ordinary neighborhood dispute explains why one neighbor accused another neighbor of murdering a little boy, we are still left with a puzzle. Why did almost every Christian resident interviewed in Velizh respond by saying that Jews were capable of committing the ritual crime? The answer has less to do with what is often referred to as anti-Semitism or with economic rivalries (although we should be careful not to dismiss the twin factors altogether) than with cosmologies of the time. Ritual murder accusations proved profoundly durable because of their capacity to mobilize fears and express popular worldviews. Most people in towns like Velizh believed in the tale not so much because of an ingrained hatred of Jews, but more often than not, because it meshed well with a wide repertoire of communally shared beliefs and practices.

2

Small-Town Life

ALL ACROSS THE EMPIRE, CHILD desertion, infanticide, and infant mortality were commonplace. Freak accidents resulted in all sorts of untimely deaths. Children could die by drowning or asphyxiation, or burn to death in a campfire or in an iron stove inside the home. They could be run over by horses, cows, and goats; left out in the elements for too long; crushed to death by household items; fall inside a well; or eat poisonous leaves, berries, or mushrooms. In Novgorod province, a three-year-old boy bled to death after he fell on a knife and punctured his throat. In Kursk province, the ceiling of a hut collapsed, crushing another peasant boy to death instantaneously. Elsewhere, two children, playing a harmless game of hide-and-seek, suffocated to death when they enclosed themselves in a chest and failed to open the latch. The spring and summer months—when children played outdoors unsupervised—witnessed a disproportionate number of deaths. In Orlov province, a three-year-old boy stumbled into a puddle of ice water and promptly drowned. Not too far away, a monstrous wind blew over a seven-year-old boy into a river just as he was crossing a bridge. As soon as the "season turns and it becomes too cold to play outside," the *Journal of the Ministry of the Interior* observed, "accidents occur less frequently, especially in the water, the most frequent cause of death."[1]

It was not unusual for newborn babies to be abandoned or murdered. In most cases, this was how young displaced women handled illegitimate or unwanted pregnancies. Less frequently, as in Iaroslav and Saratov provinces, a father could slash the throat of a nine-month-old infant boy or inadvertently stab his son with a knife in a fit of jealousy and blind rage.[2] Beginning in the eighteenth century, the Russian government allocated substantial resources to deal with child abandonment, infanticide, and senseless killings. New initiatives saved the lives of children and needy mothers and increased the punishment for killing a legitimate child. Instructional manuals alerted parents how best to care for children. Hospitals, foundling homes, and almshouses provided refuge for the poor, ill, crippled, insane, and orphaned.[3]

In spite of the growing public interest in the sanctity of children's lives, the most destitute regions continued to suffer. In Vitebsk province, hundreds of young children died each year in the nineteenth century. The most common explanations were neglect, pregnancy complications, and lack of proper medical attention. Other reasons were more traumatic and violent: infants were suffocated, drowned, strangled by their mothers, or, on more than infrequent occasions, eaten alive by boars and other wild animals. Corpses were found routinely in animal sheds, barnyards, courtyards, warehouses, and cellars. They could also turn up in woods, fields, swamps, forests, creeks, and rivers—some of the most convenient places to dispose of dead bodies.[4]

The death of a young Christian boy was, in other words, not uncommon in the life of a small provincial town like Velizh. The geography of the region proved particularly unforgiving. Much of the land in the vicinity of the town is wooded and contains large swamps that are impossible to traverse on foot. While passing through the western borderlands, the English traveler Robert Johnson remembered that the journey from the Russian interior to Belarus gradually became less hilly and picturesque. "The country suddenly loses that hilly irregularity, which so bounds in the vicinity of Smolensk."[5] Although he did not think the country presented any "remarkable feature," the physician Edward Morton recalled with some fondness how the road passed through the thick White Russian forest, "undulating, very romantically, among the trees."[6] Lined with fir, oak, and birch trees, Vitebsk province was filled with large marshy areas and as many as 2,509 freshwater lakes of different sizes.[7] An impressive number of rivers and creeks connected the lowland area. Johnson was struck by the fact that the extreme flat, open land "stretched as far as the eye could reach."[8]

Historical-demographic evidence suggests that Slavic populations had the highest rates of infant and childhood mortality in the Russian Empire. In the late nineteenth century, only about half of Russian Orthodox children survived to their fifth birthday. In Moscow and Saratov provinces, 51.6 percent of children died by age five, while in Tula and Nizhnii Novgorod the mortality rate was even higher, at 52.4 and 53.8 percent. Nearly one-third of Russians born in the Great Russian provinces died before reaching their first birthday. The rates were lower in the western and southeastern provinces and spiked in the central and northeastern parts of European Russia. Jews, by contrast, enjoyed the lowest rate of childhood mortality of any confession, and an astonishingly high population growth. Research has shown that culture, and not environment, best explains why Jewish communities had better success in keeping their children alive. Receptive attitudes toward modern medicine, in addition to personal hygiene, child care practices, and systems of support within the community, accounted for more sanitary living conditions for Jews. All these factors contributed not only to the divergence in mortality rates; they also shaped the day-to-day interactions between Jews and their neighbors.[9]

Velizh (to paraphrase Langston Hughes) was one of those miserable in-between places, just large enough to be formally classified a town.[10] It belonged to a zone known for its confessional diversity, economic troubles, paramilitary violence, and fluidity of borders. In 1772, after the first partition of the Polish-Lithuanian Commonwealth, Russia acquired a territory of forty thousand square miles, roughly the size of Kentucky. The region had long been a safe haven for runaway serfs, criminals, smugglers, and illegal migrants. One of Catherine's first proclamations was to stabilize it by dividing the land into two administrative provinces, Mogilev and Vitebsk.[11] Velizh was a typical military-administrative border town, always situated on the periphery. In the nineteenth century, it sat on the eastern edge of the Pale of Settlement. In the twentieth century, it experienced wars, occupations, and mass annihilation as armies conquered and reconquered the land. Today Velizh, a purely Russian town, sits less than eighteen miles from the Belarusian border. The last Jewish inhabitant died in 1973.[12]

Under the Polish-Lithuanian regime, Jews faced numerous restrictions on their residence. Some cities, such as Warsaw and Lublin, did not tolerate Jews within their city limits at all, while others, such as Wilno (Vil'na) and Kowno (Kovno), restricted where Jews could live. As a result of the extensive regulations outlined in the town charters, Jews in pre-partition Poland-Lithuania were forced to cluster in easily identifiable neighborhoods, districts, or streets.[13] At the turn of the nineteenth century, tsarist authorities dropped most of the burdensome statutes from the law books and permitted Jews to live, engage in trade, and build synagogues and schools wherever they wished inside the boundaries of the Pale of Settlement, provided they observed the general laws on movement and residence.[14] But long after the partitions of the commonwealth, Jews continued to live in easily identifiable streets or neighborhoods, most of which were centrally located.

The annexed territories gave Russia some 800,000 Uniates, 100,000 Roman Catholics, and 50,000 Jews, of whom 300 resided in Velizh.[15] In 1829, 90 percent of the 587,538 inhabitants in Vitebsk province lived in the countryside. Of all the places officially classified as "urban settlements," Velizh was the second largest, behind only the provincial capital of Vitebsk (14,777 inhabitants), and ahead of Polotsk (6,722), Lepel' (5,338), Dinaburg (4,646), Nevel' (4,538), and Surazh (4,270). Those decades witnessed a dramatic expansion of the Jewish population. By 1829, the Jews of Velizh comprised less than one-third of the population (somewhere around 2,000 of 6,953 inhabitants).[16]

At the time of the criminal investigation, Velizh was divided along economic, geographic, and confessional lines. Jews clustered on the right bank of the Western Dvina, in the most prosperous part of town, while the Belarusian population, comprising mainly Uniates and a small number of Catholics, lived on the left bank, in the poorest section. The Uniate Church was Eastern Orthodox in rite and Roman Catholic in doctrine. Merging Latin and Byzantine elements, it served as the building block of peasant religious identity. The mixed Uniate traditions were always in constant conflict with the Eastern Orthodox Church. Parishioners celebrated holidays according to the Julian calendar, the calendar of Orthodoxy, but learned Catholic doctrine in the catechism. They prayed to Catholic saints, while accepting the ceremonies and rites of the Orthodox Church. After the first partition, Catherine started meddling in the religious life of the Uniate community. Following the Polish Uprising of 1830–1831, Nicholas I redoubled the empress's efforts to transfer Uniate churches, clergy, and parishes to the Orthodox Church. By the mid-1870s, the Russian government succeeded in thoroughly suppressing the Uniate Church and forcibly converting all its members to Russian Orthodoxy.[17]

In the mid-1820s, the regime's campaign to eradicate the Uniate faith did little to alter the confessional landscape of the town. We could imagine Velizh as consisting of three concentric zones: the market square, surrounding neighborhoods, and suburbs.[18] An 1837 topographical survey listed 997 buildings, of which fourteen were brick structures; the rest were made of wood. The town hall—a two-story brick building—was the most visible site in the market square. This was where the municipal government, consisting of the town council, treasury, and sheriff's office, managed the town's day-to-day affairs. The post office, also a two-story brick building, stood on the eastern edge of the square, as did the courthouse. Attracting people far and wide, the market square was lined with rows of cloth stalls and shops and was the town's central gathering place. Among the many items available for purchase on good days were chickens, geese, meats, an assortment of vegetables and fruits, fresh fish, pickled herring, milk, butter, and household items. Mirka Aronson's two-story house—one of three brick town homes owned by Jewish merchant families—was on the left side of the town hall. Today the market square is a small park, with a statue of Lenin prominently on display, and Mirka

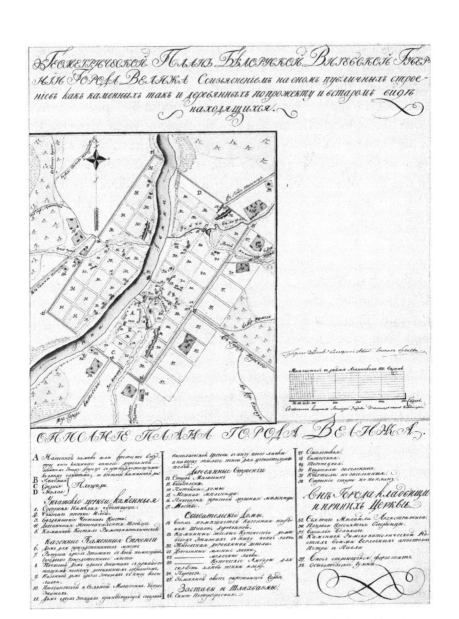

Map of Velizh in the 1830s. *Rossiiskii gosudarstvennyi istoricheskii arkhiv, f. 1293, op. 166, d. 18*

A Ruins of medieval castle

B Central marketplace

C Marketplace

D Marketplace

Brick structures

1. St. Nicholas Uniate Cathedral

2. St. Il'insk Uniate Church

3. Exaltation of the Holy Spirit Uniate Church

4. St. Trinity Uniate Church

5. Catholic church

6. Courthouse

7. Town hall

8. Post office

9. Treasury

10. General store

11. House belongs to St. Nicholas Cathedral, with trade shop on the first level and rooms for clergy on the second floor

Wooden structures

12. Old general store

13. Almshouse

14. Taverns

15. Flour mill

16. Tavern

17. Bridges

18. Primary school for Christian children

19. Two-story houses occupied by merchant families, with taverns and trading stalls on the first level

20. Jewish school

21. Meat stalls

22. Trade stalls

23. Merchant warehouses and barns

24. Ferry

25. Town boundaries

26. St. Petersburg Road

27. Smolensk Road

28. Vitebsk Road

29. Toropets Road

30. Occupied homes

31. Unoccupied homes

33. Decrepit buildings

Sites outside town boundaries

33. St. Michael's Cemetery

34. Feast of the Intercession Church

35. Vasilii the Great Church

36. Catholic cathedral

37. Fortress

38. Barn

A statue of Vladimir Lenin in the center of the town park, the site of the marketplace in the nineteenth century. With the dissolution of the Soviet Union in 1991, many cities and towns destroyed the statues. *Photograph by Jeffrey Shallit*

Aronson's house has been converted into a museum of history and local lore.

A visitor taking a stroll around town would see five Christian places of worship—four Uniate and one Roman Catholic—all of which were brick structures. The great synagogue, a two-story wooden building, located just south of the town square, across the Holy Spirit Uniate Church, played the most visible role in the religious and educational life of the Jewish community.

But there were other religious institutions, not listed in the official topographic surveys, that served important communal functions as well. The *kheyder*, a private one-teacher elementary school, was the standard institution of Jewish learning. Teachers taught little boys sacred Jewish texts in their own homes, beginning at age three. The physical conditions—poor ventilation and easy transmission of disease—were typically abysmal and the study hours exasperatingly long. The more

The Velizh Museum is now housed in the building where the Aronson/Berlin family lived in the 1820s. The structure was rebuilt after World War II. *Photograph by the author*

advanced students continued with studies of the Talmud in the *bes-medresh* (communal study hall). With a large section reserved for men and a smaller one for women, the *besmedresh* served as a place of Torah learning and worship. The furnishings were simple, consisting of chairs and tables, and most people came for several hours of part-time study and prayer.[19]

Due to the significant presence of Hasidim, it is likely that there were several *shtibls* in town. The *shtibl* was not only a place for prayer and study, as was a synagogue or *besmedresh*, but also a social and recreational center akin to a club or pub patronized by only men. Most *shtibls* were modest in size—a hall, small building, or private home—and contemporaries observed that, in addition to prayer and study, eating, singing, dancing, storytelling, and overindulgences were commonplace. Jewish law forbade levity, idle talk, eating, drinking, and sleeping in a house of prayer. Rabbinical authorities spilled much ink in denouncing the Hasidim for engaging in these activities. For their part, authorities were not so much troubled by the Hasidim straying outside the established boundaries of prayer and study. What concerned them most was the merriment, loud noise, and drunkenness that went on in *shtibls* at all hours of the night.[20]

Walking south on Il'inskaia Street, away from the marketplace, visitors would pass by the Roman Catholic church, a wooden meat stall, and a tavern. If they turned right, they would cross a small wooden bridge and stumble upon the ruins of a medieval castle on the embankment, probably built in the fourteenth century. If they made a slight turn to the left, they would see a flour mill and brewery. Only a few steps away was the general store, which occupied a two-story brick building recently erected. Just north of the market square on Il'inskaia Street was the St. Il'insk Uniate Church. A medical clinic, another tavern, flour mill, and a small primary school for Christian children were some of the other significant sites in the neighborhood.

In Velizh, as in many other towns in the East European borderlands, Jews owned almost all the homes and shops in the center, managed a sizable portion of the estates in the provincial district, enjoyed a monopoly on the marketplace, and controlled timber sales, small-scale trade, and the liquor industry.[21] A complex of wooden homes, owned mostly by Jews and a small number of humble Polish landowners, dotted the eastern and western sides of the marketplace. These were one-story structures, consisting of several rooms, with courtyards and gates. Most Jews who lived there worked as tailors, cobblers, woodworkers, soap and candlestick makers, and brush and comb makers. Some were bakers, teachers, brewers, distillers, and glaziers. In the outlying areas, the small wooden homes were occupied by peasant families, lodgers, retired soldiers, vagrants, and itinerant laborers. Soldiers' barracks, peasant huts, and other modest wooden dwellings with dirt floors, tiny windows, and damp walls could be found on the southern side of the town, on either side of the Western Dvina. The jail stood next to the woods on the outskirts of town along Smolensk Road. The Jewish cemetery was located on the northern tip, around a thirty-minute walk from the town center, and St. Michael's Cemetery was on the south side, not too far away from where the little boy Fedor was born.

Travelers took note of the miserable state of the land and the people on the western side of the Russian border. Robert Johnson, for instance, was taken aback at how quickly the "Russian character—the lively and boisterous mirth of the poor Russ—changed for the cold, calculating silence of the other." Every feature—including the countenances, costume, and cut of hair—indicated a change of tribe. Jews were the principal inhabitants of the region. And he could not believe how many there

Велижъ. Ильинская улица.

A postcard of Il'inskaia Street. The St. Il'insk Church, built in 1772 and demolished during World War II, is in the background. *Velizh Museum*

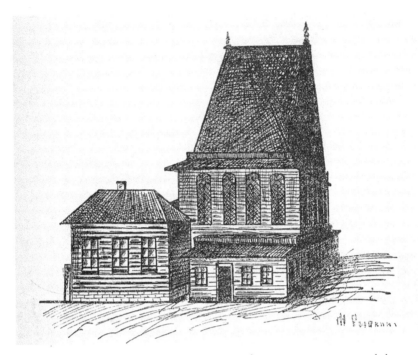

The great synagogue burned down in 1868. Male congregants sat around the spacious perimeter and on the sides of the *bimah*. Perezhitoe *3 (1911)*

were, "much more than might have been expected, so near the frontiers of ancient Russia, a country in which a Jew has never attempted to enter." "The common Lithuanians"—a reference to local Uniates and Catholics—"are poor, miserable, abject creatures," while Jews "are lanky and squalid," all dressed alike "in long tunics of black silk, with a broad silken sash tied around the waist. On the head they wear a small velvet cap, and over it a huge one made of fur."[22]

Velizh county had the lowest population density in the province. It also experienced some of the worst cases of famine, due in part to the gritty nature of the sandy soil.[23] In an assessment of the grain shortages in Belarus, the poet-cum-statesman Gavriil Derzhavin observed, after a personal tour of the region in 1799, that Vitebsk province was in much worse shape than its neighbor Mogilev. With all the grain reserves used up, the "entire northern region is suffering not only shortages, but real-life hunger."[24] For Derzhavin, the source of the problem was the unhealthy relations between petty Polish landowners, peasants, and

Jews. By allowing Jews to manage noble estates and encouraging harm-ful pursuits such as the liquor trade, Polish landowners left peasants at the mercy of the lease agents. Derzhavin spent the bulk of his lengthy *Opinion* blaming Jews for the region's economic woes.[25]

The war with Napoleon devastated the region. The Grand Armée numbering half a million men crossed the Nemen River on June 24, 1812. The French troops continued on to Vil'na (June 30), Vitebsk (July 28), and Smolensk (August 18) before marching toward Moscow and back. As the Russian army retreated, Cossacks were given the unenviable task of burning entire villages and towns, bridges, and crossways and destroying all the food and fodder they could grab. Local goods and pro-duce were burned or carried away from neighborhood stores. Desertion rates were unusually high.[26] In his reflections on the ruins he witnessed, Edward Morton noted, "All the ground was trodden by the conflict-ing armies in the memorable campaign of 1812: upon these very plains thousands and tens of thousands of the French invaders perished by the sword and the rigour of the climate, in addition to their numerous opponents who fell in the cause of their country."[27] Focusing on the situation in Smolensk, Robert Johnson remarked, "Never did the hand of destruction press more heavily than on this ill-fated city. Everything bears the mark of French devastation." After a sizable number of the inhabitants fled for their lives, "nothing but a melancholy and horrid picture of ruin is distinguishable."[28]

For more than six months, soldiers fought over and plundered the land, causing massive casualties and destruction of personal property. Witnesses observed how fires blazed through neighborhoods and, on occasion, wiped out entire urban settlements. The soldier Jakob Walter reported that many of the towns "not only were completely stripped [of provisions] but were also half-burned."[29] In the provincial capital of Vitebsk, 2,415 residents (half of them Jews) died in the war and an estimated 1.5 million rubles' worth of property was destroyed (of which 67 percent belonged to Jews). Minsk county may have endured the highest deaths, an estimated 55,500, but the numbers were not much lower in the surrounding territories. Witnesses recalled that more than 15,000 corpses were buried under the ice in the Nemen River. Roughly 1,000 charred bodies were found in Snipishki and an additional 5,000 in Antokol'. In Grodno province, the death totals exceeded 4,000 and the destruction of property was estimated at 29 million rubles, while its neighbor Mogilev endured 33.5 million rubles' worth of damage. The same was true, to a lesser degree, for the counties of Vil'na, Kovno, and Tel'shi.[30]

Velizh experienced the full brunt of the war, with 90 percent of all homes heavily damaged by fires and looting, and it continued to deal with the aftereffects for many years to come.[31] The heavy loss of livestock and repeated crop failures during and after the war resulted in diminished food supplies. In the years 1821–1822, a devastating famine swept through the region, causing widespread population loss. One provincial official reported that "many of the inhabitants [in Vitebsk province] were crippled from hunger," estimating that one hundred people died of malnutrition and ninety-eight more were on the verge of death. The loss of income due to lackluster agricultural production led to a sharp decline in living standards and life expectancy.

The famine hit the peasantry particularly hard, although it traumatized everyone, including the townspeople and nobility. It was not uncommon for people from all walks of life, dressed in tattered clothing, to beg for handouts when they could not find anything to eat. The harsh winter exacerbated the situation. In February 1822, at least forty-three peasants succumbed to hunger while huddling together in an empty provincial post office to escape from the cold. In a shelter for the homeless in Vitebsk, three or four people died every night from hunger or illness; the rest slept on dirt floors, where the air quality was particularly poor. As the province sank into despair from grain shortages, officials resorted to desperate measures to contain the crisis from reaching epidemic proportions. To stop the spread of contagion and disease, the most destitute were buried in mass graves.[32]

Provincial governors sent detailed reports of the horrors they witnessed. Initially, St. Petersburg responded by dismissing the news as "unsubstantiated rumors," but eventually it sent Senator D. O. Baranov to inspect the hungry towns and villages.[33] Baranov concluded what so many others had said before him: he blamed the deteriorating situation on Jews' exploitation of the peasantry. The moment the commonwealth was partitioned, Russia's concerns with peasant drunkenness led to a series of prohibitions on the liquor trade, with Jews as the chief targets. On April 11, 1823, Alexander I (reaffirming article 34 of the 1804 statute) forbade Jews from holding a lease on a tavern, drinking house, or inn, and selling or distributing liquor in villages. The net result of the state's attempt to legislate tavern keeping was the resettlement of tens of thousands of souls from the countryside. By January 1, 1824, authorities expelled nearly 20,000 Jews from Chernigov and Poltava provinces, 12,804 from Mogilev, and 7,651 from Vitebsk.[34] In the ensuing years, the situation got particularly bad in overcrowded towns. In a desperate attempt to make a living, hungry and unemployed Jews petitioned the governor-general's office to allow them to return to the countryside to find odd jobs in carpentry, blacksmithing, and road and canal construction.[35]

Just as the imperial administration was busy drawing distinct lines between Jews and peasants, it started to devise extensive policies to impose administrative order on its religious minorities. The conscription of Jews into the imperial army in August 1827 constituted the first successful effort to socially engineer the lives and institutions of the largest Jewish population in the world. Parents and children alike perceived military service to be a most frightening experience. For Jewish males between the ages of twelve and twenty-five, the twenty-five-year term seemed like a death sentence. The army's missionary tactics resulted in more than twenty thousand conversions, mostly of destitute and orphaned young males. In no time, Nicholas's conscription law sent shock waves throughout the Jewish communities in the Pale, but the emperor had no intention of stopping there.[36]

Nicholas's regime spent considerable energy intervening in Jewish communal affairs. Above all, it hoped to minimize the efficacy of the *kahal* (the executive board of the community) and rabbinic authority. Long before the 1844 reform officially weakened Jewish communal autonomy, the tsars, from Catherine II to Nicholas I, considered several proposals to refashion collective representation and to make the state the ultimate arbiter of individual grievances. The drive to curtail autonomous institutions represented a crucial moment in the state's efforts to forge direct links with its diverse populations. The campaigns were largely consistent with the techniques with which the state managed its vast empire. The idea was to do away with local intermediaries who presided over a variety of matters involving record keeping, census collection, and municipal administration. The reforms to destabilize Jewish communal life were felt in the domestic sphere as well, including the wildly unpopular sartorial decrees prohibiting men and women from wearing Jewish dress.[37]

In the 1820s, when the Velizh ritual murder investigation was in full swing, the state's interventionist designs had not been fully put into action. A community steeped in the day-to-day rhythms of Judaism continued to define itself according to the Jewish calendar. The Jewish spaces in Vitebsk and Mogilev provinces were populated by followers of a branch of Hasidism known as Habad. Founded by Rabbi Shneur Zalman at the end of the eighteenth century, the movement was centered in Liubavachi, only seventy miles south of Velizh.[38] Hasidism, a popular religious revival movement, emerged spontaneously. A group of pious Torah scholars, Kabbalists, and *baalei shem* (miracle workers) made mystical ethos and ecstatic prayer a central part of religious experience. The groups were headed by *tsaddikim* (righteous individuals) known for their charismatic religious leadership, folksy discussions, and supernatural powers. The *tsaddikim* established lavish courts and exerted a great deal of influence over their followers. The masses expressed their allegiance through prayer, pilgrimages, the repetition of sermons, and other religious activities. The *misnagdim*—the rabbinical opponents who elevated ascetic Torah studies—were greatly offended by the mystical prayers and communication with the supernatural realm, and disparaged the *baalei shem* as superficial mystics and quack doctors.[39]

By the turn of the nineteenth century, Hasidism was firmly established as a folk movement, which then split into numerous branches, with large and small groups flourishing in Poland, Ukraine, Galicia, certain parts of Belarus, and various other corners of Eastern Europe. For the Russian government, the Hasidim was one dark mass of religious zealots, who "at time of prayer made loud, frightening noise—crying, clapping hands together, performing somersaults, swinging arms in all directions, while distorting and convulsing their bodies," in the words of Derzhavin.[40] He compared the Hasidim to Russian Orthodox schismatics who had deviated from established religious norms and set new customs for itself.[41]

In point of fact, important regional differences shaped the lifestyles and religious activities of Hasidic communities. Shneur Zalman's principal contribution to Habad was in the form of an intellectual spirituality and emphasis on practical action. After being charged with sedition, he told Russian interrogators that the Hasidim "fulfilled the commandments of God much more punctiliously than ordinary Jews, and even more than some of the ones learned in Torah."[42] For his part, Zalman took on the role of an educator and a spiritual guide. He never claimed that the holy spirit permeated his sermons. Zalman may have distanced himself from practical Kabbala practices—the ability to influence the supernatural realm by way of charms, amulets, and mystical prayers—but his conception of Judaism was nevertheless imbued with Kabbalistic doctrines.[43]

The thousands of Jews who visited Shneur Zalman's court rarely lived above the subsistence level. They came for advice, solace, and prayer, harboring intense expectations that the *tsaddik* would help with their earthly needs. Most people in the northwest provinces of the Russian Empire, including no small number of Jews in Velizh, possessed the barest necessities to feed their families. For the better part of the nineteenth century, Vitebsk province was in desperate economic shape. The provincial governor warned St. Petersburg that the "standard of living of the population would continue to decline if a positive resolution to the situation would not soon be found."[44] In the span of thirty years, between 1822 and 1852, the province was hit with ten disappointing harvests, three of which turned into famines.[45] The scarcity of resources and large-scale outbreaks of epidemics caused widespread misfortune. After a tour of the region in 1841, one inspector found that there was little or no maintenance of infrastructure in most provincial towns, including bridges, highways, and streets. Nor was there any new construction of town squares, public gardens, inns, and bridges. The morale of the population was so low that more people died by suicide (56) than by homicide (18).[46]

Russian administrators devised plans, usually with little foresight or creativity, to increase productivity. Authorities blamed the underdevelopment on two main factors: poor soil fertility, which contributed to the inconsistency in crop yields, and the Jewish monopolization of small-scale trade. It did not help matters that excessive rains curbed grain yields and damaged plant roots and hay.[47] The bulk of the government programs, including restrictions on Jewish commercial activities, did little to ease hunger problems or advance growth. The mass population transfers—the main conduit by which the state hoped to transform agricultural settlements—resulted in a severe loss of income for Polish landlords, fueled overcrowding, and ultimately did nothing to change the functional structure of the towns.[48] The idea was to remake urban centers into active sites of manufacturing and trade by replacing the Jewish cloth stall—the principal site of exchange—with large-scale industry.[49] But for the better part of the second quarter of the nineteenth century, much of the economic output consisted of cheap goods manufactured for local customers. Nearly 87 percent of the enterprises involved the production of wine and beer, 11 percent of brick and leather, and less than 2 percent of Jewish ritual garments, linens, glass, and wax candles.[50]

The Vitebsk provincial economy displayed striking similarities to that of sixteenth century Europe, where market towns within a radius of fifty to one hundred square miles consumed the bulk of the agricultural output. With the occupational structure firmly rooted in local households and villages and semiautonomous market towns, the main problem to overcome was how to expand interregional trade.[51] In the end, the commercial activities paled in comparison to what was happening in Podolia, Volynia, and Kiev (what is now Ukraine) or Nizhnii Novgorod (the Russian heartland). On a typical day at a local fair in a Ukrainian market town, customers could acquire an assortment of locally manufactured and imported goods, such as rolls of fine silk, velvet, satin fabric, caviar, coffee, Turkish beans, almonds, Chinese tea, boots, belts, smoked fish, and tobacco.[52] The Makar'ev Fair in Nizhnii Novgorod turned into the largest gathering in all of Europe, attracting Chinese and Jewish merchants, Russian textile producers, entertainers, and more than one million visitors annually.[53] By contrast, the Vitebsk provincial fairs were so poorly attended that merchants from neighboring regions decided that it was not worth the meager payoff to haul caravans of heavy merchandise over the long distances. The bulk of the Belarusian population lived in a state of semi-starvation and had no means to buy anything of material significance. In 1848, at the annual fair in Dinaburg, less than 37 percent of all goods were sold; the total was slightly lower for Drissa, at 35 percent. With respect to Velizh, in addition to poverty, epidemic diseases such as cholera and influenza contributed to the lackluster sales. "Locals are just too poor [to purchase goods]," one official noted tersely.[54]

In the second half of the nineteenth century, improvement in communications, infrastructure, and transportation, including large-scale railroad construction, played a significant role in linking Russia's regional economies with global markets. The industrial age altered the position of the retail trader and older ways of making money. Railway lines created extraordinary opportunities to connect provincial populations with settlements in distant corners of the empire. Newly established urban markets, from Warsaw and Odessa to St. Petersburg and Kazan, gradually replaced the marketplace and the seasonal fair. With the economy growing at a brisk rate of 5 percent annually, an increasing number of Jews took advantage of the transportation revolution and the relaxation of residence laws to travel to rapidly expanding urban centers in the Pale of Settlement and beyond, where they became highly visible participants in the wholesale industry, retail trade, banking, and middle-class professions.[55]

The railroad track never made it to Velizh. But at least ten steamships owned by two different companies transported a wide variety of textile goods, grains, and timber along the Western Dvina from the Gulf of Riga to the Russian interior, with stops in Polotsk, Vitebsk, and Velizh.[56] Although Vitebsk province was not entirely bypassed in Russia's great leap forward—the provincial capital, for instance, became a hub for merchants and troupes of touring actors and artists from St. Petersburg, Kiev, and Odessa—most people lived in a world that was strikingly similar to that of the 1820s and 1830s. According to the 1897 all-imperial census, 85.5 percent of the 1,489,245 inhabitants in the province continued to reside in the countryside; Velizh county continued to rank dead last in population density. Six of the eleven settlements designated as urban had a population of less than 10,000 (five of which with less than 5,200 inhabitants). The town of Velizh may have mirrored Russia's population explosion, nearly doubling in size from 6,953 in 1829 to 12,193 in 1897, but ranked a distant fourth behind Dvinsk (69,675), Vitebsk (65,871), and Polotsk (20,294).[57]

Comprising nearly 50 percent of the population, most Velizh Jews (numbering 5,989 in 1897) died in the same place where they were born. They were unable or unwilling to leave their hometown for long stretches of time. Jewish boys received their religious education in Hebrew in *kheyders*, while girls were taught Yiddish grammar and reading by private tutors. Very few children went on to study in a *besmedresh*, which marked the end not only of their religious education but also of their education generally.[58]

At the turn of the twentieth century, as before, Jews specialized in small-scale trade and the production of clothing, footwear, and crafts. They owned nearly all the shops, taverns, and inns in town. Some found work at paper or water mills or brick and candlestick factories. Most worked as bakers, tailors, shoemakers, butchers, carpenters, and distillers. Others caught fish, traded in livestock, and loaned money at interest. Abraham Cahan, the founder and longtime editor of the *Jewish Daily Forward* who spent some time teaching at a public school in Velizh in the late 1870s, remembered Jews as extraordinarily pious, superstitious, and set in their ways. Save for a few exceptions, they knew just enough Russian to haggle at the bazaar and communicate with their Belarusian neighbors, most of whom were "close to pure Russians in their speech and dress."[59] That said, however fundamental the changes in capitalist development may have been in the late Russian Empire, Velizh Jews lived their lives in much the same way that their parents and grandparents had before them.[60]

The development of a wide range of economic relationships between Jews and their neighbors allowed social contacts to broaden. Jews played visible roles in local economies by making and selling alcoholic beverages, trading and delivering goods and products, and managing noble estates. In the Lithuanian portion of the commonwealth, a handful of noblemen owned as much as 90 percent of the land. Jews performed such vital roles in local economies that they received communal protections, privileges, and support from the noblemen on whose estates they lived and worked.[61] For those Jews who lived in small market towns such as Velizh, handicrafts or commercial trade were the preferred occupations. But no matter what economic activities they practiced, Jews and their neighbors did not live in hermetic isolation or in clearly demarcated living quarters.[62]

Economic activities had important implications for the types of social relationships Jews and their neighbors formed. Commercial exchanges led to social connections, appreciation of religious differences, and even, on occasion, friendships.[63] At the same time, economic activities helped to produce many of the conflicts between neighbors. Individuals turned to local courts to protect their possessions and commodities from unlawful abuse. Imperial institutions structured people's lives, while civil law provided the necessary framework for establishing the rules and procedures that helped to mediate conflicts.[64] For cases involving litigants of different religious origin or social status, civil courts provided the most effective means of adjudicating disagreements. People turned to district or provincial courts to settle a broad range of issues involving contractual obligations, monetary compensation, rent, inheritance rights, and property.[65] Even in those instances when two Jews could have turned to the Jewish court system, they usually opted to use civil courts. For the ordinary person, the abstract principles of Jewish law proved difficult to comprehend, while a ruling based on established commercial practices made more practical sense.[66]

Not surprisingly, lawsuits represented only a fraction of the total number of disagreements that took place between neighbors. Then as now, neighborly disputes centered on mundane things: loud noise, verbal altercations, rowdy gatherings, rude comments and gestures, perceived slights, odd or malicious behavior, or anything else that might be interpreted as particularly rude or offensive. Scholars working on civil litigation practices in other settings observe that many more disputes are resolved amicably before they ever appear in court. In whatever time or place they live, in other words, people use all possible means to settle their differences by negotiating, persuading, and reasoning.[67] While most neighborly feuds were resolved informally, individuals turned to imperial Russian courts, in part, because they had few alternatives available to them in the first half of the nineteenth century. What else could they do, to whom could they turn, if a neighbor refused to return their debt, pay their rent, or fulfill their contractual obligation?

Social tensions were a fundamental, even productive, reality of everyday life.[68] But benign annoyances always had the potential of erupting into something much larger and sinister. It was not unusual for Jews and their neighbors to get into arguments, which on occasion could turn into fistfights, or for judges to punish residents for theft, arson, personal insults, offensive threats, and vandalism. According to one sample of criminal cases, theft and robbery accounted for most crimes committed by and against Jews.[69] Although homicide by Christians against Jews or Jews against Christians turned out to be an extraordinarily rare phenomenon, it was not uncommon for spontaneous disturbances to take place during religious ceremonies, as they did from time to time during the Paschal season, with the awesome power of solidifying social boundaries.

The market town was filled with filth and disease. Poorly ventilated and overcrowded homes facilitated influenzas and measles. Animals gave humans many of the worst infections, including tuberculosis and viral pox, while poor sanitation caused waterborne bacilli to germinate with frightening speed. Feces and other water pollutants insured the spread of polio, cholera, typhoid, viral hepatitis, whooping cough, and diphtheria. People with a low standard of living had a particularly hard time fighting off outbreaks of infectious diseases.[70] In their journeys across the Pale of Settlement, travelers recounted that inns were littered with "all kinds of slop and kitchen leftovers," and that streets were typically "narrow and impassably dirty." The huts, one observer wrote, "sagging and propped up on stakes, [resembled] not so much a human habitation as a barn." The economist Andrei Subbotin was struck by the unsightly "filth and stench" in Jewish courtyards, although he conceded that the buildings "turned out to be much cleaner inside than we expected."[71] Abraham Cahan recalled that Velizh was surrounded on all sides by "expanses of mud and puddles," the size of which he had never seen before.[72] Turning his attention to everyday afflictions, the ethnographer Moisei Berlin noted that young Jewish children were susceptible to hemorrhoids (from sitting down in one place for too long), consumption (from lack of fresh air and physical exercise), and scrofula (from unsanitary home environments and poor diet).[73] Thinking back to his childhood years, the Yiddish writer Yekhezkel Kotik remembered how every year epidemics would break out in his hometown. Children would fall ill with measles, smallpox, and scarlet fever. "Diseases, people believed, were inflicted by God himself, and the brackish pool [the section of the river alongside the bathhouse] was left to spread diseases and epidemics, year in, year out."[74]

In Vitebsk province, scurvy, catarrhal inflammation, scarlet fever, and bloody diarrhea were the chief biological killers.[75] Experts touring the region determined that improper diet, caused mainly by poor harvests, contributed to the high mortality rates. Animals desperate for nourishment were vulnerable as well. To understand the complexities of Russia's life, the most capable administrators urged their subordinates to compile accurate data about the state of the province. In 1827, more than 830 livestock succumbed to disease, causing an estimated 24,900 rubles in damage.[76] Nineteen years later, more than 13,750 horses, 72,000 horned cattle, and 95,200 small livestock reportedly died from eating plant toxins and contaminated grass.[77] The health crisis, for humans and animals, was probably much more severe than the raw numbers suggest. The Ministry of the Interior had a hard time trusting the data that were being compiled at the local level. To eradicate frightful afflictions and provide medical care in a timely manner, the *Vitebsk Provincial Gazette* urged physicians to report accurate numbers. Russian authorities were particularly concerned that neither public health workers nor private practitioners bothered to "report how many sick patients they treated or who had received the vaccinations."[78]

It was one thing to know what ailed people, but an entirely different matter to treat sick patients. In the second quarter of the nineteenth century, Vitebsk province lacked the basic infrastructure—hospitals, clinics, and poorhouses—to provide effective medical services. According to one inspection report, most of the facilities were housed in primitive buildings, which often lacked beds, clean linen, patient garments, medical supplies, and dishes. Even the largest public hospital in the provincial capital of Vitebsk struggled to maintain adequate sanitary conditions. Without enough trained doctors and medical assistants, it could not keep up with the growing demand in healthcare. Predictably, the situation turned out much worse in provincial towns such as Velizh and Polotsk, where patients were given their meals in "rotten wooden bowls."[79]

By the turn of the twentieth century, the situation in public healthcare showed no signs of improvement. Vitebsk province maintained ten public hospitals and sixty-nine pharmacies. But with only one certified physician for every 9,500 or more residents, sick people chose to visit a local apothecary to relieve their pain and discomfort instead of waiting in long lines at hospitals. Housed in a private home or shop, apothecaries were unofficial laboratories, specializing in secret medical products, usually of substandard quality, and exotic powders, spices, pills, balsams, healing herbs, oils, and rubs. At least 167 apothecaries were in operation, treating everything from syphilis, scarlet fever, dysentery, and the flu to typhoid, Siberian ulcers, whooping cough, and diphtheria. Health inspectors conceded that it was nearly impossible to close down the "underground pharmacies," run by healers with no proper medical training, because they "satisfied the needs of the masses."[80]

When dealing with health and disease, Jews and their Slavic neighbors shared a common cultural frame.[81] To manipulate reality, they filtered Latin, German, Polish, Ukrainian, Belarusian, and Yiddish elements and expressions. The remarkable elasticity of this system of thought meant that Jews and Slavs employed similar magical techniques to manipulate the natural world. A network of medical practitioners, folk healers, and sorcerers relied on a regimen of potions to treat common ailments and dysfunctions. They used plants, herbs, and roots to prepare special powders. One tried and tested remedy, designed to treat fevers, called for exactly seventy-seven grains of legumes to be poured into a special pot with a lid. The owner of the pot was required to urinate on the legumes and put soft mud around the lid so that it would stick firmly to the pot. Afterward, it was to be buried deep in the ground where no one would pass over it.[82] This and many other similar remedies made it into popular handbooks, filled with Kabbalistic references, alchemical and astrological symbols, and fancy diagrams. On other occasions the do-it-yourself concoctions were preserved for posterity in a rich oral folk culture, to which both communities contributed.

The *Vitebsk Provincial Gazette* featured numerous columns with homemade recipes treating everything from Siberian ulcers and diarrhea to common headaches and eye ailments.[83] To the believers, the folk cures possessed their own inherent logic. Slavs relied on a wide range of prayer formulas, spells, and objects to protect themselves and their loved ones against hidden dangers lurking within. Men and women employed techniques that touched on all aspects of the life cycle, including predicting the length of a person's life, discovering the sex of an unborn child, and warding off hidden dangers associated with death and afterlife. They turned to icons imbued with miraculous healing powers to protect homes from fires, cure blindness, and help with difficult childbirths. They cultivated elaborate friendships with their saints in search of wondrous medical cures for paralysis or arthritis. A touch of a saint's holy body, for instance, could heal an especially piercing toothache or a severe inflammation of the nerves. Rubbing a bit of holy oil was widely considered an indispensable treatment for a wide range of afflictions. Fortune-tellers used water, fire, and mirrors to look into the future to discover marriage prospects, address an evil spirit, or find a missing person. Dream and vision interpretation was considered a particularly effective method to gaze into personal fortunes and misfortunes.[84]

Belief in the power of magical cures was widespread among common town dwellers, as well as progressively educated elites. Pauline Wengeroff, who grew up in a wealthy and very pious Jewish home in Brest, recalled how a local folk healer eased pain and affliction. To ward off the evil eye, the healer would take a piece of clothing, usually a sock or a vest, whisper a secret text, and spit on it three times. For a toothache, he would lead the sick child outside at midnight to face the moon, and would first stroke the right cheek and then the left one, all the while murmuring mystical words. From Kislev until Adar on the Hebrew calendar (usually, November until February), Wengeroff also noted, her parents roasted goose fat in complete silence, so that the evil eye would not fall on it.[85] Yekhezkel Kotik's childhood was stricken by fears of evil spirits, demons, and witchcraft. To cure afflictions associated with the evil eye, local healers would rub small bones from a human skeleton or two eggs on the spot and whisper incantations. To cure nagging ailments, for both Jews and Christians, they would apply cupping glasses, administer enemas, and perform bloodletting.[86]

Attitudes toward the supernatural realm were eclectic and attracted a diverse group of practitioners. Tales of spirit possession—the phenomenon that an alien spirit, either a dead human or departed soul, entered a person and controlled that person's actions—enjoyed immense popularity.[87] Hasidic parables and tales, as told by *tsaddikim* to their followers, revealed how wandering souls entered the body of a living person to either fulfill a mitzvah or atone for a sin. They described the proliferation of dark forces in everyday life and the triumph of *tsaddikim* over the powers of impurity.[88] Kotik recalled how everyone in his hometown believed in the existence of demons, devils, and evil spirits. The teachers would "stuff the heads of their pupils with innumerable tales of devils' doings." They knew exactly what awaited a man as soon as he entered the world to come, and how he ascended to heaven. When someone would die that person would be "laid out on the floor, not on the bare floor, but on straw, so that each wisp pricks him a thousand needles. Then evil spirits surround him during the funeral procession. And when the body is lowered into the grave, the Angel of Dumah ... rips open his belly, plucks out his guts, and flings them into his face. He then turns the corpse over, strikes it with a white-hot iron rod, subjects it to excruciating torture, and finally tears the body to pieces."[89]

The power to heal and to harm developed in relation to one another. The invisibility of demons was their most frightful attribute. Jews experimented with an eclectic mix of magical practices to counteract elements deemed harmful or suspicious. To protect their earthly possessions, they wore protective amulets containing biblical texts, numerical and alphabetical codes, and precious stones. They hung mezuzahs outside their doors and recited the Shema (the oldest fixed prayer in Judaism) into their children's ears while they were asleep.[90] No less significant were the ways in which the diabolical anti-world played in creating strains, divisions, and fears in daily life. Since the late Middle Ages, an extensive Christian folklore had told elaborate stories of Jewish sorcery, the potency of blood, and the salvific powers of human sacrifice. The conviction that Jews deployed magic to inflict harm on their neighbors ran deep in the popular imagination. In Velizh, as in so many other small towns in the borderlands, tales about evil Jews and ritual murder circulated by word of mouth in streets, taverns, and courtyards.[91]

3

Tsar Alexander Pays a Visit

IN APRIL 1825, TSAR ALEXANDER I and his wife, Elizabeth Alekseevna, decided to take a holiday somewhere warm before the start of the autumn rain. They talked of Germany and Italy but in the end agreed on Taganrog, a quiet port town on the Azov Sea. Elizabeth's health had deteriorated, and she often took to her chamber for days at a time. The route Alexander chose ensured that every arrangement had been made to guarantee her rest and comfort. They would avoid major urban centers, where there would be official processions and exhausting religious ceremonies. From St. Petersburg, they would proceed due south to Velizh, turn southeast by way of Dorogobuzh, Roslavl, Novgorod-Severskii, and Belgorod, and pass through Bakhmut before reaching their destination. After months of careful planning, Alexander left the imperial capital on September 1, three days before Elizabeth. Traveling some 1,400 miles at a reckless pace in a carriage drawn by three horses, Alexander took exactly thirteen days to reach the Azov Sea.[1]

The tsar tried to keep his travel plans a secret. In the last years of his life, dissatisfied with himself and his accomplishments, Alexander preferred to spend his days in solitude and quiet. News, however, not only reached the diplomatic corps in the capital but the provincial towns along the mapped out itinerary as well. The moment he set foot in Velizh on September 4, Alexander was handed a complaint by none other than Maria Terenteeva:

> In the year 1823 (I can't recall the exact month and date) a misfortune befell my son. In the town of Velizh, in Vitebsk province, the Jews, residents of that town, stabbed my son Demian Emelianov [*sic*] to death on the Slobotsky Bridge. I only recall the names Iuzik and his wife Khanna who grabbed [my son] on the bridge and killed him. Because of this incident, I personally asked the chief of police, whose name I don't know, to grant me legal protection, but he declined my request. I've seen him six times to demand my rights, but instead he ordered that I be kept under police watch and be given twelve kopeks a day. Although I'm free now, I want to live without harassment in my town of Velizh. The Jews told me repeatedly that they're planning on kidnapping me, and I'm still running away from them. Now, as a result of the loss of my son by people who don't believe in Christ our lord, I've come running to the feet of your imperial majesty, begging for your royal protection.[2]

Notwithstanding Terenteeva's far-fetched claim that the boy in question was her biological son or the fact that she did not even get the name right, Alexander took the murder charge seriously. He immediately forwarded the complaint to Nikolai Nikolaevich Khovanskii, the governor-general of Vitebsk, Mogilev, Smolensk, and Kaluga provinces, who was residing at the time in the provincial capital of Vitebsk.

Like so many talented young noblemen, Khovanskii began his career in the military. He swiftly rose through the ranks, distinguishing himself for his meritorious duties in the Russian-Turkish War in 1810 and once more in the Napoleonic Campaign. In 1813, he was promoted to lieutenant general. Eight years later, he relocated to St. Petersburg to serve as senator in the First Department. The same year that Fedor's body was found in the woods, Khovanskii was promoted to full general with an appointment as the governor-general of the northwest provincial region, a post he held until 1836. As part of a transformation of government in the late eighteenth century, the office of the governor-general served as the most important intermediary between the imperial center and the provincial world. His duties included promoting agriculture,

industry, and economy; keeping roads in working order; providing for the poor and needy; and maintaining law and security. Most important, the statesman enjoyed extensive policing authority over the region he governed. Although Khovanskii did not have formal judicial powers and could not receive appeals against provincial court decisions, he could order criminal investigations and interfere in both civil and criminal procedure as he saw fit.[3]

Terenteeva's complaint set off a chain of events that resulted in an extraordinarily complex criminal investigation. Alexander I died suddenly on November 19, 1825. The accession of Nicholas I to the throne signaled the beginning of an aggressively conservative political agenda. The Decembrist Rebellion of December 14, 1825, created an atmosphere of fear, hostility, and crisis that would dominate Nicholas's reign. To promote his supreme authority, Nicholas championed military discipline and the official defense of the Russian Orthodox Church. In the second quarter of the nineteenth century, Nicholas received disturbing reports from all corners of the vast empire: of religious perversion, spirit possession, and rebellion.[4] Dedicated to policing the boundaries of true belief, the regime threw its moral weight into imposing harsh penalties for behavior deemed especially dangerous to the social order. Efforts to suppress sectarian communities who deviated from established religious doctrines resulted in dozens of arrests, trials, and forced resettlements. Given the wider preoccupations with strange and unnatural activities, the Russian government saw no choice but to respond to blood libel allegations in a most serious manner. After all, even the Skoptsy, considered the most pernicious of the sects for dismembering their bodies, was not accused of practicing cold-blooded murder as a religious rite.[5]

On November 4, 1825, nearly twelve months after the Vitebsk provincial court wrote off Fedor's death to the "will of God," the governor-general reopened the case. Khovanskii's first order of business was to appoint inspector-councilor Vasilii Ivanovich Strakhov as the lead investigator to the case. Trained as a civil servant, Strakhov had climbed to the respectable rank of fifth grade. His assignment was straightforward: to follow routine administrative procedure, question every individual linked to the crime, and bring the investigation to a timely resolution.

The criminal file before him totaled nearly one thousand pages, containing, among other things, police and autopsy reports, material evidence, and dozens of depositions. A survey of the town revealed that there was no shortage of witnesses to interview, even though several individuals who played a key role in the case had died. Fedor's mother, Agafia Prokof'eva, passed away approximately four months after her son's body was found in the woods. In less than twelve months after the Vitebsk provincial court acquitted the Jews of the ritual murder charge, Mirka Aronson had passed away as well. Several other important suspects, including Shmerka Berlin and Iosel' Glikman, would die long before the investigation was completed.

Strakhov realized that the events in Velizh were extraordinarily confusing, and that first he needed to get the facts of the case straight. With the presumption of guilt running against Jews, the inspector-councilor decided not to jump to hasty conclusions. Instead, he talked at length to several Christian residents who were either directly related to Fedor, such as the father and aunt, or had served as important witnesses in the case, but no one revealed anything different from what they testified originally.[6] Strakhov then turned his attention to the star witness, Maria Terenteeva, at which point the investigation took an unexpected turn. Why did the beggar woman refer to the boy as her own son? Surely, Terenteeva did this for good reason, and Strakhov had every intention of getting to the bottom of things as quickly as possible.

Strakhov summoned Maria Terenteeva for an interview on November 22, 1825. Terenteeva, encouraged to speak freely and at length, began her story just as she had in 1823. On Easter Sunday at noontime, she explained, she was walking back home from the town center. After passing a castle and several empty storefronts, she descended a small slope to the Slobotsky Bridge. "At that very moment, I heard a little girl call out something to a little boy. I noticed Khanna Tsetlina standing nearby. She gave the boy a piece of sugar and grabbed him by the arm and escorted him to her cottage." Fearing that something was terribly amiss, Maria decided to follow Khanna. She clearly remembered, as if it were yesterday, that Khanna's housekeeper, Avdotia Maksimova, and three Jewish women, none of whom she had seen before, opened the front door when they came inside the courtyard. Avdotia said something in Yiddish to Khanna, which she could not understand, and motioned everyone inside.[7]

What happened next Maria observed with her own eyes. In hopes of protecting the child, Maria told the people around her that Fedor was her son. "No one paid any attention to me," Maria explained. "Instead, they proceeded to do unimaginable horrors to the boy. Avdotia locked the boy inside an adjoining chamber. Khanna fed me wine until my head began to spin and then told me to leave." Inebriated, Maria did not have the strength to walk back home, so she curled up on the porch and slept for several hours. It was late in the evening when she finally woke up. Khanna gave her vodka and two silver rubles, and they all walked across the market square to Mirka Aronson's large brick house. One of Aronson's servants opened the gate and immediately ushered the boy down to the cellar, at which point Aronson handed Maria two more silver rubles and vodka and made her promise not to say a word to anyone about what she had witnessed. Maria did not know what the Jewish women intended to do with the boy, but she warned them, "If I find out whose boy this is, I'll reveal everything."[8]

It turned out that this was not the first time that Khanna Tsetlina asked Maria to "bring back" an innocent child. Even if Maria could not recall the precise date, she distinctly remembered Khanna asking for a "good Christian boy," to which she responded by saying that she "didn't know of such a boy." Now, after having witnessed a most disturbing scene unfold, her mood changed for the worse. On her walk home—she rented a small room on the outskirts of town across the river—she felt as though the entire town was watching her every move. She recalled that a little white dog, or perhaps a rabbit, ran between her legs. "I fell flat on my face," she went on, "and as I was lying on the ground, such a tremendous burden weighed on me that I wasn't able to stand up for quite some time." When she finally made it home, Maria told her landlady everything that she witnessed, but decided to keep quiet about what happened inside Mirka Aronson's house. To her surprise, her landlady revealed that the Jews had ritually murdered Emel'ian Ivanov's little boy.[9]

On the third day of Easter week, Maria was walking around town begging for alms when she decided to stop by Emel'ian Ivanov's cottage. She found both parents in tears. They had searched everywhere for their son, so they told her, and even used a special map and magic straws to help them locate their son. Not knowing what else to do or whom to turn to, they decided to visit a local fortune-teller. But the fortune-teller was not very helpful. "What kind of a fortune-teller can't predict where your son is?" Maria fumed. "Besides, how can a young boy suddenly disappear in such a small town?" She offered her services and asked them to bring her wax and a cup of water. Later that week, Maria went over to the cottage to see if they were able to locate the boy. "Why didn't you go out to look?" Maria inquired. "How can we?" Ivanov shouted back. "It was you who killed him!" But no matter how awful Ivanov's accusation may have been, Maria maintained her innocence. She emphasized that she had no intention of "spreading wild rumors or saying anything objectionable about anyone" and that she visited Ivanov "without pretense or ill will."[10]

The moment Maria left Ivanov's cottage, she walked directly to Mirka Aronson's brick house. Together with five other Jews, all of whom she could easily identify, Maria went down to the basement and saw the boy on the ground wrapped in linen. A basin filled with blood stood nearby. The body and the head were pierced all over, the nails on the hands and toes trimmed to the very tips, the tongue completely severed, as was his penis, directly at the scrotum. Surprisingly, Maria did not see blood on either the body or the cloth. The moment that Jews "screamed for her to get out of the cellar," she decided to go back home. The next day one of Maria's neighbors informed her that the body had been found and the police were looking for her. "If they are looking for me," Maria snapped, "then I'll go talk to them myself." She told Strakhov that she described everything just as she did in the summer of 1823 save for two important details: that she took money and spirits from Mirka and Khanna and that she helped Khanna transfer the body to the woods in a spring britzka.[11]

To the question of why she referred to herself as the boy's mother, Maria had a simple explanation. "Ever since Agafia Prokof'eva passed away, I considered the boy my own. When the father, Emel'ian Ivanov, didn't make the slightest effort to search for him, I decided to take matters into my own hands and [to seek justice] myself. When Tsar Alexander passed through Velizh, I seized the opportunity to deliver the petition. And just as Alexander was leaving the St. Nicholas Cathedral,

I got down on both knees and placed the piece of paper on his crown. A man by the name of Luk Oleinikov wanted to take it away from me, but the crowd that had gathered around didn't let him." "But why call the boy Demian?" Strakhov inquired. "For the simple reason," Maria reasoned, "that she had forgotten his name; it was a mistake."[12]

Maria concluded the testimony by describing how unbearable life had become because of dealings with the Jews. The first incident took place when she purchased a piece of herring from Avdotia Maksimova. One Sunday morning, at the beginning of the Lenten season, she noticed Avdotia sitting at a stall at the marketplace selling herring. Avdotia immediately ran up to Maria to see if she was interested in buying a nice fatty fish. Maria, deciding to do her acquaintance a favor, bought the herring. But when she tried to clean it that afternoon, the fish inexplicably slipped out of her hands, falling flat on the ground at least four times. Maria finally got a hold of it and managed to tear it in half with her bare hands, giving a piece to her landlady and saving the rest for herself. The landlady, fearing that someone must have contaminated the fish, ate a small bite and immediately felt sick to her stomach; the vomiting continued all day and night. After finishing her portion, Maria did not feel anything unusual, but the moment she woke up the next morning her stomach began to cramp. For three days and nights, she vomited blood with such intensity that she thought she would die right there and then. Her landlady instructed her to tell the authorities what had happened, but the only thing the town mayor did was "to warn Maria not to buy anything from the kikes."[13]

The final episode occurred around twelve months after little Fedor's death. Maria was certain that, if she ever tried to leave town, the Jews would find a way to harm her. It was late in the evening when she decided to fetch fresh water from the river. The moment that she passed by Gavrilov's house, forty Jews, none of whom she had ever seen before, encircled her and grabbed her violently by the hair. When she began to scream, they all hid inside the house. A few days later (it was the Jewish Sabbath) the Jewess Leia asked Maria if she would be interested in milking her cows. Maria agreed to perform the deed, and while she was milking the cows, the Jew Abram and two Jewesses, none of whom she had ever seen before, entered the courtyard. They all went inside Leia's house, at which point Abram's wife Nakhana [Khanna Tsetlina's sister] revealed the real reason they summoned her. They wanted to dress Maria in Jewish clothing and take her "somewhere important." Maria explained that the Jewesses "ordered her to take off her simple peasant blouse and handed her a dress, two sheepskin overcoats, and two Jewish-looking shawls." And as they were walking down to the river, they ran into an old acquaintance who asked where she was going. "My God, I don't even know myself," Maria responded, "apparently to the very same house where they murdered the soldier's boy." Lots of people had gathered on the street that day. Maria recalled that two clergymen came over to warn her that she should never "trust the kikes," and so she promptly undressed and went back home.[14]

Jews, at all levels of society, employed Christians as drivers, wet nurses, watchmen, cooks, governesses, and maids. The reasons had to do as much with economic considerations as with pressure to conform to halakhic traditions. It was not uncommon for a well-to-do family to employ half a dozen or more Christian servants, the vast majority of whom came from the margins of society and were usually homeless and without permanent employment.[15] In addition to working around the clock, they labored on the Sabbath and on holidays when Jews were prohibited from carrying objects from one domain to another, preparing fires, traveling outside boundary limits, delivering letters, fetching beer and bread, preparing the samovar, transporting freight, and buying goods on market days.

Since early modern times, the Catholic Church had spoken out against arrangements involving direct physical contact between Jews and Christians. Sexual relations between Jewish employers and their Christian maids were not uncommon, and authorities viewed poor maidens as particularly vulnerable to temptations. Cautioning against the Jewish employment of Christian wet nurses, governesses, and servants, the Catholic Church threw its moral power into imposing strict cultural boundaries.[16] To avoid violent religious encounters, including blood accusations, Jewish councils imposed the ecclesiastical legislation on their own communities.[17]

The realities on the ground made it nearly impossible to limit social interactions.[18] Nevertheless, long after the partitions of the commonwealth, Russian authorities tried to regulate Jewish-Christian domestic arrangements.[19] Sensational stories of conversions, secret liaisons, and sexual transgression heightened fears of young maidens falling prey to Jewish influence. In 1817, for instance, two Catholic domestic servants decided to secretly convert to Judaism in a Jewish cemetery so as to escape notice. Subsequently, one of the women agreed to marry a Jewish man. The Jew forced his young impressionable wife and her friend to relocate to a nearby province to start a new life, where he eventually abandoned both women, leaving them to their own tragic fate.[20]

As this and other similar cases were being adjudicated, the Russian government passed a series of laws that banned peasants from working for and with Jews in almost every capacity (from transportation to construction to domestic service): Jews who maintained post offices were not permitted to reside in buildings occupied by Christian workers, Jewish artisans could work with a Christian apprentice only when one other Christian worker was present, Christian wet nurses were banned from feeding Jewish children under any circumstances, and Jews were prohibited from employing Christian servants in intimate domestic spaces. All these prohibitions emerged out of fears that young Christian women would develop intimate ties with Jewish men and be tempted to convert to the Jewish faith.[21]

Concerns over proselytism and debauchery intensified as communities of ethnic Russians known as Subbotniks (or Sabbatarians) appeared in the 1820s in Astrakhan, Riazan, and Saratov provinces. Although their beliefs and practices varied widely, Subbotniks generally followed Jewish teachings and ethical traditions, with some going so far as marrying Jews, observing Jewish dietary customs and holidays, praying in Hebrew, and wearing fringed garments and phylacteries. Almost always, officials attributed the growth of the sectarian communities to pernicious Jewish influence on Russian peasantry. In an effort to limit boundary crossings, the Russian government took drastic steps by uprooting and banishing Subbotniks to the far corners of the empire.[22]

The story Terenteeva told thus resonated with profound anxieties of Jewish enticement and transgression that were being discussed in administrative circles. Strakhov understood that female domestic servants played an important economic role in the Jewish household and that they had access to its most intimate quarters. It was not unusual for servants to eat with Jewish families at the same table, instruct Jewish children in their languages, and sleep with Jews in the same room.

The intimacy of the domestic arrangements meant that impressiona-ble young women would invariably learn Jewish customs and rituals not only by observation but also by active participation.[23] Terenteeva's confession revealed many new insights, although on occasion she said things that directly contradicted her previous statements. Strakhov was well aware of this fact. But at this point in the investigation, he showed no interest in forcing his star witness to resolve the ambiguities. Instead, what he decided to do was to push ahead with his work. He summoned two crucial witnesses, Avdotia Maksimova and Praskoviia Kozlovskaia, into the interrogation chamber, both of whom, it turned out, had direct knowledge of Jewish ways of life.

While working as a domestic servant for the Tsetlin family, Avdotia Maksimova was able to learn Yiddish quite well. Although she had a hard time expressing herself in the language, she had no problem under-standing everything the Jews talked about. This is why Strakhov con-sidered Avdotia a particularly important witness in the case. Strakhov talked with her on December 4, 1825, almost two weeks after he first interviewed Terenteeva. In painstaking detail, she described how for four straight days she transferred the boy back and forth between Khanna's and Mirka's homes. At times, she made the short walk across the mar-ket square under the cover of darkness. On other occasions, she did so during broad daylight. One day in particular stood out for her. Khanna asked Avdotia to go over to Mirka's tavern to purchase a glass of red wine for her ill son. When she went down to the cellar, she "saw something covered in linen lying on the ground." She immediately walked over to the spot, unwrapped the cloth, and to her surprise saw the dead body. A Jew she had never seen before yelled at her to mind her own business, while someone else handed her another glass of red wine and told her to get out of the cellar. Everything happened so quickly, as if in a dream, that she did not even have time to notice if the body was punctured. When she finally made it home, Avdotia told Khanna Tsetlina every-thing that had taken place that night, but the only thing Khanna did was give her a five-ruble coin, making her promise not to say a word to anyone about what she had seen.[24]

The longer Avdotia talked, the more confusing her story became. Strakhov quickly realized that Avdotia's linguistic abilities proved sounder than her recollection of the events. In the second interview,

which took place the next day, on December 5, Avdotia not only impli-
cated herself in the case, but also contradicted several important assertions made by Terenteeva. It was Avdotia (and not Maria) who helped
Glikman and his son Abram deposit the body into the woods. So certain
of this fact, Avdotia testified that she would have no problem pointing
out the very spot where they buried the body.[25]

Avdotia went on to describe how on Easter Monday Glikman and
Abram came over to Khanna Tsetlina's to ask where they should dispose of the body. The Jews posed the same question to Avdotia as well.
"Sooner or later," Avdotia told them, "they'll find out who spilled
Christian blood." She suggested that they take the body to the outskirts of town and hide it in the thick woods. Late that evening, Iosel'
and Abram came by the house in a spring britzka. Khanna woke up
Avdotia and ordered her to wash off all the blood that had dried up
on the body. And as she was performing the task, Avdotia noticed that
the entire body was covered with "tiny little wounds, as though [it] was
pierced with a knife, with the member severed." Afterward, she finished
off all the wine that Khanna offered her and set off in the britzka in a
drunken state. "After all," she testified, "a servant is obliged to follow
her mistress's orders." Avdotia admitted that much of what she had
disclosed contradicted her initial statement, but she was convinced that
the discrepancies were due to memory lapse, confusion, and the fact that
she was frightened the Jews would harm her.[26]

The twenty-two-year-old Praskoviia Kozlovskaia (née Pilenkova)
worked as a domestic servant for Mirka Aronson in the spring of 1823.
A Uniate by birth, she received the sacrament of confession every year.
When the boy disappeared, Praskoviia lived in Aronson's attic with two
other domestic workers, a young Jewish girl from Velizh and an elderly
Jewish woman who hailed originally from Vitebsk. Praskoviia worked
for Mirka Aronson until the autumn of 1824, when she moved out to
a nearby village to live with her uncle Luk Oleinikov (the same man
who had handwritten the complaint Terenteeva presented to the tsar).
At some point before the investigation was reopened in the fall of 1825,
she married a Polish nobleman, and the couple decided to move back
to town.[27]

At Mirka Aronson's, Proskoviia's domestic duties did not include anything out of the ordinary. She lit and maintained the fireplace, brought

fresh water from the well, swept and cleaned the rooms, and prepared the samovar. Most days she cleaned the front chambers of the house, where Shmerka and Slava Berlin and their children resided. Rarely did she visit the rooms in the back of the house. She distinctly remembered, however, that a townsman and his daughter of either Russian or Polish origin rented one of the back rooms, while the upstairs was reserved for guests who would come to town on business. From the attic window, Praskoviia had an excellent view of the market square, from where she was able to observe everyone who entered and left the building. Significantly, although Praskoviia testified that Glikman and his son had come by the house, she did not detect any unusual activity. From one of the other domestic servants, she learned that two Jews had come to town to purchase hay, but she did not know whether they were successful in their endeavors. She recalled that they went somewhere every day, but she had no idea where exactly they went or if they ever left town. She also could not recall seeing anything suspicious in Aronson's cellar. In fact, Praskoviia maintained that she did not know very much about the murder—only the fact that she had heard rumors that Jews were responsible for the boy's death. In closing, Praskoviia revealed that she had been acquainted with Maksimova for a long time but crossed paths for the very first time with Terenteeva at the magistrate's office the day she was brought in for questioning.[28]

The inspector-councilor understood all too well that the criminal law code called for firm empirical evidence to establish the crime of ritual murder. He did not need to be reminded that provincial courts had summarily dismissed all the accusations that had popped up in recent years or, for that matter, that a careful review of the case by the highest court in the province did not net anything conclusive. History may not have been on Strakhov's side, but the stories he heard proved too disturbing not to take seriously. The oral interrogations brought an entirely new perspective on the case. How could he overlook the confessions? After all, Terenteeva and Maksimova did not only claim to have witnessed the murder firsthand; they also admitted to having actively participated in the ritual of blood sacrifice.

Thus, no matter how contradictory the testimony may have been, it seemed to point to one thing: that the Jews sacrificed the little boy to mix his blood with matzo. An impressive collection of materials—vivid eyewitness testimony, forensic-medical evidence, material proof, and community report of reputation—helped substantiate the charge. Inquisitorial procedure called on investigators to work on the assumption that, where a crime was committed, a criminal must be punished.[29] But who killed the little boy? What motives were behind the diabolical crime? And how far had the conspiracy run? Strakhov had no easy answers. "From the very beginning of the investigation," Strakhov reported to the governor-general, "not one hour has been wasted." But instead of bringing the case to a timely resolution, as he had hoped to do, the inspector-councilor had become increasingly perplexed by the stories he heard, as the women "first confessed to one thing and then to something else entirely."[30]

Determined to solve the case, Strakhov took all three suspect-witnesses into custody: Terenteeva on November 19, 1825, Maksimova on December 1, and Kozlovskaia on December 15. That December he took in two additional suspects: Anna Eremeeva, the homeless girl with psychic powers who played such an important role in the first stage of the investigation, and an eighteen-year-old servant named Melania Zhelnova who worked for the Tsetlin family. Strakhov concluded that Eremeeva had learned the details of the crime from Terenteeva, most likely when the outcasts were walking around town begging for alms. Zhelnova, for her part, did not reveal anything of significance in a preliminary interview. Although both women were placed under house arrest for the duration of the investigation, they wound up playing an insignificant role.[31]

Having become convinced that Jews committed premeditated murder with ritual intent, Strakhov focused his energies on obtaining an airtight confession. Working late into the evening, the inspector-councilor pressed for more information and the clarification of crucial details. All evidence suggests that the interrogation sessions were unusually long and strenuous. In all probability, so Strakhov reckoned, the Jews first tortured the little boy and then, shortly before conspiring to commit the murder, forced all three women to renounce the Christian faith and convert to Judaism. Like any seasoned criminal investigator whose ultimate goal is to ensure the conviction of the suspects, it seems reasonable to conclude that Strakhov not only formed a theory of the crime, but also played a central role in shaping the narrative.[32]

Inquisitorial procedure involved the collection, interpretation, and weighing of a sequence of legal proofs. The courts gave predetermined weight to testimony based on the social and religious status, age, and sex of the witness. As exclusive arbiter over the collection and interpretation of evidence, Strakhov was keenly aware that prisoners could construct a false confession or maintain their claims to innocence. According to the sequence of proofs, voluntary confession stood at the very top, followed by medical and witnesses' testimony, written statements, community report of reputation, and the purifying oath.[33] Bearing a special stamp of authenticity, confession articulates unrealized truths and inner secrets, without which Strakhov would not have been able to establish guilt or move forward with the investigation. As the lead investigator in the case, Strakhov worked hard to create a special bond between the confessant and confessor. By controlling the conversations, he hoped to activate elements of dependency, subjugation, and fear.[34]

Strakhov could have applied any number of coercive methods to get Terenteeva, Maksimova, and Kazlovskaia to open up. But the inspector-councilor had no intention in distancing himself from the most important witnesses in the case. More than anything else, he wanted to gain their trust in the hope they would reveal the hidden truths of the crime and name all the co-conspirators in the affair. Experimenting with several different techniques, Strakhov eventually settled on the most merciful approach in his arsenal. Following the first principle of the inquisitorial mode, he instructed the women to attend church services, with the expectation that the liturgy would stir emotions and induce confession. Markelom Tarashkevich, the Uniate priest at the St. Il'insk Church, played a decisive role in getting the women to talk. At the outset, Tarashkevich made it clear to the suspect-witnesses that he wanted them to tell "only the truth," while admonishing them of the consequences if they decided to resist.[35]

In the end, the visits to Tarashkevich proved invaluable. Although they did not agree on all the details of the crime sequence, Terenteeva and Maksimova confirmed their role in the murder conspiracy quickly. At first, Kozlovskaia gave Strakhov an unusually hard time, but the longer they talked, the more coherent was her narrative. Strakhov spoke with Terenteeva on no fewer than seven occasions, with Maksimova nine times, and Kozlovskaia six times.[36] In the spring of 1826, Strakhov announced to the governor-general that "Maria Terenteeva's and Avdotia Maksimova's confessions revealed that the boy Fedor Emel'ianov had been abducted because of Jews' beliefs and enticements."[37] By April 1827, after several more rounds of interviews, Strakhov was able to obtain a full confession from Kozlovskaia as well.

After many months of intense work, Strakhov was able to get Terenteeva, Maksimova, and Kozlovskaia to corroborate each other's testimonies to the last intimate detail. The richly textured story contained all the salient tropes of the ritual murder drama as enacted in settings around the world: of deceit and conspiracy, sexual transgression and apostasy, and shockingly cruel actions inspired by fanatical rituals. It also contained many familiar motifs and stock characters such as the Christian maidservant who was intimately familiar with Jewish affairs and religious rites.[38] Ultimately, what began as a set of discrete, highly fragmented testimonies turned into a tightly controlled confessional narrative, with four principal elements: abduction, torture, conversion, and aftermath.

In the final form, Khanna Tsetlina masterminded the affair, and Maria Terenteeva, contrary to previous accounts, was the one who enticed the boy with the sugar. On Easter Sunday the beggar woman came by the Tsetlin home for a visit, as she did on occasion. Khanna gave her wine and a five-ruble silver coin and instructed her to bring back a Christian boy. Although Maria refused at first, Khanna reassured her that the boy would be loved and cared for, at which point she gave her two additional silver rubles, more wine, and the sugar. Avdotia Maksimova overheard the entire conversation. Later that afternoon, she greeted Maria and the boy at the gate. There were many Jews at the Tsetlin home, including Khanna and Evzik Tsetlin, their daughter Itka, and nanny Risa. The moment that Maria and Avdotia were safely inside, Khanna offered more wine, making them promise not to say a word to anyone.[39]

Under cover of darkness, they sneaked the boy across the marketplace to Mirka Aronson's house, where Shmerka and Slava Berlin enclosed the child in a tiny little room. Maria spent Holy Week (excluding Saturday, the obligatory day of rest for Jews) transferring the boy back and forth between the two homes. That Wednesday, Khanna instructed Avdotia to place the boy in an old chest that was used to store bottled preserves. To make sure that no one would locate him, they decided to wrap him in linen. So the boy would not suffocate, the door of the chest was left slightly ajar to let in a bit of air. Maria noted that this was why the investigators were not able to locate the boy when they searched Aronson's house. Avdotia observed that Jews "withheld food and drink the entire week," while Praskoviia revealed that "special guards were stationed outside the house the entire time the investigators conducted the investigation."[40]

At the back of the house, in the middle of a large chamber room, a wooden barrel lined with steel nails hung on a rope directly from the ceiling. A table covered with a white tablecloth, with a large candelabrum and candlesticks, stood adjacent to the window facing the courtyard. To get them in the mood, Khanna and Mirka offered Maria and Avdotia wine and an assortment of snacks and afterward told them to throw the body in the river as soon as they collected the blood. At that point, Maria and Avdotia went down to the cellar to fetch the boy. While they were undressing him, Praskoviia walked in and mumbled something under her breath. Avdotia immediately told Slava not to let Prakoviia leave the room, warning her that she would meet the same fate if she dared disobey. Praskoviia fetched a copper basin and fresh water. Maria grabbed the boy by his face, placed him on the table, and carefully washed the body, from head to toe, before enclosing him in the wooden barrel. All the Jews who had gathered around took turns swinging the boy back and forth; the ritual lasted nearly two hours. When he was finally taken out, the entire body looked bright red, as if the skin had been burned. Fedor was placed on top of the table, at which point Shifra Berlina trimmed the boy's nails and Poselennoi circumcised him.[41]

The time had now come to take the boy to the "great Jewish school" or "synagogue," as it was called on occasion. Located on Shkolina Street, around a two-minute walk from the marketplace, the school was taller than all the buildings in its vicinity and played a central role in Jewish communal life. It was still dark outside when the boy was brought to the school, where a large group of Jews had gathered. Maria covered the boy's mouth with a handkerchief to prevent anyone from hearing him scream. Fedor was placed on another table covered with a white tablecloth with both of his legs and hands firmly bound together with a leather belt. Maria started the ritual by softly slapping the boy's cheeks two times. Avdotia and the Jews took turns doing the exact same thing. Poselennoi handed Maria a steel object that resembled a nail, and ordered her to puncture the skin just below the boy's left nasal passage.

The thought of injuring the boy frightened Maria, and when she saw blood, she threw the nail on the ground. Poselennoi handed the nail to Avdotia who pierced the right side in the same exact manner. For the next several minutes, Maria, Avdotia, and the Jews took turns stabbing the boy's body. The boy screamed in pain, but after a few minutes passed, offered a timid smile until he finally lost consciousness and died. When Maria took him out of the basin, the entire body was pierced with tiny little holes covered in blood. Avdotia cleansed Maria with a special liquid, and then proceeded to dress the boy in the same exact clothes he wore when he set out on his walk on Easter Sunday.[42]

Fearing that their secrets would be exposed, the Jews forced all three women to convert to the Jewish faith. Whereas Praskoviia converted to Judaism only a few hours before the boy was tortured and ritually sacrificed, Maria and Avdotia partook in an elaborate conversion ceremony several days before the kidnapping. It was Holy Wednesday when the medical healer Orlik Devirts invited Maria to his home. Offering her wine, he warned her that authorities would exile her to Siberia if she refused to convert. Maria did exactly as she was told. Orlik led her to the Jewish school, where a group of Jews had gathered, many of whom she had never seen before. Maria drank a glass of bread wine and immediately became inebriated. Three Jews proceeded to take off all her clothing, and as she sat drunk and naked on the floor, they washed her with wine or some special liquid that stung her skin. Afterward, so as to mask her identity, they dressed her in a man's overcoat and took her to the river, where she was immersed in the water. Before bringing her back to the school, the Jews sprinkled warm water on her.[43]

In a ritual resembling the witches' sabbath, Maria passed through a fire ring and stood on top of a sweltering hot iron pan. The Jews encircled Terenteeva so that she would not be able to escape. They covered her mouth so she would not be able to scream and ordered her to swear allegiance to the Jewish nation, renounce her Christian beliefs, and accept the tenets of the Jewish faith. Only after she agreed did they permit her to step down from the hot iron pan. Afterward, Maria put on a special blouse and rubbed her burned feet with yellow ointment.

She then stood in front of a wooden cabinet (Torah ark), where the Commandments (Torah scrolls) were hidden behind a curtain.[44]

As Maria sat in front of the Torah ark on the very tips of her fingers, covered in a black and white prayer shawl, Iankel' Chernomordik, the schoolteacher, came over and sat next to her. Iankel' placed a piece of paper on her knees with the image of the Holy Spirit, calling it "the gods of the Christians," and put a similar piece of paper on his own knees. Maria then spit on the image, renounced her beliefs, and recited several strange words. The schoolteacher proceeded to spit on the image as he instructed Maria to open the cabinet with her left thumb. And as she was holding the Commandments in both hands, he kissed her and called her by her new name, Sara.[45]

In no time, Chernomordik (who also went by the nickname Petushok or Cockerel) kissed her and informed her that it was now time for the wedding ceremony with Khaim Khrupin. Maria was led into a special chamber where there were two beds, one of which was designated for her. The moment that Khaim lay down next to her, he "caressed her in the same exact manner he would caress his wife." When they finally returned to the school, the Jews offered her an expensive dress and a nice pair of shoes. Khaim warned her that she should continue to wear her simple peasant clothing so that no one would be able to recognize her. All the Jews began to kiss and congratulate her for converting to the Jewish faith, although Maria "knew deep down in her soul that she remained a devout Uniate."[46]

A similar religious ceremony awaited Avdotia. Khanna offered Avdotia plenty of wine to drink, making her promise not to say a word about anything she had witnessed. To be certain that none of the secrets would be revealed, Khanna wanted Avdotia to convert to the Jewish faith. It was nearly nightfall on Low Monday when the ceremony took place. That day, Avdotia was given more spirits to drink than usual and was sent over to Petushok's cottage. Avdotia told Petushok that she did not know why she was required to convert. But Petushok reassured her that he would teach her how to pray and that she would become a faithful Jew. He brought her to "the school where all the rich Jews came to pray," wrapped her in a plain white shawl, and brought her in front of the Torah ark. Petushok opened the curtain and explained that this was where the Jews kept the Commandments.

As she stood in front of the ark, Petushok took out a special note-book and told her to repeat strange words after him. Afterward, he spat nine times, telling her that "in the sky, land, and water there's only one God. And even though every person in the universe prays to their own God, there's only one eternal truth." He then handed her a whisk to hold in her right hand and a citron in her left hand, and made her bring her hands directly to her mouth. After kissing the tips of her fingers, he placed them on the Commandments, called her by her new Jewish name Risa, and offered her a glass of red wine.[47]

After Praskoviia Kozlovskaia's conversion ceremony, Iosel' Glikman led all three women to the Torah ark. As he was taking a big book from behind the curtain, Iosel' reminded them not to tell a single soul what they had witnessed. He then recited several passages from the book. And once Glikman stopped, a group of Jews walked in with the antimins—a rectangular piece of linen, decorated with representations of the entombment of Christ, the four Evangelists, and inscriptions related to the Passion—that they had stolen from the St. Il'insk Church. In Eastern Orthodoxy, the antimins is used to celebrate the Eucharist and is unfolded only during the Divine Liturgy.[48] Only after Maria and the Jews took turns doing unimaginable horrors to the sacred piece of cloth did they dispose the body in the river. It was early in the morning and the sun was about to rise. Fearing that someone would see them, the women reasoned that the most inconspicuous thing to do was to dump the body in the woods on the outskirts of town.[49]

It was now time for the most important part of the ritual: the distri-bution of the blood. All the blood was collected in a special basin and stored in three large glass bottles. While the women were busy dumping the body in the woods, Iosel' Glikman took one bottle to the town of Uly. Fratka Devirts took everyone back to the school, where a table with two glass bottles and a basin stood in the middle of the largest room in the building. Her husband, Orlik, divided the blood into two bottles and soaked up what remained of the liquid with a large piece of linen that measured around four and a half feet long. The cloth was cut evenly in small pieces and distributed among the Jews. The bottles were stored under lock and key in a special closet in Mirka Aronson's house. The following year, at the time of Passover, Orlik Devirts took Terenteeva to Vitebsk. They went directly to a house made of bricks, where two

Jewish women greeted them at the door. The older one knew just what to do with the blood, and immediately took the bottle inside and mixed it with an unidentified liquid. On their way back home, Terenteeva and Devirts stopped by Liozno, a neighboring town, to drop off the third bottle. Kozlovskaia testified that she witnessed Mirka Aronson's cook, Basia, mix small drops of blood to bake *krendels* (pretzels).[50]

The confessional narrative provided authorities sufficient grounds to move forward with the criminal investigation. It remains unclear what Terenteeva, Maksimova, and Koslovskaia hoped to gain from implicating themselves in the murder conspiracy. Perhaps they thought that Strakhov would release them as soon as they told what he wanted to hear? After all, was it not the Jews he was really after? Or perhaps jealousy and greed motivated them to tell their tale? Whatever the case, Nicholas's paranoia with the dangers of religious sectarianism meant that authorities responded to the allegations in a most serious manner. The idea was to uncover the conspiracy and remove once and for all the socially harmful elements from public view. In April 1827, nearly nineteen months after the case was officially reopened, Khovanskii sealed shut the great Jewish school and ordered Strakhov to "get to the bottom of things as quickly as possible."[51] To expedite matters, the governor-general sent officer Zaikovskii of the Vitebsk provincial treasury, collegiate-assessor Khrutskii of the Vitebsk provincial court, and general-major Shkurin to assist Strakhov with the case. Although the crime was most serious, punishable by the harshest penalties in the Russian criminal law code, convicting Jews of ritual murder was an entirely different matter.[52] To establish a foolproof case, Strakhov and his team of inquisitors would need Jews to confess to their darkest secret: that a Jewish cabal had in fact conspired to sacrifice a Christian boy for his blood.

4

The Confrontations

DURING HIS FIRST FEW MONTHS in Velizh, Vasilii Ivanovich Strakhov resided in a modestly furnished apartment in the very center of town. It did not take long for the inspector-councilor to set up a regular harem in his home. Women of ill repute, disguised in black cassocks, with cups of wine or vodka in their hands, were reportedly spotted there at all hours of the night. The word on the street was that Strakhov paid handsomely for their company, and that he, too, could be seen in the sort of large flowing garment usually worn by priests, bishops, and monastics.[1] As time went on, Strakhov realized that he needed a larger venue to carry out an elaborate criminal investigation. In July 1826, he found just the place he was looking for. This wooden house, located on Bogdanovicheva Street, was spacious enough to comfortably accommodate all the members of the inquisitorial commission. The local jail, with space for no more than six inmates, was in a state of disrepair. Strakhov wasted no time in transforming the remaining rooms of his new home into a makeshift place of detention.[2]

The Bogdanovicheva house played a central role in the criminal investigation. This was where the commission carried out the bulk of its inquisitorial work, and where most Jews, along with their accusers, were held under lock and key. There was nothing particularly unusual in Strakhov's decision to transform a private residence into a jail. Small provincial towns did not have the infrastructure to accommodate more than a handful of prisoners at once. With limited funding, lax security, and endemic overcrowding, the Russian government rarely used provincial prisons as long-term solutions for punishment and incarceration. Before the second half of the nineteenth century, Russia maintained few large-scale prisons; the individuals convicted of serious crimes were exiled for hard labor to remote parts of the empire.[3] As in other times and places around the world, most Russian prisoners were not convicted offenders but suspects under preliminary arrest awaiting trial and interrogation. Retired military officers, with little training in prison administration or sense of purpose beyond custodial maintenance of the building, usually took on the tedious task of administering the holding cells and looking after the prisoners.[4]

By April 8, 1826, Strakhov felt that he had accumulated enough evidence to begin the arrests. Slava Berlina and Khanna Tsetlina were the first people taken into custody. A week later, Itsko Nakhimovskii, Abram Glushkov, and Iosel' Turnovskii were locked up as well. By the time the inquisitorial commission wrapped up its work, at least forty-three Jews were charged with, among other things, ritual murder, providing the necessary tools and supplies to carry out the murder conspiracy, theft and desecration of church property, and the forcible conversion of Maria Terenteeva, Avdotia Maksimova, and Praskoviia Kozlovskaia. Thirty-eight Jews were permanent residents of Velizh; the other five lived in surrounding towns and villages.[5] Of all the individuals taken into custody, nearly 60 percent were men, and 85 percent were in the prime of their lives, in their thirties, forties, and fifties. Although a staggering twenty-nine families were caught up in the ordeal, around 45 percent of those imprisoned came from five of the most prominent families in the town: the Tsetlins, the Chernomordiks, the Devirtses, the Rudnikovs, and the Aronson/Berlin clan (see Appendix).

Working under the rules of the inquisitorial system, Strakhov and his team conducted the interrogations in the privacy of a guest room. It was the investigator's task to systematically interrogate the suspects, and it was the suspects' duty to either refute the allegations or recount what had happened to the best of their ability. Even though Russia had officially abolished torture, Strakhov relied on a variety of confrontational, manipulative, and psychological techniques to get the Jews to talk. In his quest for a total confession—what was regarded as the queen of proofs in the law—he brought Jews for face-to-face confrontations with the accusers.[6] In Russia, as in other places in early modern Europe, this interrogation technique was used primarily to resolve conflicting testimonies by confronting the accused with their witnesses.[7] The confrontations were designed to be highly emotional, drawn-out ordeals, testing the patience and fortitude of everyone caught up in the case. Standing directly in front of the accusers, the suspects were given a chance to refute the charges made against them and to pose their own questions to the accusers.

The criminal investigation had taken quite a toll on Shmerka Berlin. Four years had passed since little Fedor's body was found in the woods. The most prosperous merchant in town had now become a shadow of his former self. Over the years, Shmerka had suffered a series of financial setbacks. By the summer of 1827, after he had been locked up for nearly twelve months, the trauma of detention had exhausted him. As he stood in front of the inquisitorial commission, rationalizing that Jewish religious law firmly forbids Jews from using blood for religious rituals, the recording secretary noticed that Shmerka's face suddenly turned pale and his hands began to tremble. Doing his best to stay faithful to the original testimony, Shmerka explained that he did not know the exact cause of the boy's death or who was responsible for the murder. "Neither Jews nor Christians had any reason to commit the dreadful act," Shmerka continued, "and this is why I first testified [in 1823] that someone must have run him over with a carriage and dumped the body in the woods." As far as he could tell, there was no other reason to kill an innocent child. Afterward, perhaps out of spite for the Jews, "someone must have stabbed the boy to death and blamed them for the murder."[8]

When Maria Terenteeva opened the door and walked into the room, Shmerka immediately cried out in a sharp tone, "This plague of a person would say something like this!" Maria responded by describing in vivid detail how Jews tortured the boy. To this, Shmerka only waved his hand, telling her that he had gotten tired of hearing the same story over and over. As the session progressed, Shmerka remarked that he had run into Avdotia Maksimova on numerous occasions, but that he had not seen Terenteeva before the spring of 1823. In fact, he could not understand why anyone would believe that Jews were capable of ritually murdering the boy or, for that matter, that so much blood could flow from such tiny wounds. Shmerka went on to explain that neither he nor his family had set foot inside the Jewish school when the boy was said to have been murdered. This was why he had no idea if the alleged blood was poured into the bottles or if the pieces of linen had been saturated in the blood.[9]

Sitting at the edge of the table, holding herself up with her elbows, Shmerka's wife, Slava, barely had the strength to make it through an interrogation session. Disoriented and frightened, Slava finally appeared before the inquisitorial commission, but no sooner than she answered a question, she changed her mind. Slava nonetheless managed to confirm many of the same details that her husband had described: that she had known Avdotia Maksimova quite well, but could not remember of ever encountering the beggar woman Terenteeva before, that no one tortured a Christian boy in their house, that she had not set foot inside the school, and that she knew absolutely nothing about the murder conspiracy other than what she heard by way of the rumors that were circulating around town.[10]

Slava somehow gathered enough strength to challenge the accusations. Looking directly into Maksimova's eyes, she lashed out, "Tell me, who actually carried the boy to the school? Did anyone see this take place? Whose dress did you put on that day? And where exactly did Khanna keep the boy in her home? Were there any witnesses who can confirm this [allegation]?" Slava went on, "Lies, lies! It's all lies! She made everything up from beginning to end, nothing but lies!" When confronted with Terenteeva, Slava screamed that the beggar woman told only lies and that she had never met her before. To this, Terenteeva responded in a calm voice, "How dare you, aren't you afraid of God's wrath?" The inquisitors reminded Slava that her skin color, especially of her face and neck, had changed dramatically during the interrogation session, turning exceptionally pale one moment and visibly red the next. So that she would notice the remarkable change in her complexion, the commission forced her to stand in front of a mirror, but Slava stood by her testimony and affirmed her innocence.[11]

On June 9, 1827, long after the sun had set and the candles had burned out, Slava was asked to sign a written statement. But as the ink was drying, she noticed that the recording secretary was not faithful to her words. She requested to make several "corrections," but the commission denied her request, declaring that the statement was "complete." In hopes of clearing her good name, Slava sent a complaint to the governor-general's office, describing how Strakhov had forced her to

"sign the written statement" and that he intimidated her by screaming
obscenities and threatening to strike her with his bare hands. Strakhov
did not waste any time calling Slava's credibility into question, making it
clear that she "changed first one answer and then another one, and then
demanded, with the utmost impudence, for the statement to read just
the way she wanted it." From this pattern, Strakhov intimated, it was
self-evident that Slava made things up and had sent the complaint in the
most hysterical state just to get back at him for taking her into custody.[12]

Shmerka's son, Hirsh, could not think of any reason why anyone would
want to kill the little boy. Jews certainly would not stand to profit, Hirsh
reasoned. "The boy may have died of natural causes, or perhaps someone
could have killed him, if for no other reason than to cast blame on the
Jews." He remembered that the shoemaker Filipp Azadkevich frequently
walked around the marketplace with old books in his hands, telling anyone who cared to listen that Jews needed Christian blood for religious rituals. Furthermore, he explained that he hired Abram Glushkov to guard
the house only after he was summoned for questioning. In a confrontation with Terenteeva, Hirsh remarked, "Why are you lying? I've never
known you. You've never stepped inside our house."[13] Hirsh's wife, Shifra,
was panic-stricken when she was brought in for questioning. The recording secretary observed that she was "crying, smiling, and sighing heavily
all at the same time," while trying her best to refute the accusations.[14]

The entire Berlin family, including Shmerka's brothers, Meir and
Noson, were under immense psychological pressure to confess. But no
matter how difficult the circumstances may have been, the brothers did
not budge. As his face "twitched nervously," Meir stared down Terenteeva,
telling her that "he had never met her before and that he had no idea
what she was talking about." Terenteeva quickly objected, "Don't lie. You
knew me when I was called Sara." At that moment, the recording secretary noted that Meir's face "turned pale." Pulling his beard as hard as he
could, he leaned against the wall and began to hit it furiously with his
bare hands. He started to cry. "How dare you say this?" Meir responded.
"This never happened. You have no idea what you're talking about. You've
been brainwashed!" During his confrontation with Terenteeva, Noson
also appeared to be visibly distraught. He complained that his head hurt
badly and that he was barely able to stand up and answer the questions.
According to the recording secretary's observations, Noson's body "shook

as though he was having a seizure." After an hour or so had passed, Noson was finally able to speak, but could not remember certain words and had a generally hard time answering the commission's questions. When the exceedingly lengthy interrogation session came to an end, Noson refused to sign the written statement, because, he later explained to the governor-general, Strakhov dealt him two strong blows to the chest.[15]

Evzik Tsetlin had been acquainted with Shmerka Berlin all his life. They lived only a few doors from one another. From time to time, the men collaborated on business ventures, including, most recently, the construction of a glass factory in the provincial district. As two of the most prosperous families in town, the Tsetlins and Berlins frequently socialized together as well; the wives were especially on good terms. But when the ritual murder rumors started circulating around town, Evzik and his wife Khanna were not in any mood to socialize. The Tsetlins lost a sizable amount of the capital they had invested in the factory. Evzik spent much of his time at home in distress, thinking of ways to get back his money, while his wife Khanna was busy tending to their ill son. Evzik remembered that one of his neighbors had informed him that a dead boy was found in the woods, but he never bothered to inspect the body and he had no idea who had committed the crime. Although the word on the street was that Jews did this for demonic reasons, Evzik reassured the commission that Jews would do no such thing. "Jewish religious law," Evzik explained to Strakhov, "forbids us from eating or drinking Christian blood or any blood for that matter."[16]

Like Hirsh Berlin, Evzik theorized that the shoemaker Azadkevich had orchestrated the entire affair, turning Terenteeva, Maksimova, and so many other Christian neighbors squarely against the Jewish community. Evzik remembered that since the day he was elected town councilor, Azadkevich had held a grudge against him. One day the townsman asked Evzik to mediate a disagreement with two other Jews. It turned out that a financial transaction had gone terribly wrong. Azadkevich wanted nothing more than for Evzik to discipline the Jews. But in his capacity as town councilor, he did no such thing. Instead, he promptly threw Azadkevich in jail and put him on a bread and water diet. While behind bars, Azadkevich threatened Evzik that he would get his revenge one day. In the spring of 1823, it appears the moment had finally arrived: shortly after the boy was found ritually murdered, Azadkevich boasted to everyone around town that Khanna and Slava would "languish in prison for at least five years."[17]

As the interrogation session intensified, Strakhov went over his copious notes and noticed an apparent contradiction. Why did Evzik claim that he had not encountered Terenteeva before, when Khanna originally testified that the beggar woman was run out of the Tsetlin home on several occasions? Strakhov reminded Evzik that his wife had recounted in detail why Terenteeva should be blamed for the murder. Evzik reassured Strakhov that there was a simple explanation. Lots of different folks, from all walks of life, frequented the tavern; there was no way he could keep track of all of them. Perhaps his wife insisted that Terenteeva leave the property, but he could not remember when this happened or why. Evzik explained that he knew absolutely nothing about the murder. Of the three accusers, he was acquainted only with Maksimova, and he knew for a fact that she had not converted to Judaism. Not only did Maksimova go to confession regularly, but on Jewish holidays and on Saturdays she sold wine and beer at the tavern, handled money, fetched water from the well, and lit the stove—all things Jews were strictly forbidden from doing.[18]

By November 1826, Evzik had been locked up in his room for nearly five months. One evening, around thirty minutes after dinner was delivered to his room, he threw off his robe, tore his shirt into tiny pieces, and began to scream at the top of his lungs for Strakhov to come see him. The guard on duty saw Evzik without any clothes on, running hysterically around his room in circles. The guard rushed over to Strakhov, telling him to come quickly; "Evzik Tsetlin has just lost his mind." When Strakhov finally showed up, he witnessed quite the scene. Evzik was visibly agitated and did not want to answer any questions or even acknowledge Strakhov's presence. After some time had passed, the guards restrained him by tying his feet together. But subduing Evzik was not easy. For several minutes, he continued to kick and scream, until he fell off the bed flat on the floor. By this time, Evzik had lost what little strength he had left and finally managed to calm down. Several days later, he explained to an officer that the "interrogations had taken a real toll, making me feel increasingly hopeless." Strakhov had lied to him on numerous occasions. In the middle of the night when no one would see him, Strakhov changed the signed written statement, making it appear that he had confessed to one thing when in fact he said something different entirely. Evzik hoped that one day everyone in town would find out how unjustly he had been treated.[19]

Khanna Tsetlina was also in a state of deep despair. Strakhov's questions frightened her. As her face turned "deathly pale" and her "body trembled from exhaustion," Khanna did her best to reassure the commission that she did not make up anything. She denied of stepping inside Mirka Aronson's home or the Jewish school. She had no idea if the bottles of blood were distributed to Jews or if the cloth was saturated in the blood and then cut in tiny little pieces. The only thing that she knew for sure was that Avdotia did not bring the bottles to the house. Although Khanna remembered making honey at the time of the Passover holiday, she denied ever mixing Christian blood in rolls and pretzels and arranging for the deliveries to Vitebsk. In her confrontation with Avdotia, Khanna yelled, "Lies! Lies! You have forgotten everything, you madwoman."[20]

On another occasion, Khanna told Strakhov that Avdotia Maksimova should have known better than to accuse her of ritual murder. Avdotia lived with them for ten years. At one point, the Tsetlins had even vouched for her innocence when she was charged with theft and faced exile to Siberia. Khanna remembered that Avdotia looked "happy and content" when she worked for them, reminding Strakhov that, in the spring of 1823, Avdotia testified that she knew nothing about the murder. And therein lay the absurdity of the case. "What hope do I have when three women accuse me of such awful things? Even if ten women would say the same thing, I would still maintain my innocence: that I know absolutely nothing [about the murder]."[21] Khanna's daughter, Itka—who was only twelve years old when the scandal broke out—also had a hard time rationalizing why Avdotia would make up such dreadful accusations. Itka spent most of her time outdoors, playing games with her friends, and did not pay much attention to the investigation. Itka told Avdotia when they confronted each other, "Remember what you used to tell me: the truth will always come to light. It was you who raised me. How many times I played at your feet as you watched over me!"[22]

There are other stories like Khanna's and Itka's. For the duration of the interrogations, Zusia Rudniakov refused to make eye contact with Strakhov. Zusia looked "disoriented and frightened," and the more questions he was asked the harder he breathed. When Strakhov showed him what appeared to be bloodied rags of some sort, Zusia turned pale and wept. Terenteeva turned in the rags as proof of ritual murder, but Zusia had no intention of inspecting them. Instead, he continued to rub his forehead in disbelief. The moment Terenteeva walked into the room, the recording secretary noted that Zusia paced nervously around the room, taking deep breaths every few minutes and scolding her in a very loud voice.[23] Itsko Beliaev called Terenteeva a "swine and madwoman." When Terenteeva recounted how she was forced to stand on top of a sweltering hot iron pan during the conversion ceremony and how her feet still hurt to this day, the only thing Itsko could do was cry. He asked Terenteeva, "Are you saying that in three whole years your feet haven't been able to heal?[24] Another prisoner, a man by the name of Abram Kisin, screamed loudly as he hit his arms and legs against the bed. He threw himself in all directions and called for his father, wife, and children to save him, because he felt "all was lost."[25]

At the time of the investigation, Basia Aronson got into an argument with her sister-in-law Slava Berlina over an unpaid debt of 1,000 rubles. The women were on such bad terms that they had turned the matter over to the *bet din* (rabbinic court). While the case was being adjudicated, Basia avoided Slava. For this reason, she had no idea who allegedly tortured the boy because, she explained to Strakhov, "the last thing I wanted to do was see or talk with Slava."[26] Iosel' Glikman, the man who was accused of transporting the boy's body to the woods, threw out yet another theory: "Somebody must have stabbed the boy as a cruel joke and then blamed the ritual murder on us. If Jews had killed the boy, [we] certainly would not have dumped the body two miles from town, but found another place, closer to town, to hide the body." As he stood on his knees in front of the inquisitorial commission, he repeated several times, "My lord, forgive me, forgive me!" Glikman would not explain what he meant. Instead, he paced nervously around the room, breathing deeply on occasion, rubbing his face and head with his hands, all the while complaining that he was not feeling well.[27]

Several other prisoners also had a hard time comprehending why anyone would believe that Jews forced Terenteeva, Maksimova, and Kazlovskaia to convert to Judaism. "Jews don't convert Christians," Iankel' Chernomordik explained to Strakhov, "and even if [we] did, shouldn't all three [women] be wearing Jewish clothes?" During the confrontation with Terenteeva, Iankel' wasn't able to articulate his thoughts clearly. The only thing he could do was cry and mutter under his breath,

"God has struck me down. My lord, please forgive me! I have no idea what she's talking about."[28]

Iankel's thirty-year-old daughter Khaika also had no idea what the three accusers were talking about. Shortly after Khaika got married, she and her husband moved out to a neighboring village. Her husband found work managing an estate for a nobleman, and she hardly spent any time in Velizh, coming only on occasion to see her parents. The entire village of Safanovoi, where they resided, could attest to this fact. For this reason, Khaika had no idea who killed the boy or whether the women were forcibly converted. She too had never set foot in the provincial capital of Vitebsk before, as Terenteeva had alleged. When they confronted one another, Khaika gave Terenteeva a disparaging look and then lowered her gaze and proceeded to pace around the room just as Iosel' Glikman and her father had done before her. When Strakhov pulled out the bloodied rags and placed them on the table, the recording secretary noted that "Khaika's entire body trembled in agitation." But even in this worked-up state, she had no intention of inspecting the rags. Khaika "stared directly in her accuser's eyes for a long time," as though, the recording secretary noted, she was trying to frighten Terenteeva.[29]

Unlike the prisoners who were born and raised in Velizh, Khaim Khrupin had come to town when he was twenty-six years old. After finding work as a tutor, he decided to stay. Together with his wife and children, he resided in a modest wooden home located across the river at the very edge of town. The house had two separate entrances and a common courtyard. Khaim and his family occupied one half of the home, while Maria Terenteeva and her Christian landlady lived in the other half. Although Khaim had run into Terenteeva on numerous occasions, he remembered one day with particular clarity, when he caught Terenteeva rummaging through his belongings. He was certain that she wanted to steal something—such was her reputation around town—and so he told her to leave immediately. Why did Khaim not reveal this crucial detail before? Khaim had a simple explanation, "I was frightened by the stories circulating around that Jews were getting punished in the interrogation chamber."[30]

As a language teacher with limited knowledge of Russian, Khaim "doubted that he revealed everything that was necessary for his acquittal." This is why he did not hold back when he was brought in for a second round of questions. He firmly denied of having set foot inside the Jewish school during the conversion ceremony or lying on the same bed with Terenteeva. Khaim told Terenteeva when they confronted each other, "You've never been a Jewess, just as I have never been a Gypsy." He felt that Terenteeva had accused him of all this "nonsense" because she held a grudge against him when he threw her out of his home. "Terenteeva can say whatever she wants but no Jew will affirm her testimony," he went on. Regarding the allegation that he had intimate relations with her, Khrupin pointed out that Jewish law strictly forbids this. "A Jew is not permitted to lie on the same bed with anyone other than his wife. I was never married to Maria, and the *kahal* scribe never signed the *ketubah* [marriage contract]. Since Terenteeva lies unceasingly, I ask God that she continues to live." "There will come a time when Terenteeva will reveal the truth," Khrupin predicted, "perhaps not to the commission but to someone else. If Terenteeva would die for some unexpected reason, then the truth would be lost eternally. ... If I were brought in [the interrogation chamber] on a daily basis, I would say the exact same thing: that Terenteeva is lying."[31]

Almost always, the Jews stood their ground in face of tough and exceedingly hostile questions. Not only did they refuse to tell the inquisitors what they wanted to hear, countering any possibilities they were involved in the crime, but they repeatedly refused to sign the confession statements. With tears running down both of his cheeks, Ruman Nakhimovskii, for example, clutched his stomach and "shook feverishly" when Strakhov displayed the bloodied rags. Ruman was the custodian of the Jewish school, repaired things when they were damaged or broken, and walked around town collecting candles on Fridays. As the interrogation session progressed, Ruman took his time answering the questions and appeared "visibly frightened." At one point, he leaned against the fireplace in the corner of the room and stared at the door, as though he was waiting for someone to enter. Later in the day, Maksimova told him, "Don't hold back, Ruman, there will come a time when you will reveal the truth. I didn't say one word in vain." Ruman replied, "No, I would never confess to having committed the crime. It never happened." Terenteeva also pressed Ruman to confess, "You don't know me? We stabbed the boy together, and you were the one who converted me—don't deny this. The boy's blood will not be wasted. God will not permit this." "You're lying," Ruman responded, "You've been brainwashed. Jews don't need Christian blood." Ruman then turned to the inquisitors, "I have no strength left. I'm not capable of confessing [something I didn't commit]. I'd rather die."[32]

More like a late-medieval holding facility than an institution of incarceration, the Bogdanovicheva house was not impermeable to the stream of small-town life.[33] The house was located in the very center of town, only a short walk from the marketplace. Like any other institution of confinement, it was governed by its own distinct rules and systems of exchanges. On any given day, a host of administrators, family members, translators, and medical practitioners frequented the house. The stream of visitors delivered warm meals, water, tea and coffee, clothing, candles, medical supplies, and reading materials. Prisoners also could purchase certain items such as flour, beef, fish, eggs, and milk.[34]

The inhabitants of the house—the inquisitors, guards, and inmates—had no choice but to adapt to the vagaries of prison life. This was a world where everyone lived in cramped quarters, where it was not extraordinarily difficult to overhear conversations or communicate with family and friends on the outside. The rooms on the first floor had better heat and lighting. One prisoner, for instance, was grateful that he was not locked up in the attic, where the light was particularly poor. "Thank God," he observed, "that they decided to be nice to me and not put me … in the darkest place in the house, where two other Jews are locked up, and where it's impossible to see a thing."[35] Nevertheless, the "darkest place in the house" had its rewards. Whereas guards patrolled the rooms on the first floor, the attic was generally left alone for long stretches of time. Prisoners could open the tiny windows with ease and communicate in special coded language—a practice used in many European prisons—with people standing in the marketplace.[36]

In the summer of 1827, Strakhov ordered a new round of arrests. With both the Bogdanovicheva house and the town jail filled to capacity, the inspector-councilor was forced to improvise. The inquisitorial commission did not have the resources to build a new holding cell; it quickly needed to come up with a place of temporary custody. On July 15, Strakhov found another house, only a short walk from the marketplace, which had enough space to accommodate the growing number of inmates and guards. It remains unclear if the home was unoccupied or if the commission forced the residents to vacate the property. Whatever the case, this turned out to be the most cost-effective solution to the problem of overcrowding. The commission felt that it need not worry about food, linens, and supplies; all these items could be delivered from home by family and friends at the inmates' request.[37]

A cache of writings—some of which were mere fragments—smuggled in and out of the two homes and town jail provides an intimate glimpse of daily life. With ink and paper hard to come by, the prisoners jotted down notes in minuscule Yiddish on whatever objects they could find: on wooden chips, scraps of cloth, and even on the edges of spoons and forks.[38] The inquisitorial commission was not capable of controlling all aspects of the daily routine. No matter how hard the inquisitors tried to limit communication, the prisoners managed to see and talk with one another and to exchange notes.[39]

Relying on hand gestures and signs, prisoners acquired tidbits of information about what was going on around them. They learned of recent arrests, the health and safety of loved ones, and if their messages were successfully delivered. Before her arrest, for example, Evzik Tsetlin's daughter, Itka, "would come by the house and make strange signs with her hands and post occasional notes on her [father's] window."[40] Some prisoners communicated with friends, family, and neighbors at prearranged times. Others waited until the guards on duty were not around to open windows so they could talk with people who happened to pass by. Frequently, prisoners sharing a wall talked with one another "by praying or singing in a loud voice inside their rooms."[41]

The fact that the prisoners enjoyed a modicum of social ties with the outside world did not mean that they did not suffer from loneliness, boredom, and melancholia. Khaim Khrupin wrote to his wife in desperation of news of his young children, "I beg you to tell me if my son has started to read. I would also like for you to bring my son along when you deliver the meals. Tell him to stand by my window. Tell my daughter to stand by the window, as well."[42] With his mental and physical state deteriorating, he tried to allay his wife's fears, "I beg you, dear wife, not to worry about me. I'm perfectly healthy, without an attack of the nerves, thank God."[43] Khrupin followed up with a note to his mother: "Please don't miss me too much. What good would that do? Perhaps God will allow me to stand one more time before the inquisitorial tribunal. I'm hopeful that the last round of interrogations would give them enough evidence to set me free and that, most importantly, all the foolish things that they've tried to accuse me of would come to light. I pray that the uncircumcised one [Strakhov] would finally come clean and admit that he personally signed the interrogation documents."[44]

Khrupin's wife tried to reassure her husband that everyone at home was doing just fine. "For God's sake, don't worry about us. We have nothing to fear. Not because the most dangerous time has passed, but because I assure you that we have nothing to fear. Also, don't worry about our expenses." The Jewish community provided charity for the destitute and needy, and from that little bit of money, Khrupin's wife noted that she was able to pay the tutor to the last kopek. In fact, she was certain that the money would last her a few more weeks, and she should have enough to buy a fur coat at the fair. "I pray that you not worry about us and turn melancholy," she concluded the letter. "Save your health, otherwise you'll fall ill. Why haven't you sent back shirts to wash? Why haven't you sent back the dirty dishes?"[45]

On another occasion, Khrupin's wife wrote with news of their son, expressing fear that their correspondence would be discovered:

> Your son misses you terribly. In the coming days, he will study at home … He has already started to read the *siddur* (prayer book) and is getting pretty good at it. Don't worry about me or about our household expenses, nothing has changed. But I miss you. I have no idea if you've received all the food and drinks that I've sent you. I also can't understand why you don't finish your meals—just so that you send back a note? I'm extremely afraid [the guards will discover our correspondence]. I don't advise you to send notes this way. Don't worry that they've locked you so tightly. They didn't do this because you did something wrong, but because Nota [Prudkov] escaped from prison. … The investigation is making all of us [in town] terribly frightened. It's wartime here. They've just conscripted several of our brothers [into the cantonist battalions]. If it's possible to send a note by way of your [trustworthy] contact, please do so, but don't ask anyone else."[46]

Prisoners fought the grinding idleness and boredom in a variety of ways. Khanna Tsetlina, for example, asked for yarn and needle and some books; another prisoner requested reading material, including two Talmud volumes, and ink.[47] When distractions failed to produce the desired results, religious faith helped ease the emotional stress of separation. Blessings over food, recitations and prayers, and the observance of fasts and feasts on the Jewish calendar helped structure daily life. One prisoner, for example, requested an assortment of items from home for Passover, so that he could "read the history of the Israelite exodus from Egypt by candlelight." He asked for the Seder wine, a clean white tablecloth, and a small handkerchief to cover his head. Several days later, the same prisoner followed up with a more detailed list: unleavened bread (to be delivered before the start of Passover), horseradish tops, baked wings (any bird sufficed), onion sprouts, a mix made of crushed nuts and apples, English pepper, cinnamon, Rennes wine, a drink made with honey, and a glass for the wine. "Praise be to God that he hasn't deprived me of his mercy, and I haven't been sent to the dark place, the attic, where it's impossible to see a thing, with the other two Jews." He concluded, "I ask that you also bring me tea and sugar for the holiday, and eggs and fish for the holiday dinner, if they aren't too expensive. I don't have any more news. God have mercy on me."[48]

Invariably, the imprisoned Jews suffered from poor health and hygiene. The correspondence offers a graphic record of their ailments: of chronic illnesses, nervous spells, and stomach ailments. Jews described their health in unusually candid terms. "I'm very sick," one prisoner wrote. "My arm, side of my body, and head all hurt badly. The doctor prescribed me medicine, but now I have none left. I tried to inform [the inquisitorial commission] of how awful I feel, but no one pays attention to me." He continued, "The doctor used to come by every other day, but now visits once a week and this is why my health has deteriorated so quickly. God only knows what will happen to me. I am sick, and it's impossible to get through to anyone."[49] Medicine was not always available or effective. One prisoner, for example, asked for better food to relieve the pain. "I'm not well," he wrote, "I took some powder, but it didn't do me any good. It seems I have hemorrhoids. ... Today I also took a cocktail of pills to help the constipation. It's really bothering me. I have a good appetite, thank God, but I'm having a really hard time."[50] At a later date, the same prisoner reported that he wasn't able to control the illness: "I'm very sick, God have mercy on me. I'm suffering from constipation for a long time now. I've tried medicine, but the powder doesn't seem to work. I have stools filled with bloody water nearly twice a day, but I'm still bloated like a barrel. I feel the blood pulsating inside me and on top of that there's the constipation. I beg you, my merciful brothers, pray that I come out alive. Although I have an extraordinary appetite, I've assumed that I shouldn't eat when taking medicine. That didn't help; the doctor finally instructed me to eat."[51]

More than anything else, the Jews wanted to get out. They scribbled notes at great personal risk in the hope that someone would save them from their predicament. Khaim Khrupin implored his wife to help spread the word. "I write to you, dear brothers of Israel, to come to our rescue. Woe is me! Woe is me! Take pity on us. Hurry, come quick, they're doing terrible things to us!" Khrupin was convinced that it was just a matter of time before Terenteeva's accusations would be discredited. "If they find even a smidgen of truth in anything she says about us, I'm ready to be hung by a noose in the middle of the market square."[52] Other prisoners appealed to friends and family members to take their pleas seriously. One prisoner, for instance, described how the inquisitors made her sit in a room in front of the three accusers. "The women talked until I blacked out. I have no idea what happened afterwards. From the very beginning [of the confrontation], I stood my ground and denied everything until they decided to bring me back to my room. I'm telling you one more time that the situation is really bad here. Take pity on us, do something for God's sake! You have nothing to fear. You should know that we're losing hope. Don't think for a moment that I'm writing this note because I'm feeling sorry for myself. We're all in this together."[53]

In no time, communication turned into an elaborate game of concealment.[54] Although the guards were generally receptive to black-market dealings with the prisoners, there were plenty of occasions when they managed to confiscate personal correspondence in search of Jews' dark secrets. "A few weeks ago a guard walked into my room and found two wooden chips under my pillow," one unidentified prisoner remarked. "He grabbed both pieces of wood and immediately threw them into the fire."[55] When bribes proved dangerous or ineffective, Jews passed notes in bowls and pots, inside beef and fish dishes, in bottles of wine and water, in the linings of dresses and caftans, and in women's hairpieces.

No matter how hard Jews tried to conceal their intentions, the highly elaborate schemes were not always successful. Prisoners expressed frustration that their messages were falling on deaf ears. "I have already written to you regarding the troubles I've experienced," Iankel' Chernomordik wrote to an unidentified friend or family member. "You don't bother to look for scraps of wood [that is, the handwritten notes] in the items that I'm sending back to you." Chernomordik tried to attach short notes in a teapot, stockings, spoons, clothing, and *tzitzit* (pieces of knotted ritual fringes). "You're as slow as an ass, and for some reason can't seem to comprehend my signals," he remarked. "I told you to tie the string into a knot and look carefully at the dish I'm sending back to you."[56] In another message, this time to a different friend or family member, Chernomordik did not hold back, "It pains me that I haven't been able to eat all this time. I've tried to instruct him to hook a piece of string inside the dish [to retrieve my note]. I'm sending back the fish one more time, but he can't seem to comprehend why I'm doing this.[57] Writing in a similar vein, another prisoner could not understand why all of his notes have gone unanswered. "It's as if I'm throwing a stone into the sea."[58]

For the inquisitors, the confiscated notes offered additional proof of Jews' complicity in the ritual crime. Linguistic experts, most of whom were apostates from Judaism employed by the state, observed that Jews encrypted the texts with "special coded Hebrew words, making it extraordinarily difficult to understand their real meaning."[59] Strakhov was convinced that Jews were manipulating the criminal investigation and that they were sending secret messages to prepare their friends and family in case they too were summoned to the interrogation chamber. How else to explain why Jews went to such great lengths to communicate with one another?[60] To expose the depth of the conspiracy, the inquisitors confronted the prisoners with the notes, but the prisoners caught on to the tactics. Khaim Khrupin acknowledged that he had written the letters so that his wife would "run to the capital and appeal to the emperor." "You're a bunch of liars," he exclaimed. "You're breaking the law. I'll reveal everything to the emperor!" Itka Tsetlina reassured the inquisitors that she had no idea what the notes meant because she had no recollection of having written them. Another prisoner acknowledged that the notes could be his, but he could not remember for certain. "This is not my handwriting; these are not my letters. Hit me! I'd be better off if you struck me down! What will happen to me [if you do]? All of you officials are breaking the law. We Jews are trying to tell the truth, but no one's listening to us."[61]

Given the harsh realities of confinement, it is remarkable that so many Jews stood their ground as firmly as they did, although, as might be expected, this was not the case for everyone. At least a handful of people felt that by telling the interrogators what they wanted to hear they would be afforded judicial leniency. Itsko Nakhimovskii, for example, was imprisoned for almost two years when he finally broke down, promising to "reveal the truth." For ten or twelve years (he could not remember for sure), Itsko rented two rooms from Shmerka Berlin, from where he operated a small tavern and sold oats and hay. Itsko told Strakhov that he was left with nothing more than his memory, soul, and ability to communicate: "My memory would recall what really happened, my tongue would describe the events just as they had occurred, and my soul would make sure that I reveal the entire truth about my sufferings and torments and the murder case, even though I didn't have anything to do with it. Only I would be able to save my people." Nakhimovskii never did come up with a satisfactory explanation. As the months went by, solitary confinement made Itsko increasingly prone to fits of nervous rage. The slightest sound frightened him. The only solace he found was looking out of a small window of his room at the people walking around the market square. One day Strakhov unexpectedly transferred Itsko to a room with a view of the courtyard. At that point, Itsko's mood changed for the worse. He felt increasingly hopeless and decided to try his luck and escape. He waited until no one was looking and ran out past the gate onto Il'inskaia Street, screaming as loudly as he could, "Help! Help! I can't bear to be in my room any longer. I will go crazy. I will kill myself." He made it as far as the St. Il'insk Church, at which point he was apprehended by a security guard and escorted back to his room.[62]

In the spring of 1823, Nota Prudkov went on a business trip to Riga to purchase lumber. When he returned in either June or July, the town was abuzz with ugly rumors. Prudkov was arrested on February 4, 1828. Standing in front of the commission, trembling in fear, Prudkov could not understand why Strakhov targeted a poor, illiterate man like himself, when so many "rich" Jews remained free. The surest way to get released, Prudkov reckoned, was to offer a "full confession." Although he did not agree with all of Terenteeva's assertions, Prudkov disclosed that a small number of "wealthy" Jews had committed the ritual act. He did not know if they cut or stabbed the body or their precise motivations. It could have been done for "religious" reasons, but if that was the case, Prudkov reassured the commission, only "the wealthiest, most educated Jews in the community knew these highly esoteric practices and customs."[63]

With his confession falling on deaf ears, Prudkov decided to try something different. One thing he knew for sure was that he could not be confined to his room any longer. He waited until everyone was asleep before he broke the hardwood floor with his bare hands, took a wooden stick from underneath the bed, which he had saved for that purpose, and dug a small tunnel underneath the wall of the house. As soon as he reached the other side, he headed straight to the embankment, at which point he smashed his leg irons into tiny little pieces with a boulder. It does not appear that he made it very far. The very next day a guard found him hiding out in a neighbor's cottage. Prudkov explained that he escaped in order to convert, something that he had "intended to do for a long time now," but the inquisitors did not buy this justification either.[64]

The most sensational confession came from Fratka Devirts. Fratka was arrested on July 11, 1827, almost five months after her husband, the pharmacist Orlik, was taken into custody. At first, Fratka denied all the accusations that were leveled against her. The moment she set foot in the interrogation room, she cried out, "I don't know a thing [about the murder] nor was I a witness to anything that had happened. Why was I brought here? I don't know these beggar women! Are you really going to believe their stories?" Fratka walked around the room, screaming as loudly as she could, that she would be rather whipped by the knout than forced to answer any more questions. "If the commission believed that they found a fool, then they had another think coming. I'm not afraid of being rude, to say what's on my mind, and I will not stop for any reason!" Fratka snapped.[65]

But it did not take long for solitary confinement to get to Fratka. On August 22, 1827, she asked to use the outhouse, and when no one was looking, she decided to make a run for it. She climbed over the fence and made it as far as the neighbor's courtyard before a soldier apprehended her. In an attempt to explain her mother's erratic behavior, Rieva Kateonov pointed out that Fratka "had a weak temperament" and was predisposed to fainting spells. It did not help matters, Rieva went on, that Fratka was confined in a dark, unheated room. Rieva petitioned, unsuccessfully, to hand deliver a candle, which she hoped would brighten her mother's spirits.[66] As the days went by, Fratka felt increasingly hopeless about her predicament. She tried to escape one more time, and when that attempt also failed, she requested a meeting with the inquisitorial commission. One of the security guards observed that

Fratka was in the "most indecent state" when he came to her door: she was walking in circles around the room, swinging her arms wildly from side to side while uttering all sorts of obscenities.[67]

In a highly sensational account, Fratka revealed crucial details about the murder conspiracy. One day she ran into Ruman Nakhimovskii, the hump-backed custodian of the Jewish school, while taking a stroll in the courtyard. To her surprise, Ruman whispered in her ear that all the rumors circulating around town were true and that he had personally witnessed the murder. Ruman saw "the entire Berlin clan, Evzik and Khanna Tsetlin, and many other Jews take turns stabbing the boy with a knife. And when the boy took his last breath, Evzik hid it in his caftan and left somewhere in a hurry." Fratka wanted Ruman to tell her more, but she was afraid that a soldier would overhear their con-versation, even though they were speaking in Yiddish. On another occasion, Ruman told her yet another disturbing story that confirmed both the demonic and curative powers of Christian blood. As the Jews took turns stabbing the boy, Slava's daughter and son-in-law, Lanka and Iankel' Hirsh, fainted from fear. All the Jews were immediately taken by surprise. Slava was especially wor-ried that her daughter and son-in-law would reveal the gruesome details to the authorities. So she dipped her index finger in the boy's blood and rubbed it on both of their bare chests. Lanka and Iankel' began to sneeze uncontrollably, and shortly thereafter they lost consciousness and died. Ruman explained to her that Slava also planned to use the blood to treat her husband's tuberculosis, but he did not know how or when she planned to do this.[68]

Fratka realized that Ruman would deny everything. Jews are strictly forbidden from shaming God's name, and no one, especially such a pious and respectable Jew as Ruman, would admit that he was a witness to ritual murder. "If the *kahal* learns what I had just told you," Fratka warned the commission, "it would immediately pronounce *herem* against me, cut off all relations with the Jewish community, includ-ing the purchase of kosher meat." Fratka insisted that this information needed to be kept strictly confidential. In a face-to-face confrontation, she not only reminded Ruman what he had whispered, but disclosed yet another crucial detail: that a Jew by the name of Hirsh, who lived on the outskirts of town, had in his possession the knife and razor blade the Jews used to murder and circumcise the boy. Fratka pleaded with the officials to take Ruman "somewhere far away," because if they let him go free, the Jewish community would immediately suspect that she had informed on them. And if that were to happen, Fratka was certain that she would be treated worse than a *meshumad*, an apostate, someone who was rejected by the Jewish community because she had abandoned the Jewish faith. Along with her children, Fratka would need to "hide somewhere faraway or have no choice but to commit suicide."[69]

Sensing the inquisitors' skepticism, Fratka decided to throw out a bombshell. Berka Zarkha, the *shochet* (kosher butcher), had hidden the knife in the courtyard of the *kahal* building, in a secret storage shed, with around twenty other knives, all of which were enclosed in beautiful cloth-covered cases. Fratka explained that the knife could be "easily distinguished from the others because it was enclosed in a red Moroccan leather case, engraved in silver with Hebrew letters, although there was nothing unusual about it, save for one small detail: unlike an ordinary shaving blade, it could not be folded in half." To make matters even more interesting, Fratka produced two more pieces of evidence: the *izmel* (circumcision knife), as well as the dried-up foreskin, which she insisted was Fedor's. Fratka recounted that an old Christian woman whom she had never seen before handed her both the circumcision knife and the foreskin when she went outside one winter day to relieve herself. Afterward, she hid both the knife and foreskin under her mattress for "safekeeping."[70]

In the end, Strakhov did not find Fratka's sensational account very convincing. The problem of establishing the truth was well known in

These knives were collected by the inquisitorial commission as evidence of Jewish ritual murder. *Rossiiskii gosudarstvennyi istoricheskii arkhiv, f. 1345, op. 235, d. 65*

criminal procedure. Confession may have been the queen of proofs in the law, but the inquisitors recognized that suspects could easily invent their tales to avoid interrogation and punishment. Not knowing what else to do, and preparing herself for the possibility of sitting in isolation for years to come, Fratka decided to end her life. So she slit her throat with a sharp piece of glass, but it turned out that the cut was a superficial wound, which produced little, if any bodily damage or blood.[71]

5

Grievances

ON APRIL 8, 1826, THE day that their wives, Slava and Khanna, were taken into custody, Shmerka Berlin and Evzik Tsetlin sent a desperate complaint to the governor-general. They wanted nothing less than for Nikolai Nikolaevich Khovanskii to dismiss Strakhov from his official administrative duties. Two of the most respected residents of the town, they pleaded, were imprisoned without "any tangible evidence," on the basis only of "vicious, weak-minded, and completely fraudulent accusations." The men noted that their children were forbidden from having contact with their mothers, and that Slava and Khanna sat in prison deprived of the most basic necessities of humanity. They argued, "Like malicious criminals, they are harassed daily to the point that they may soon die from illness and emotional exhaustion. The investigation is proceeding slowly and without the supervision of a Jewish deputy who would have made certain that their oral statements were accurately recorded in official notebooks."[1]

To make matters worse, Shmerka and Evzik went on, "one of the women knows very little Russian, while the other one is completely illiterate." Fearing that the case could spiral out of control at any moment, they pleaded for the governor-general to exert his influence and end the senseless criminal investigation. "Our wives are suffering from having been confined to such a small space and have recently fallen ill." At the very least, they hoped that they would be "treated more charitably and relocated [to a place] where they would be able to breathe fresh air and where we, along with our children, would be permitted to visit them." In order not to arouse suspicion, they proposed to speak only in Russian. "We ask that they be given an opportunity to prove themselves in their innocence against such baseless accusations—the shedding of Christian blood—so that their own Jewish blood would not be shed in vain."[2]

For hundreds of years, Jews in Poland-Lithuania achieved their political ambitions by bribery, the gathering of intelligence, and the timely intercession of royal or imperial courts. The strategy of maintaining political influence with those in power was coherent and, at times, highly successful. But by the 1820s, with the gradual disintegration of Jewish self-government, Russian Jewish communities were left largely to their own devices to defend common political interests and express their claims to basic civil rights.[3] In the second quarter of the nineteenth century, a new mode of political activity was being worked out in Western Europe. Voluntary associations, the mass circulation press, and pamphlets gradually displaced intercession as the key tools to mobilize resources and political influence. In places with a developed Jewish public sphere, it became increasingly easy to coordinate an organized international response to prevent widespread suffering and human rights abuses. Newspapers, in particular, helped galvanize the support of the global community in a Jewish cause. This was the case not only because of their unparalleled power to disseminate disaster news, including to well-positioned diplomats and activists, but also because of their ability to unite populations separated by vast geographic space.

The Jews of Russia, however, stood outside the orbits of the new Jewish international.[4] They did not have access to newspapers published abroad or well-positioned diplomats who could disseminate disaster news and intervene on their behalf. Frustrated and isolated, Shmerka and Evzik did not have very many options at their disposal to protest what they perceived to be a grave social injustice. They did the only thing that subjects of the Russian Empire could do: they filed a formal grievance.

The moment Strakhov learned of the complaint he denied everything. What was the fuss all about? "[Slava and Khanna] talk in Russian like all other Russians," he reported to Khovanskii. The inspector-councilor felt that he had good reason to assume total control of the investigation. Russian law did not permit outside observers such as Jewish deputies to oversee criminal investigations. By proceeding "cautiously and in secret," he hoped to uncover the "truth of the crime" and, most significant, the work of what he perceived to be "an elaborate Jewish conspiracy." The last thing he wanted to happen was for vicious rumors to circulate beyond the confines of the provincial town. "Those Jews who are familiar with the secrets [of blood sacrifice]," Strakhov confided to Khovanskii, "use all available means to disrupt the investigation in hopes of saving the suspects from their deserved punishment in order to undermine the reality [of a highly malicious criminal act]." Instead of responding to the complaint, Strakhov felt that the best course of action was to arrest both complainants before they interfered with the detective work.[5]

And so on June 20, 1826, less than one month after they filed the grievance, Shmerka and Evzik were taken into custody. At that point, the investigation was just beginning to unfold. The governor-general did not see any reason to take Jews' grievances seriously. In fact, there was no doubt in Khovanskii's mind that Strakhov would complete the work in a timely manner and that the guilty would be brought to justice. Together with their wives, both men were imprisoned for their alleged role in the blood sacrifice.[6] The arrests put the entire Jewish community on high alert. How many more Jews was Strakhov planning to arrest? Who was going to be the next victim? What could the Jewish community do to defend itself from the allegations?

It did not take long for Evzik's brother, Sheftel Tsetlin, and Itsko Nakhimovskii's father, Berka, to formulate an official response. On August 27, they sent a second complaint to Vitebsk. Hoping to rescue the Jews, they decided to reason with Khovanskii by describing the absurdity of the accusations. They explained that a local schoolteacher named Petrishcha was the main culprit behind the affair. Everyone saw him "walking around town with some kind of book in his hands," spreading vicious rumors about Jews. Based on translations and explanations of relevant Talmudic passages, Petrishcha "managed to convince all the town residents that Jews consume Christian blood." To make the accusations sound even less plausible, they added that the physician

Levin played no small role in validating the charge by providing "false expert testimony." After all, if the body was actually pierced with a dull nail, why did Levin not detect any swelling on the body? They emphasized that, after the most powerful court in Vitebsk province had made the initial review of the testimony and material evidence in November 1824, it decided to acquit the Jews of the crime.

Strakhov, convinced of the Jews' guilt, did not pay any attention to this important detail. "He arrested the Jews in a most malicious manner," they wrote, "and locked them up in his home without any contact [with the outside world] or access to fresh air. He relies on coercive methods of interrogation, does not permit a Jewish deputy to supervise his work, and is not concerned with conducting an honest criminal investigation or uncovering the perpetrators of the crime." They petitioned the governor-general to replace Strakhov with a new investigator who, they hoped, would abide by proper rules and procedures.[7]

Sheftel and Berka did not reveal anything that the governor-general had not heard before. Khovanskii's office was stacked with grievances, petitions, and appeals on all sorts of topics, many of which were from Jews. Ever since assuming administrative control of the northwest provinces, Khovanskii had developed the habit of not taking Jews' complaints very seriously. The ritual murder case confirmed all his initial suspicions—Jews, he believed, were a particularly cunning folk—and he was not in any hurry to formulate an official response. How was he supposed to dismiss such convincing medical and material evidence? One thing he knew for sure was that he had no intention of replacing the inspector-councilor with someone else. To his mind, Strakhov was a capable investigator who dutifully abided by the rules of the inquisitorial process. As far as all the other claims, the best course of action, he reasoned, was to wait patiently for Strakhov's report.

Previously, Russian officials never went so far as to accuse all Jews of supporting, let alone engaging in, ritual murder, although they did believe that individual "fanatics" practiced the malevolent rite.[8] Based on everything that he had read and heard, Strakhov had become increasingly convinced that the Velizh case was different. The denunciations served as powerful blows of Jews' guilt. Strakhov wanted nothing less than to utilize his investigative powers to preside over what he surely thought would be a landmark conviction.[9] On November 17, 1826, he sent a lengthy memorandum to Vitebsk, proclaiming that he had compiled enough preliminary evidence to place Jews in detention: "I do not have medical training, so I am not in a position to comment on the accuracy of Levin's forensic evaluation. I am certain, however, that Terenteeva's and Maksimova's confessions justify all of my initial suspicions: that the Jews tortured the boy under the express guidelines of their superstitious beliefs and practices."[10]

Whatever his own personal biases may have been, Strakhov insisted that he treated the prisoners fairly and with respect: "They all sleep in their own individual rooms on cots equipped with mattresses and blankets. The warden delivers three warm meals per day, as well as essential personal items, including medicine, directly to the rooms. Some prisoners such as Evzik and Khanna Tsetlin and Shmerka and Slava Berlin are permitted the luxury of drinking tea and coffee [in their rooms]." For a short time, Strakhov explained, the prisoners were even allowed to exchange notes with their family and friends, although he decided to put an end to that practice fairly quickly. The severity of the crime, the inspector-councilor emphasized, required that "authorities take all possible precautions to minimize social contact among prisoners."[11]

Like all other subjects of the empire, Jews had the legal right to obtain redress against corruption and tyranny. They could do this by sending personal or collective complaints either to provincial governors or directly to the Senate or one of the chancelleries in St. Petersburg. After the partitions of Poland-Lithuania at the end of the nineteenth century, Jews turned in increasing numbers to the imperial government to voice individual grievances and resolve neighborly conflicts. Strakhov insisted that Jews had every right to petition the state and that he had no intention of taking this right away from them, even if the added paperwork slowed down the investigation. As far as the pivotal question of the Jewish deputy, Strakhov replied unequivocally, "Jews have no right to make this demand [on the commission]." The delicate nature of the case meant that he needed to proceed with caution and circumspection, to guard against false statements and deception, and to execute his duties in the privacy of the inquisitorial chamber. If the governor-general approved Jews' request and permitted a deputy to supervise the criminal investigation, there was no doubt in Strakhov's mind that Jews would obstruct justice by planning their answers well in advance of the oral interrogations.[12]

Strakhov addressed the complaints the same way he handled the case—methodically, point by point, leaving no question unanswered, no detail overlooked. He spent countless hours producing a series of inquiries, communications, and reports. Such was his training; such were the expectations of all civil servants in the service of empire. "Jews have every right to petition the governor-general to remove me [the chief investigator] from the case," he explained to Khovanskii. "They also have every right to be displeased with the inquisitorial techniques and administrative procedures that I use, but this does not mean that I did anything wrong," he pointed out. "Unrestrained emotions should not serve as grounds for dismissal."[13]

With the edifice of self-government slowly crumbling, the Jewish communities of Russia were structurally weakened, making it extraordinary difficult for them to defend common political interests. "There is no [central] council and the provincial council is no more," wrote the communal leader R. Hillel b. Ze'ev-Wolf about the state of Jewish communal politics around 1804. "With no conferences of elders, there is no one to plan ahead and to go before the officials or petition the king. . . . Today transgressors have multiplied. . . . Each one is for himself, so that no common counsel is taken to find a remedy in the face of harsh decrees."[14] The problem of coordinating a broad-based response to a political controversy was heightened not only because of communal fragmentation (the divisions between the Hasidim and their orthodox opponents) but also, and perhaps more important, due to the disciplinary efforts of the imperial regime.

In early modern Poland-Lithuania, the practice of *shtadlanut* (lobbying of authorities or the crown) to achieve a political objective was well established. Intercession required good knowledge of languages and skills of diplomacy. Jewish communities appointed exceptionally capable men with connections to powerful figures to lobby on their behalf. In addition to a nice salary and tax exemptions, the *shtadlanim* were entrusted with large sums of money that were earmarked as the chief instrument for "political action" (that is, bribery).[15] Russian rulers may have had no intention of recognizing an official collective representative body on the model of the Polish and Lithuanian Council of Four Lands, but in the first two decades of the nineteenth century, Alexander I did permit a group of delegates known as the deputies of the Jewish people to submit formal complaints.[16] Deputies drafted a wide range of memoranda to protect the internal interests of their communities. Usually, they did so to protest what they perceived to be malicious actions of the government such as the expulsion of Jews from the countryside or the confiscation of Jewish religious property, or particularly debilitating economic sanctions. Merchants relied on the deputies' rhetorical skills to request permission to travel and trade their ware in the interior provinces. During the war against Napoleon, two especially well-to-do contractors, Liezer Dillon and Zundel' Zonnenberg, submitted these and other similar requests directly to the highest levels of government in St. Petersburg.

At the height of the system, between December 1817 and July 1818, almost every province in the Pale of Settlement participated in the election of official deputies and designated alternates. The deputies enjoyed a life of unparalleled freedom and social privilege: they were permitted to travel beyond the geographic confines of the Pale and reside for extended stretches of time in the imperial capital, where Dillon, Zonnenberg, and other representatives received occasional audiences with the wealthiest and most powerful administrators in the empire, including Tsar Alexander I himself. But privileged status did not mean that Russian administrators looked favorably at the requests presented before them. In fact, as special agents of the Jewish community with discreet knowledge of sensitive information, the deputies aroused suspicion: not only because they traveled with large sums of money in their pockets, but also because they carried precious letters, petitions, and other communication written in Hebrew or Yiddish—languages that no one in the government could read. On more than an infrequent occasion, the authorities seized and translated the letters in search of Jews' dark secrets.[17]

This does not mean that the deputies were entirely powerless in their advocacy. After several Jews were blamed for the ritual murder of a young peasant girl in the provincial town of Grodno in 1816, Dillon and Zonnenberg exerted their political influence to undermine the credibility of the charge. In January 1817, they appealed to Alexander I to denounce what they regarded as "medieval Christian prejudices." To their delight, Alexander immediately turned the case over to one of his highest-ranking officials, Count Aleksandr Golitsyn, who at the time was the dual minister of the interior and popular enlightenment. Golitsyn rewarded the deputies' efforts by instructing provincial governors and governors-general to treat skeptically the "medieval superstition" and not charge Jews with the crime without firm empirical evidence.[18]

The Grodno case was the pinnacle of the deputies' success. In the ensuing four years, they lost what little clout they possessed, operating with little financial or political support.[19] In fact, by the time Shmerka Berlin and Evzik Tsetlin had sent their appeal to Vitebsk to protest the blood libel charge, the Russian government refused to acknowledge the legitimacy of the institution. The political circumstances made it structurally difficult for Jewish communities to work together to defend common political interests. But all was not lost. It so happened that Slava Berlin's sister and brother-in-law, a man by the name of Hirsh Berkovich Brouda, were residing in St. Petersburg. In the 1820s, a tiny Jewish colony of no more than several hundred souls, composed of well-connected communal advocates, well-to-do merchants and contractors, dentists, skilled artisans, and the occasional foreign national, enjoyed temporary residence privileges in the imperial capital.[20]

Brouda made his fortune trading and selling timber, and it appears that he had what it took—the linguistic skills and rhetorical flair—to agitate on behalf of the Velizh Jewish community. The Jews asked Brouda to plead with the higher authorities for justice—just as the deputies Dillon and Zonnenberg had done in the wake of the ritual murder accusation in Grodno. Between January and September 1827, Brouda filed no fewer than six formal complaints with the Second Section of the Fifth Department of the Senate.[21] These were extraordinary detailed letters written on official stamped government paper, describing the trauma and passions of imprisonment. Brouda began by reminding the authorities that Strakhov relied on the "most oppressive measures" to torture Jews with the sole purpose of getting them to confess to a crime they did not commit. As a particularly alarming example, he pointed out that, on the night of November 18, "wild screaming and unrestrained commotion" could be heard from the place where they locked up the Jews. In fact, the noise got so loud that "numerous neighbors from various parts of the town could hear the dreadful cries." One of the neighbors remembered a prisoner screaming out loud: "They hit me! They hit me! They tried to strangle me to death. He [Strakhov] lied to me." "I have no doubt," Brouda remarked, "that Strakhov uses the investigation to vindicate himself in the eyes of the state ... despite the fact that such a vindication undoubtedly destroys the lives of a million [*sic*] Jews."[22]

In dealing with a charge that appalled the conscience of mankind, Brouda appealed to the higher organs of government to stop the unnecessary suffering.[23] First, he wanted to make sure that the inquisitorial commission was abiding by proper rules and procedures as outlined in the 1817 circular. To minimize irregularities, Brouda requested that the most powerful procurator in the province be assigned to the case. His duties would include supervising Strakhov's work and reporting to the Ministry of Justice at every stage of the investigation. He also wanted the Senate to authorize an official deputy who would work with the Jewish community—to make sure that the commission did not stray outside the boundaries of the law. Meanwhile, Jews would be allowed to complain to the Senate when they found good reason to do so.

Second, Brouda felt that Strakhov was stalling on purpose. His actions only increased the prisoners' misery: "My relatives, Shmerka Berlin and his wife and their [grown] children, and all the other poor Jews [locked up in prison], were torn from their own young children and bound in leg-irons like hardened criminals. Strakhov's tyrannical actions have exhausted their bodies to the point that they have contracted the most debilitating illnesses." Brouda felt that Slava Berlina was in particularly bad shape: "Strakhov locked her up in his own bedroom and interrogated her in private [without the presence of a recording secretary or other members of the investigative commission]. As a result of all the cruelty, Slava suffers from hysterical-spasmodic attacks, which the town doctor Levin was in no position to treat."[24]

Although Brouda did not use the phrase, the circumstances he described in his letters resemble what might be termed a humanitarian crisis, that is, an egregious government action that threatened the safety and well-being of a group of people.

When Strakhov decided to imprison the Jews, he had no compassion whatsoever for their humanity. Fathers and mothers were captured from their very own homes and escorted under armed guard to [the house] where they continue to sit in solitary confinement to this very day, as if there was no doubt whatsoever that they had committed the crime. ... On some occasions he arrested the wives, at other times, he took away the husbands, and then there were instances of small help-less children left to their own devices to look after their own fate.[25]

If nothing else, Brouda hoped the higher authorities would intervene in the case by stopping the inhumane treatment of Jews. "[Strakhov] applies torture in any manner he sees fit, without concern for the evi-dence before him and established criminal procedure." Not only "does he treat the Jews poorly by chaining them in leg-irons," but he also "takes into custody completely innocent people who sit behind closed doors at the investigator's mercy." To put it in slightly different terms, Brouda felt that the tragedy had grown to unprecedented proportions: "Strakhov wants to unmask something that had never and will never be proven [in a court of law]."[26]

Brouda reminded the Senate that all of this was taking place at the same time that Jews were filing official complaints with the gover-nor-general's office. The Jewish community had sent several formal grievances, including a lengthy letter by the Velizh *kahal*, shortly after the emperor decided to reopen the criminal case.[27] Khovanskii repeatedly ignored the Jews' pleas, refusing to discipline the chief investigator for his actions. Instead, he gave Strakhov the freedom to do as he pleased. If the goal of the investigation was to locate the perpetrators, why did Strakhov interrogate only the Jews, and none of the other Christian residents, in the town? "Where's the mystery?" Brouda asked in desperation. "It appears to be nothing more than an ordinary crime."[28]

From a very early date, sometime in the sixteenth century, a series of treatises authored by an international team of writers expounded an ideology of resistance to monarchical abuse. *Vindicae contra tyrannos*, first published in Basel in 1579, declared that "if a prince were to gov-ern with violence and disregard for divine and human law, and thus tyrannically, another prince, with perfect justice and legality, [may] take military action."[29] In subsequent decades, devising action against events that appalled the conscience of mankind gained traction in the international community. The idea behind humanitarian intervention, as it was first conceived and practiced in early modern Europe, was to change the regime's policy toward victims of abuse. A humanitarian public—comprising diplomats, scholars, and sophisticated pressure groups committed to ameliorating the plight of subjugated peoples—helped mobilize public opinion and generate support for action.[30]

No event better illustrates how Jewish communities were able to shape public opinion than a ritual murder charge in Damascus in 1840. There, only five years after the Velizh case was officially settled, an Italian monk and his servant disappeared. Shortly thereafter, a large number of the wealthiest Jews in Damascus were charged with and convicted of ritual murder. News of the case quickly spread across the Middle East and the entire Western world. The most respected newspapers in England, France, and Germany published dozens of articles and polemics of the case, many of which presented the alleged murder of Father Tommaso as part of a wider Jewish cult of human sacrifice.[31] At first, the crisis produced great confusion in the Jewish community. In due time, however, Jews were able to mobilize an extraordinary and unprecedented response: lobbying at the highest levels of government, international press campaigns, parliamentary debates, well-publicized meetings, fundraising initiatives, and a diplomatic mission to Egypt by two of the most esteemed personalities in the Jewish philanthropic world, Sir Moses Montefiore from England and Adolphe Crémieux from France. In the end, the lobbying efforts proved to be a partial success: Although the imprisoned Jews were ultimately released, the sultan refused to formally repudiate the ritual murder charge.

In direct contrast to the Damascus situation, news of the Velizh case failed to circulate beyond the well-guarded circles of the imperial bureaucracy. It is highly unlikely that Brouda or any other member of the Velizh Jewish community attempted to reach out for help to politically influential activists in England, France, or Germany. If they did, the correspondence—on either side of the border—has not surfaced. In terms of its global reach, the Velizh case caused barely a ripple. On his visit to Russia in 1846, it does not appear that Moses Montefiore was aware of the case.[32] In the mid-1840s, newspapers all across Europe covered Russia's terrifying measures against Jews. Conscription brought fears of mass conversion. "Half a million Jews may haven fallen as martyrs to their faith," warned the *Jewish*

Chronicle, "and another half a million may have gone over to the Russian Church." The expulsion of Jews from within fifty versts of the Prussian and Austrian borders served as yet another painful reminder of Nicholas's draconian policies. According to the *Journal des Débats*, Russia had "declared war against the civilization as well as the generous and philosophic spirit of our age. ... Every day the German journals bring us accounts of persecutions exercised by order of the Emperor against the Jews."[33] In his long and distinguished career, Montefiore took great pride in agitating on behalf of Jewish humanitarian causes. While traveling in Russia, he gave much of his time and money to Jewish charitable foundations. At a later date, he also offered several recommendations to Count Pavel Kiselev, the minister of state domains, on how to tackle the most pressing questions of the day concerning Jews.[34] Yet there was no mention in his diary or letters of the cruelties that blood accusations had wrought on Russia's Jews. It appears that the Third Section's efforts of keeping the blood libel case a well-guarded state secret had worked.

In this political climate, the Ministry of Justice came to the conclusion that the complaints filed against Strakhov were unfounded. On March 19, 1827, after reviewing the weighty dossier, it felt that the case was legitimate enough to move forward with the criminal investigation. The state's wider concerns with regulating the boundaries of religious belief played an important role in the decision. At the same time, the justice ministers knew all too well that, no matter how impressive the empirical evidence may have been, convicting Jews of the crime of ritual murder would set an extraordinary historical precedent. Although instructed to move forward with the case, Strakhov and his team were reminded to observe the principles of the 1817 circular. According to criminal procedure, all internal correspondence, depositions, interrogations, petitions, material evidence, and other paperwork needed to be forwarded directly to the Senate. Most important, the justice ministers emphasized that Jews had the legal right to petition the Senate and present any counterevidence for official review by the most powerful judicial institution in the empire.[35]

For years, scholars argued that Jewish life during Nicholas's reign was marked by persecution and the arbitrary dispensation of justice. The ukase—or the special edict of the Russian government—served as the key tool by which the tsar disciplined its subjects.[36] Nineteenth-century critics of Russia's legal system noted how provincial governors meddled freely in court decisions, changed verdicts at will, and initiated investigations in cases where there was not a hint of a crime.[37] To be sure, the imperial law code was full of contradictory statutes regulating all facets of daily life. Based on privilege and difference rather than uniformity and transparency, Russia's legal system was designed to take away the population's rights at a moment's notice. Recent research has shown that, although imperial Russian law was not founded on equitable principles, it nevertheless enabled all imperial subjects to articulate claims on the state by invoking the protection of established legal norms. When an individual filed an official grievance, Russia's judicial machinery was obligated to respond to the claims of its public.[38]

By April 1827, Berka Nakhimovskii and Sheftel Tsetlin became increasingly anxious about the latest developments in the case. With their complaints officially dismissed, and with communication to the outside world firmly sealed, they had every reason to believe that the Velizh Jews' collective fate rested in the hands of the criminal justice system. And so Berka and Sheftel decided to follow the Ministry of Justice's guidance by appealing directly to the Senate. The best course of action, they reasoned, was to continue writing formal grievances. What else could they do to escape imminent danger, to whom could they turn to express their frustration? Perhaps some of the most esteemed bureaucrats and military officers in the empire would see the light of day. Perhaps someone in the imperial capital would comprehend the absurdity of the allegations. This time, they decided to enlist the help of Shmerka Berlin's brother, Biniamin, one of the most capable and articulate men in the provincial district, in writing the complaint.

In a long, flowery letter, Biniamin, Berka, and Sheftel enumerated a list of administrative abuses they witnessed. Among other things, they pointed out, Strakhov had placed Iankel' Hirsh Aronson "in leg-irons when he was severely ill." Some prisoners "were kept in dark filthy rooms without fresh air and, as a result of the unsanitary conditions in which they lived, one Jew [Aronson] died and several others managed to contract deadly diseases, all the while the Christian women were held without the slightest harassment and personal injury." All this was happening at the same time the governor-general was violating the laws of the land. In the past two years, they noted, Jews had sent several complaints to Vitebsk detailing Strakhov's "unlawful activities," and to their disappointment, the governor-general "deliberately ignored all their pleas." There was no doubt in their minds that Strakhov had no intention of altering his tactics or behavior and that he would continue to "humiliate Jews" for the duration of the criminal investigation. Echoing past grievances, the men came to the conclusion that the best course of action was to "remove the chief investigator from the case."[39]

As soon as it received the complaint on April 27, 1827, the Senate called on the governor-general to respond to the allegations. Although powerful provincial officials such as Khovanskii could ignore laws or fail to maintain standards of honesty, the language of due process and equal justice gave all imperial subjects the legal right to petition the state.[40] No matter how slow or clumsy the judicial system might have been, every subject in the empire had the right to have her or his voice heard. The imperial ministries—including the Chancellery for Receipt of Petitions—usually took the communications seriously. In the first half of the nineteenth century, the state responded to nearly every request—no matter how mundane or outlandish—sent its way. Like so many other imperial subjects, Jews turned to the judicial system because it worked at a significant level and because it proved to be the most effective way of negotiating the hazards of daily life.[41]

In a direct rebuttal of the criticisms, Khovanskii insisted that he had no intention of taking away this right away from the Jews, although he was certain that they did not have good reason to file the grievance. How in the world did Berka Nakhimovskii, Sheftel Tsetlin, Biniamin Berlin, not to mention the advocate Hirsh Brouda, know what was taking place behind closed doors? Khovanskii went to great lengths to point out the fact that just because the commission worked in strict secrecy did not mean that it had deliberately mistreated the prisoners. The town doctor was always on call when an imprisoned Jew required medical care. On several occasions, they even summoned the most esteemed physician from Vitebsk to tend to the prisoners' needs. When Jews felt tired or restless, they were given "ample opportunity to take walks in the courtyard." When they "felt hungry and thirsty, they were brought all the food and water they requested, usually directly from home." Khovanskii clarified that the commission decided to seal the bottom half of Evzik

Tsetlin's window with dark green paper not to make the room dark or inhabitable, as the petitioners had asserted, but to stop him from communicating with friends and family on the outside. The precautionary measure was necessary from the very first days. Tsetlin "was able to communicate with Jews who passed by [the house] what was being discussed during the interrogation sessions. Because he was able to open the window it was easy for him to talk with Jews who were standing outside his room. And [even when the window was closed shut], it was possible to know what was going on inside the room, especially when Tsetlin decided to raise his voice." On many occasions, "Tsetlin's servant stood outside his window with tea, coffee, and food, and they talked so loud, as if they were engaged in a shouting match."[42]

Furthermore, Khovanskii was convinced that the Christian inmates were kept "in much worse circumstances than the Jews." All the Jews, save for Iankel' Hirsh Aronson and Shifra Berlina, were in perfectly fine health. On several different occasions, the governor-general made the journey to Velizh, and each time, he observed, he did not encounter any evidence that justified the complaints in any way. "I've been to the house where the interrogations are taking place," the governor-general reported to St. Petersburg, "and not only did I not witness suffering or distress, but I also found the [Jewish] prisoners to be in fine health. They all reside in comfortable rooms and are given enough of everything to subsist just fine." Khovanskii observed only one important difference: unlike their coreligionists in town, the Jews locked up behind closed doors "are deprived of the freedom to go wherever they wish." The preventive measure was necessary, he warned, because of the severity of the criminal charge. "If the prisoners were allowed to roam freely, they would [no doubt] conceal the truth and undermine the sanctity of the investigation."[43]

Regarding the claim that Strakhov mistreated Aronson, Khovanskii came up with a sound explanation. The moment that Aronson—who, along with several other Jews, sat in solitary confinement in the town jail—started to feel sick, the warden did everything in his power to look after his needs. Khovanskii could not understand why Jews got so angry. "He [Aronson] was given two nice cells, all the food that he wanted to eat, as well as other basic necessities delivered straight to his cell from home. The town doctor called on Aronson daily. Even a physician from the provincial capital of Vitebsk came by [for a visit on occasion]." The problem was that Aronson was weak from tuberculosis; there was little, if anything, the doctors could do for him. As a rule, the inquisitorial commission forbade the prisoners from having direct contact with any-one in the town, but it made an exception for Aronson, allowing "his mother to see her sick son on a daily basis." In the final weeks of his life, Aronson was even given a choice: "Did he want to be transferred to the house with all the other prisoners or to a special house where he would live on his own with a watch guard?" Aronson refused both offers. Instead, he petitioned to die in his own home among his family (he suc-cumbed to tuberculosis on April 21, 1827, only five days after he filed the request). As far as Shifra Berlina, Khovanskii noted that no matter how hard the commission tried to make her feel comfortable, the merchant's daughter continued to suffer from "hysterical spasmodic attacks."[44]

In the spring of 1827, the governor-general warned St. Petersburg that the investigation would not be complete for "some time." He asked for more time because, he felt, the case was troubling on several differ-ent levels. Although the inquisitorial commission had every reason to believe that Jews bore full responsibility for the ritual crime, it still had not put together a complete list of names. That was reason enough to proceed slowly and with meticulous care. "Some Jews have yet to be arrested," Khovanskii explained, "but there were plenty of names the accusers had not recalled, and several others they've conspired to hide [from us]."[45] To get to the bottom of things, the inquisitorial commis-sion needed to resolve the troubling inconsistencies in the testimonies, examine the empirical evidence for additional clues, and go over the murder sequence by sequence, fact by fact, until it established the true depth of the criminal conspiracy.

6

The Investigation Widens

IN THE SUMMER OF 1827, the investigation took on a bureaucratic life of its own. The work was long and exhausting. Most days started promptly at seven o'clock in the morning and continued until nine o'clock in the evening, with a three-hour break in the afternoon.[1] Shortly after the inquisitorial commission was given approval to forge ahead, Strakhov ordered a new round of arrests and pleaded for additional reinforcements. On July 6, 1827, three high-ranking military officers, eleven noncommissioned officers, three musicians, and seventy-five soldiers arrived to help.[2] By the fall of 1827, Strakhov sealed shut five synagogues, and ordered a mass of privates and noncommissioned officers to guard the perimeter of the only synagogue that remained open.[3]

Strakhov and his team of inquisitors worked diligently to come up with a complete list of names involved in the murder case. Time and time again they brought Jews for confrontations with their accusers, rendering pain at will and exploiting the psychological weaknesses of the prisoners as they saw fit. But the longer the investigation dragged on, the harder it was to establish a seamless narrative of what really happened. As with mass witch-hunts, there were always pieces of the story left unfinished, contradictions and unanswered questions in the testimonies, and the specter of additional details or names of accomplices.[4] At some point in the summer of 1827, Strakhov became increasingly convinced that

Fedor's murder was part of a wider conspiracy not yet uncovered. The operation of secret, mysterious, and unseen powers has played a fundamental role in ordering human experience. Conspiratorial ideas—on the articulation of political power, the spread of contagion, and the control of the world's money supply and banking—have had broad appeal all around the world. With great interest and apprehension, authorities in different times and places consumed reports of new threats lurking in the social fabric. For the judicial powers at hand, the evil intrigues operate on a grand scale, even though the fantasies reveal themselves in particular sites, such as, in our case, the sleepy border town of Velizh, where a Jewish cabal threatened to condemn the entire Jewish nation.[5]

On September 9, 1827, Governor-General Nikolai Nikolaevich Khovanskii departed to St. Petersburg to appear before a committee of senators. Although appointed by the emperor, the governor-general was a delegate of the central government, required by law to be in constant contact with the imperial capital.[6] As any highly ambitious official who wanted nothing more than to climb the administrative ladder, Strakhov was well aware of the governor-general's responsibilities. If the Senate were to fine or castigate Khovanskii for a dereliction of duty, Strakhov's own future would surely be on the line. Given these high stakes, the inspector-councilor spent several long nights preparing an exhaustive report, explaining in minute detail what the commission had accomplished and listing the complex reasons why it required more time to complete the investigation.

To limit corruption, the Russian law code outlined the rules of the inquisitorial process: how exactly the interrogation process was required to proceed and how officials were expected to write, sign, assemble, and store legal records. To ensure that administrative procedures were followed correctly, the commission needed to inform the governor-general of its progress. Provincial governors were required to send updates to St. Petersburg at key stages of the case. The tsar and his ministers tried to control the investigation of high crime to the last intimate detail. Commissions were dispatched routinely to provincial towns and villages to take over the judicial process. Not only did the imperial center want to prevent abuse at the local level, but it also wanted to do everything in its power to quash heretical or politically dangerous behavior before it could spiral out of control.[7]

The slowness of the Velizh case began to sound alarms in St. Petersburg. Why was it taking so long to complete the investigation? When did the commission plan on wrapping up the case?[8] Khovanskii had no easy answers. In painstaking detail, he went over the commission's findings with the Senate. The interrogation sessions were clearly paying off, he pointed out: Terenteeva and Maksimova were naming more names and revealing, however gradually, the hidden dimensions of the murder conspiracy. Khovanskii emphasized that several hurdles impeded the swift resolution of the case. First, not all the suspects lived in the surrounding region. This was why the investigators were spending considerable energy and financial resources tracking everyone down. It also did not help matters that the Jews used a variety of different strategies—including "trickery and cunning"—to slow down the investigative process. Furthermore, there was the problem of time and memory. Several years had passed since the little boy was found in the woods. In the meantime, both the suspects and their accusers had forgotten crucial details. Given all the contradictions and lapses in testimony, it was nearly impossible to speed up the investigation. What it needed was more time.[9]

The Senate not only granted the governor-general an extension, but it also gave him absolute oversight over what it characterized to be an "extraordinary criminal case."[10] In the fall of 1827, with the investigation expanding in scope and intensity, Khovanskii urged the inquisitorial commission to come up with a complete list of names as quickly as possible. Less than a week after Khovanskii left for St. Petersburg, Strakhov summoned the accusers for more interviews. On several different occasions, Maria Terenteeva hinted of wider conspiracies, but she was unusually vague on the details. Then, on September 15, 1827, Maria broke down after a particularly painful session. Not only did she name more names, but she admitted to helping Jews kill two more Christian boys.[11] The murders allegedly occurred in the spring of 1813. Once again Mirka Aronson's two-story brick house was at the center of the diabolical events. One day, Maria explained, she went out to the marketplace to purchase a besom, a broom made of twigs, when she ran into an old acquaintance and her two sons. As they were chatting, Shmerka

Berlin "came out of the shadows, grabbed both boys by the arms," and "whisked them away inside the house."[12] When Maria came over to the house the next day, Mirka Aronson, Shmerka and Slava Berlin, and various other Jews from all walks of life were there, as well.

"The boys were crying uncontrollably," Terenteeva went on, but after the Jews fed them "several drops of liquid from a glass bottle on a tiny silver spoon," they suddenly fell silent. Terenteeva recounted a well-rehearsed plot. She described how Jews undressed both boys, enclosed them in a barrel lined with steel nails, and shook it from side to side for several hours. She talked about how she washed the bodies in a special liquid, trimmed the fingernails to the very flesh, and cut off the foreskin. The great Jewish school was once again at the heart of the frightful tale. Avdotia Maksimova, in hopes of "cleansing her conscience," wasted no time retelling much the same story that Terenteeva had described: how she stabbed both boys with a nail, washed off the blood, and helped deposit the bodies in the river.[13]

Not wanting to slow down the judicial process, Strakhov nevertheless proposed to broaden the inquiry. The first order of business was to talk with the domestic servant Maria Kovaleva, who, it turned out, was able to corroborate the account, even while embellishing it with surprising new details. In the spring of 1813, Kovaleva explained, she was an "impressionable young girl." As she stood inside the Jewish school, Kovaleva remembered that she saw something long and round with two long pointers resembling the devil's horns. "Iosel' Glikman told me that this was the Jewish god who does only good things for the Jewish people and no one else." Kovaleva went on to describe another incident that connected ugly rumors with past events. About a year after the two boys were murdered, Kovaleva was cleaning Mirka's floors when she spotted a little red wooden chest hidden in the corner of the room. Curiosity got the best of her, and she opened the lid and saw what appeared to be "three dark red pancakes and a large silver cup." She remembered, as if it were yesterday, that the thick dark red substance floating in the silver cup gave off a heavy nauseating smell resembling that of rotten flesh.[14]

"Why did she not come forward earlier?" Strakhov inquired. Kovaleva's face turned visibly agitated. "I was afraid that the Jews would deny everything and that authorities would whip me with the knout and send me off to Siberia." Kovaleva was convinced that her life would end right there and then. She realized that the Jews wanted to frighten her into silence. And now—years later—Kovaleva felt the time had finally come to "reveal everything." But disaster struck quickly. Only a few days after she told her tale, Kovaleva decided to end her life by hanging herself. In the last moments of her life, it appears that Kovaleva was certain that her confession would come back to haunt her. On the eve of her suicide, the guard on duty noticed that Kovaleva was in a state of hysteria. He confirmed that "Kovaleva was crying uncontrollably, pacing around the room, mumbling under her breath that she had revealed the entire truth" and that she missed her husband and children.[15]

In the meantime, Jews were summoned for more interrogations. When she was brought before the inquisitorial commission, Khanna Tsetlina opened up to the possibility that Terenteeva purchased a besom at the marketplace, but she flatly denied that Jews locked up the boys in Aronson's house. Khanna assumed that Kovaleva was brainwashed. How could it be otherwise? After all, Kovaleva repeated—word for word—the same exact tale that Maksimova and Terenteeva had recounted.[16] Other Jews shared similar thoughts. No matter how serious the crime may have been, Slava Berlina, for instance, flatly denied the allegations leveled against her. Evzik Tsetlin told the inquisitors that they had no legal right to question him or any other Jews, while Orlik Devirts wondered why Kovaleva did not turn to the police. "It's evident that she's been brainwashed," Orlik insisted. "Surely, the boys had family and friends in town. Wouldn't somebody have said something by now? Wouldn't they have searched for the young children [as soon as word got out that they went missing]? Lies! Lies! It's all lies! These events [supposedly] took place years ago. But if they did in fact take place, wouldn't a neighbor or perhaps someone else in town said something by now?"[17]

In the winter and spring of 1828, the entire town was throbbing with vicious rumors. The inquisitorial commission hoped to wrap up the case, but the interrogations only added to the complexity of the investigation. At a meeting with the Uniate priest Tarashkevich, Terenteeva confessed that not only did she assist with the death of two Christian boys, but that she took part in yet another ritual murder, of a noblewoman named Dvorzhetskaia in December 1817. Terenteeva explained that she had been acquainted with Dvorzhetskaia for "quite some time."[18] One day, Terenteeva and Dvorzhetskaia decided to walk down to the river when they ran into a local moneylender who was holding a bottle of spirits. She recalled that they took turns drinking from the bottle "until their heads began to spin." Afterward, they made their way to the home of a Jew who lived next to the police station and the Holy Spirit Church, only a few steps from the Jewish school. There, they passed around another bottle, and the moment that Dvorzhetskaia became completely inebriated, four Jews grabbed her by both arms and dragged her inside the school, where five more Jews were waiting for them. One of the Jews undressed Dvorzhetskaia, took fifty rubles from her pocket, and shoved her inside a barrel that was hanging by a rope from the ceiling.[19] Although Terenteeva described the diabolic ritual on several different occasions, the inquisitors pressed her to repeat the tale one more time. Terenteeva went to great lengths to recount how they shook the barrel from side to side for "three full hours" and how they took turns "slapping Dvorzhetskaia's cheeks, tying rope around her knees, and stabbing the body with a shiny nail."[20]

The inquisitors immediately found inconsistencies in Terenteeva's testimony. Given the opportunity to explain herself, Terenteeva testified, "The events took place a long time ago. I consumed large amounts of wine that night. I visited several different [Jewish] homes." To resolve the contradictions, Strakhov summoned Orlik Devirts for a confrontation, but the old man refused to stand face to face with Terenteeva. "Was [Dvorzhetskaia] really killed at the school?" he asked. Then, as his face changed color, Orlik squeezed his hands firmly together, took a deep breath, and told the inquisitors in a depressed voice, "My life is wasted. I am done for." "I haven't done anything wrong," he continued, "and this is why I have no interest in confronting her anymore. You can do with me as you please. She is a mean, dirty woman. She lies continuously, repeats everything you [the inquisitors] tell her."[21]

The commission concluded that Orlik Devirts was not within his legal right to refuse a confrontation. By not standing face to face with Terenteeva, Strakhov warned Orlik, he was admitting to his own guilt. But Orlik, paying no attention to the legal justification, maintained that Terenteeva's confessions were false. "When exactly did the [murders] take place? I don't know anything about them. Why would I take part in such things, when, God only knows, I can barely feed my children?

You're distressing me in my old age." When Terenteeva walked in the room, Orlik didn't hold back. "Is there anyone in town that can confirm what you've said is true? You've been taught to say this." "Yes, Orlik, I've been taught to say this," Terenteeva replied, "but you're the one who taught me everything I know. Who else knows [how to perform a ritual murder] ... the time has come to reveal the truth."[22]

In hopes of making sense of the allegations, Strakhov summoned Terenteeva to clarify the gaps and the discrepancies in her story, but she suddenly shifted the focus of the conversation by revealing more dark secrets.[23] It was around the time of the Passover holiday, "one or two years after Dvorzhetskaia's death," when Orlik Devirts took her to a tavern in the village of Semichevo. He left her there for three or four days and came back with two peasant girls. The younger girl was immediately escorted inside a special chamber and given a piece of bread to eat, while the older one spent the night in the adjoining room with Terenteeva. And the longer Terenteeva talked, the more she embellished the story with new details: how she mixed the blood with water and a handful of wooden chips, poured the mixture into exactly three glass bottles, soaked a piece of linen in the blood, cut it into small pieces, and then distributed a tiny piece to the Jews. When Strakhov pointed out the inconsistencies, Terenteeva turned visibly angry. Why was the inspector-councilor taking the Jews' side? "If Maksimova hadn't lured me into committing the crime," she asserted, "I would never have done such a thing."[24]

The Jews could not believe what they were hearing. Slava Berlina did not deny that she was acquainted with the old man Sholom, the owner of the Semichevo tavern, for "some time." The old man made frequent trips to Velizh to purchase groceries and other small items, but Slava was certain that she never set foot in the tavern. For this reason, she believed that the ritual murder allegations were beyond absurd. "Don't even bother writing anything down," Slava maintained. "What the accusers are saying is a bunch of crazy lies." When Terenteeva walked into the room, Slava did not hold back, repeating several times, "All you do is tell lies! I'll take you to court. You'll see what lies in store for you for making false accusations [against us]. You'll be sent away for a lifetime." Terenteeva did not pay any attention to Slava, telling the commission in a face-to-face confrontation, "It was Slava who taught me the diabolical rituals. If she didn't make me drink so much wine or force me to pierce the bodies, then I would have never learned to torture Jews." By this time, Slava had worked herself into a state of frenzy. "The commission is composed of con-artists who do their work deceptively, falsify papers, don't listen to a word I say. There will come a time when I'll stand in front of the tsar, mark my words, and I'll reveal everything. I'm afraid of nothing!"[25]

Just before her death, Shifra Berlina told the commission that the "accusers could say whatever they wanted because they stood nothing to lose. They drink wine from morning to night. Terenteeva is poor and lives on the streets." Orlik Devirts confirmed that he knew Sholom and that on several occasions he even passed by his tavern on his way to Semichevo. He was adamant, however, that he did not have any business relations with the old man. If Terenteeva was telling the truth, why did more witnesses not come forward? "Why doesn't a respectable towns-man—someone everyone knows and admires—say something [against us]?" The only folks who talk, he emphasized, are "those people that live on the streets and wander from courtyard to courtyard in search of handouts."[26] When Terenteeva was summoned into the interrogation room, Evzik Tsetlin refused to talk with her. The recording secretary noted that he "pretended to be sick to his stomach." "You're not allow-ing me [to] talk," Terenteeva thundered back, "I am telling you that it was you who killed the two girls, the year after you murdered the two boys." But the only thing Tsetlin did was wave his hand at Terenteeva, refusing to sign the interrogation papers.[27]

However fantastic the accusations may have been, Maria Terenteeva had no intention of stopping there. Two or three years after she claimed to have helped murder the girls, Terenteeva insisted that she took part in yet another diabolic ritual.[28] Once again she provided a long, rambling account, with the exact details impossible to confirm. At the time of Passover, she said, a Jew named Zeilik Brusovanskii knocked on Evzik Tsetlin's door. The old man lived in the village of Suslinoi along Smolensk Road around two or three miles from town. Terenteeva happened to be sitting in the front chamber of Tsetlin's home when Zeilik came by and convinced her to go back home with him. "When we were walking along Smolensk Road," Terenteeva explained, "we saw four children, two boys and two girls, standing on a bridge. Zeilik forced me to abduct the children. I did not have the strength to say no." The very next day Maksimova and a handful of Jews from Velizh came to Zeilik's tavern and promptly went to work on the children.[29]

Maksimova confirmed the tale in broad outline but added terrifying new details, many of which directly contradicted Terenteeva's account. When Strakhov confronted Terenteeva with this information, Terenteeva's behavior changed for the worse. Without pause or explanation, she stopped answering the commission's questions. In no time, Terenteeva called Maksimova "abusive names" and claimed that she had masterminded the entire affair. Not knowing how to proceed, Strakhov decided to give Terenteeva time to cool off, to remember the events as they had "really happened."[30]

Not surprisingly, the allegations provoked an outcry from the Jewish prisoners. Strakhov summoned Zeilik Brusovanskii for a series of questions, but Zeilik was not very helpful: "I've been inside Aronson's house before, but I didn't instruct anyone there to ritually murder the children. I couldn't have been very friendly with [the Aronson family]. They're important people, while I'm just a miserable old soul who's no use to anyone. Although I know most of the Jews in town, I've never met Maksimova or Terenteeva before. They've never set foot in my tavern." The recording secretary noticed that Zeilik "stared at the floor the entire time" he was questioned. Breathing deeply, as if he was in great pain, Zeilik's body shook feverishly, and he did not know what to do with his hands. Zeilik concluded the deposition by stating the obvious: "I know absolutely nothing [about the murder]. Why would I want to stab to death poor innocent children? When one of my family members confesses, that's when I'll confess, as well. But until then I have nothing more to say. We [Jews] don't need [Christian] blood. Perhaps in other parts of the world Jews ritually murder children, but I don't know anything about [those crimes]."[31]

Although he admitted that he "frequented Zeilik's tavern on numerous occasions," Iosel' Mirlas refused to entertain the thought that he had taken part in the murder conspiracy. The recording secretary noted that Mirlas began to "weep uncontrollably." When he was asked why his face turned different colors, Mirlas replied, "It's not only my face that changes color or my body that trembles. After I talk with the commission, my head hurts for two straight days, as if I've lost my mind." Khanna Tsetlina was not very helpful either. When Strakhov asked her to recount the details of the murder, she replied, "I've never visited [Zeilik's tavern]. I don't know anything about the murder. If Jews need to kill [Christian] boys, we would have found them right here in town."

Evzik Tsetlin seemed to be in an agitated state the entire time he was questioned. The recording secretary noted that he looked "deathly pale." "I only have Avdotia to thank for feeling so well," he replied sarcastically. "I would have felt much better, if you never lived with me," he told her. "I have no doubt the other one [Terenteeva] would have said such dreadful tales. Why are you destroying my family? You've torn the entire town to pieces. But don't think that it will always be like this. You'll see what will happen. I've already told you: you'll never be able to prove anything incriminating [against us Jews]."[32]

With so many irregularities in the testimonies, the commission determined that the only way to prove the veracity of the accusation was to uncover the dead bodies. So the delegation followed Terenteeva to Zeilik's tavern, the site of the alleged crimes, but to their dismay the only thing they found was four rotted wooden columns. Maksimova proclaimed that she would be able to point out the grave. As the delegation was walking back to town along Smolensk Road, she suddenly darted inside the thick woods and began to dig up dirt and old twigs in search of the bones. Maksimova offered all sorts of explanations: that they were drunk at the time of the murder, that it was difficult to locate the spot because they were there only once, and that it happened such a long time ago. The inquisitors walked in circles for several more hours, but decided that it was best to return to town to conclude the investigation rather than waste more time walking aimlessly around the woods.[33]

In the span of eighteen months, Terenteeva and Maksimova recounted an assortment of fantastic tales, including host desecrations, or some variant thereof.[34] Perhaps the women overheard neighbors gossiping on a street or inside a church or tavern. Or maybe they remembered a case when a Jew was charged with stealing liturgical objects, desecrating the host, or murdering Christian children. Whatever the explanation, it seems reasonable to conclude that the women developed their plots from the narrative fragments in circulation at the time. Drawing on oral and written traditions, as well as a wealth of signs and symbols, plots and subplots, the stories they told worked because they were embedded in local memories and rooted in the real world.[35]

The host—the consecrated Eucharistic wafer—was believed to be the body of Christ himself. Eucharistic tales of abuse claimed that Jews captured and desecrated the most important symbol of Christian identity. As the consecrated wafer came to represent the body and blood of Christ, anxieties about the desecration of the host resulted in anti-Jewish campaigns and elaborate trials. Since early modern times, host desecration narratives had become enshrined in local traditions and liturgical practices. Devotion to the miraculous workings of the host was instrumental to the popularization of the blood libel. When they abused the host by throwing it in boiling water or piercing it with knives, or when they killed Christian children for the ritual use of their blood, Jews turned the blood of Christians into demonic material.[36]

Maksimova talked about how she hid the host in a handkerchief, while Terenteeva confessed that she did the same thing on at least three separate occasions. Both women described in fantastic detail how they helped Jews desecrate the Eucharist: how they mixed together water, wheat flour, blood, and sacred mysteries in a special basin; how they rolled the dough into buns, cut off the crust with a *treyf* (nonkosher) knife, and threw a tiny morsel into the fire; and how everyone gathered around to pierce the bread and smash it to pieces. Although they contradicted themselves on several occasions, and at one point Terenteeva got so angry at Maksimova that she refused to talk with her any more, it appears that they did agree on the salient elements of the narrative.[37]

"We have no need for sacred mysteries. What would we do with a crumb of bread?" Khanna Tsetlina explained to the inquisitors. "It may have lots of significance to you [Christians], but it means absolutely nothing to us [Jews]. How is it possible to disrespect a piece of bread?" With respect to Maksimova, Khanna did not hold back: "She likes to drink wine, for which she'll gladly sell her soul. She's a filthy whore. I don't want to see her anymore. I have nothing to say to her." Evzik Tsetlin could not agree more. "If it wasn't explained to me that Christians consider bread a sacrament, then I wouldn't have known this to this very day." "How is it possible to disrespect a piece of bread," Tsetlin wondered. "I've never read about such things in books. Not everyone is able to understand [what's printed there]. We have many types of books, and it's not possible to read them all. I'm not educated enough to understand them." Shmerka Aronson said something similar: "For 1,800 years, they've talked about how Jews use [Christian] blood. I heard that they even found printed works that document why Jews need blood. But it's all lies. I know for a fact that none of it is true."[38]

"How is it possible to desecrate sacraments?" Orlik Devirts asked. "Every month there are new developments [in the investigation]." Slava Berlina had no idea what Terenteeva and Maksimova meant by "sacred mysteries." "When did the desecrations occur?" she asked. Refusing to sign any papers—even though the inquisitors confirmed that all her words and actions would be dutifully recorded in special notebooks—she told the commission, "Write what you like, it makes no difference to me. I won't sign any papers." The moment Maksimova walked in the room, the recording secretary noted that Slava's entire body began to shake. She screamed as loudly as she could: "You've come here to tell lies. Do you know who I am? I'm Slavka Berlina. Don't think for a minute that I'll let things go ... you'll see what will become of you. Why don't you just admit that Strakhov taught you everything?"[39]

While the commission was busy interrogating the suspects, Terenteeva spent several long sessions recounting what turned out to be the last of the confessions: a horrifying tale of theft and defilement of church sacred property.[40] In late medieval and early modern Poland, the theft of Catholic Church objects was classified as the most sacrilegious of crimes. Although the Eucharistic wafer was considered the most sacred of all, courts routinely punished Jews for stealing, trading in, or defiling chalices, silver knobs, crosses made from precious metals, chrismatory (vessels containing consecrated oil), silk curtains, and tablecloths. In early modern Poland, trials and public executions of the criminals were public spectacles, and those individuals convicted of sacrilege were routinely burned at the stake. As news of the executions spread by word of mouth, large crowds gathered to witness the executions.[41]

Conflating the host desecration tale with church robberies, Terenteeva drew on a long tradition of recounting crimes that were deemed by state and church authorities alike as most serious. In this instance, the focus of Terenteeva's confession was on the antimins, which was stolen from the St. Il'insk Church. A meeting with the Uniate priest Tarashkevich brought Terenteeva to her knees. "I would have revealed everything to you a long time ago, Holy Father, but I was terrified of your response." She recounted how Jews handed her a carafe of vodka to drink and ordered her to steal the antimins. Terenteeva stood at the church doors at the twilight hour, just as everyone was leaving the building after Mass. She waited until everyone left, and as soon as the priest walked away from the altar, she ran inside the building and grabbed the sacred cloth. "The decorated towel wasn't very large," Terenteeva explained. With the towel in hand, she walked directly to the Jewish school, where a group of Jews wasted no time committing sacrilege. First, they took turns spitting on the cloth. Afterward, they stomped on it with their bare feet until it was torn into shreds, burning the remains, to leave no trace behind.[42]

This time, General-Major Shkurin took it upon himself to investigate the veracity of the accusation. To be certain that the "decorated towel" was in fact the sacred cloth, he asked for Terenteeva to demonstrate how she sneaked inside the church and stole the antimins. So Terenteeva, Shkurin, and several other members of the commission walked over to the St. Il'insk Church. The recording secretary noted that as soon as Terenteeva stepped inside the building, she threw herself down on the ground and started to cry uncontrollably, taking deep breaths intermittently, begging for the "Almighty God to forgive her for all the crimes she had committed." While prostrating herself on the ground, Terenteeva did not pay attention to Shkurin's entreaties. Finally, after an hour or so, "fearing that God would strike her down and she would die on the spot," Terenteeva declared that she would not be able to demonstrate to the inquisitors how she stole the antimins.[43]

Several days later, Tarashkevich went through the St. Il'insk Church's files and discovered that one of the antimins was in fact missing.[44] Avdotia Maksimova confirmed that the antimins was stolen in 1823, at roughly the time Fedor's body was found in the woods. Maksimova explained that, shortly after the boy was ritually murdered, Khanna Tsetlina handed the antimins to Iosel' Mirlas, who did unimaginable horrors to it. After carefully smoothing out all the wrinkles, Iosel' spit on the towel and wiped his hands with it. All the other Jews allegedly took turns doing the same exact thing. At the conclusion of the ritual,

Orlik Devirts picked up the towel from the floor and tore it into four equal pieces, with which he made a cross. Ruman Nakhimovskii wasted no time burning the towel and depositing all the ashes in a little copper basin, which he promptly took to the Jewish school. After Praskoviia Kozlovskaia confirmed Maksimova's account to the last detail, Shkurin was satisfied that he had assembled enough evidence to convict the Jews.

Evzik Tsetlin, among other prisoners, wasted no time denying the allegations. "What's an antimins, anyway? Avdotia, how long are you planning on telling these tales?" Then, turning to the commission, he burst out, "I don't want to listen to any of this anymore. I don't want to talk to her anymore." Later that afternoon, he continued, "You've completely ruined our town, destroyed our homes, our families. We're wasted, done for!" Khanna Tsetlina also could not comprehend the significance of the towel. She told Avdotia, "Avdotiushka, Avdotiushka, God only knows, you need to remember that the time will come when you too will die and enter the next world. You need to be honest about everything that has happened [here in town]. Did we really do all those things you've described?" To Kozlovskaia, "It's not true, it's not true! Praskoviia, you know this never happened. The towel was never spit on, stomped on, or burned. I was never with you at the school; you never worked for me." And to Terenteeva, "I never sent you over to the priest with a bottle of vodka. Why would I do something like that? Why would I ask you when I have my own domestic servant? I never even knew you [at that time]."[45]

Shkurin questioned many other prisoners, but they all stood their ground. Slava Berlina, for instance, told the inquisitorial commission that she had no interest in signing the confession papers. "I'm a woman. I don't know the laws of the land. The governor-general is not the emperor. . . . But I'm certain that I along with [all the other prisoners] will be proven innocent in due time."[46] Another prisoner claimed that she never lived in Velizh before and therefore had no idea why she was asked to testify. With tears in his eyes, Iosel' Glikman got down on both knees, explaining to the general-major, "God knows, Your Excellency, I know absolutely nothing [about the murder]. If something does come to light in the criminal investigation, then all Jews will be found guilty [of ritual murder]." Zusia Rudniakov remarked, "Perhaps it's true. I'm just a poor peddler, what do I know? I don't associate with the wealthy

Jews in town. I've never been [to their homes]. They don't ever talk with me. I don't know how to read or write. The only thing I know is that I've never heard of such things before." Nota Prudkov (before he confessed to the alleged crime) said that he could not agree more. "Go talk to Beniiamin Solomon, he's a learned Jew, ask our rabbis, all the apostates [in town]—they'll all tell you that this couldn't have happened. Jews don't need blood. The antimins and the blood is one and the same thing. This is a church towel, for God's sake, they hang people for stealing these [types of sacred objects]."[47]

In 1827 and 1828, at the height of the panic in Velizh, fears of mass Jewish conspiracies to murder Christian children spread across the northwest provinces of the Russian Empire. The interrogations revealed that little Fedor's murder was of a much wider problem. It was not just that Terenteeva and Maksimova confessed to helping Jews kill the noblewoman Dvorzhetskaia and eight more Christian children. No less disturbing were the reports of cases that suddenly popped up in nearby towns. First, a seven-year-old boy was found near a lake in Tel'she, Kovno province. Shortly thereafter, residents claimed to have witnessed two Jews kidnap and kill the farm boy. A lengthy criminal investigation ensued and as many as twenty-eight Jews were arrested on mass suspicion of ritual murder. Then, in Grodno, authorities decided to reopen a criminal case that had been closed for more than a decade. In light of the Velizh investigation, they wanted to be absolutely certain that Jews did not cover up the murder.[48]

There was nothing remarkable about the intensification of the criminal investigation. In different global locales, the pursuit of transparency prompted passionate crusades to uncover destructive hands of evil agents.[49] In villages and small towns of the Swabian-Franconian borderlands, for example, rumors of monstrous conspiracies of mass poisons, fantastic tales of murdered babies, and macabre accounts of atrocities led to widespread arrests of alleged witches. Merchants, peddlers, wandering craftsmen, and itinerant preachers passed on the local gossip as they traveled from town to town and region to region.[50] The fears quickly spread through different parts of early modern Europe. All in all, by the end of the seventeenth century, the great witch-hunts resulted in more than 110,000 arrests and 60,000 executions, with many more individuals forced to live their daily lives under constant threat of suspicion.[51]

Although the Velizh case did not spread to such depths, the pressure to accuse generated a powerful dynamic of its own, until more and more members of the community were drawn in. Connecting the past with the present, rumor with real-life historical events, Terenteeva, Maksimova, and Kozlovskaia lashed out at those people who stood the most to lose in a confrontation that threatened to destabilize the town's power structure. Without a firm social basis—without, in other words, so much support from the Christian residents—it seems highly unlikely that the accusers would have targeted so many persons of respect, responsibility, and authority. Here, too, the local currents conformed to patterns that played out elsewhere. But whereas certain individuals—at the height of the witchcraft accusations, in seventeenth-century Salem, Massachusetts, for example—remained off limits, all the Jews in Velizh were fair game.[52]

7

Boundaries of the Law

TO BRING ITS INVESTIGATION TO a resolution, the inquisitorial commission needed to establish with certainty that Jews played a formative role in the murder conspiracy. To do this, the inquisitors needed to elicit a full confession from the Jews themselves: that they had taken part in the affair in all its grisly details. In the early modern world, authorities could choose from an extensive repertoire of instruments to establish what really happened in a case: the tying of hands and the application of hot pincers to the soles of feet, stretching on the rack, ankle presses, metallic braces or screws to crush legs, sleep deprivation, cold water drips, knouting, and the strappado. The strappado was the most popular method of forcing people to talk. The accused's hands were tied together and attached to a rope; the rope was thrown over a beam, at which point the person was hoisted high into the air, brought down for a short period of time, and raised again.[1] All these techniques were used to get criminals to confess to their dark secrets, to provide more information, or to affirm a recantation.

As surprising as it may seem, Russia followed what might be termed the basic principles of Confucian justice, applying torture sparingly and discriminately.[2] But in contrast to the Chinese legal system, the Russian government had no interest in sanctioning the use of pain solely to make the victim suffer. In early modern Russia, judicial torture was prescribed only to double-check the veracity of the confession and the names of the co-conspirators. Muscovite courts went to great lengths to limit the use of unregulated torture, stipulating when and how much pain could be administered at any given time.[3] In fact, torture was an exceptional procedure in the criminal law, reserved for crimes such as witchcraft, religious dissent, espionage, and urban uprisings. On those rare occasions, the guilty were subject to mass spectacles of punishment—flogging, branding, beheading by ax and sword, bludgeoning on a large wooden wagon wheel, and public executions.[4]

In the eighteenth century, the Russian government further limited the use of state-sanctioned violence, reserving judicial torture and capital punishment for extraordinary crimes such as premeditated murder and homicide.[5] As the logic of cruel bodily punishment came under restriction, Russia—in comparison to other European states and China—was among the front runners in reducing the violently physical element. On September 27, 1801, Tsar Alexander I formally abolished the use of torture, declaring that "nowhere in any shape or form should anyone dare to permit or perform any torture, under pain of inevitable and severe punishment ... that accused persons should personally declare before the Court that they had not been subjected to any unjust interrogation."[6]

This does not mean, of course, that the Russian law code prohibited the application of various other tactics to compel people to talk. During the reign of Nicholas I, it was not unusual for suspects to be flogged and harassed, set in pillories, and confined in damp and dark cellars.[7] The inquisitorial records—and especially Jews' personal correspondence—demonstrate in extraordinary detail the methods that the inquisitors used to exploit prisoners' weaknesses. Operating in the privacy of a room, relying on a variety of confrontational and manipulative strategies to uncover the depth of the conspiracy, Strakhov and his team worked the prisoners into a state of frenzy. Jews were placed in semi-solitary, indefinite detention and interrogated for hours on end. Some were humiliated, restrained in leg irons, and threatened with coercion. Others were slapped and beaten at will until they agreed to sign written statements.

The inquisitors used the threat of pain, false-evidence ploys, and lengthy questioning to lower the Jews' psychological capacity for resistance.[8]

In addition to rendering pain and emotional desperation, something else was driving their actions. Strakhov knew all too well that, if the Jews failed to provide a fundamentally convincing narrative of what happened in the spring of 1823, the chances of successfully resolving the case were radically diminished. Time and time again, the inspector-councilor decided to put Jews through particularly grueling sessions designed to break down the human spirit by assaulting the victim's dignity.[9]

In the initial stages of the investigation, Strakhov shrugged off the reports of abuse, telling the governor-general that "not one prisoner has required even the slightest medical treatment."[10] But even if the inquisitors did not stray outside the bounds of the permissible (a highly unlikely proposition), confinement not only made the prisoners physically weak; there were emotional consequences as well. Shmerka Berlin suffered from tuberculosis, and it did not take him long to have trouble breathing and eventually fall into a state of hysteria. Shifra Berlin passed away from poor health not long after she was taken into custody. Evzik and Khanna Tsetlin and their daughter Itka suffered mental breakdowns from induced debilitation and repeated abuse.

Imprisonment took a physical and an emotional toll on the prisoners. Standing in front of the inquisitorial commission, many Jews found it difficult to cope with the trauma of the oral interrogations. Some individuals had a hard time getting their point across in a language only a handful of people knew reasonably well. Others succumbed to depression from which they never fully recovered, and often lost their train of thought in mid-sentence during the interrogations. In this respect, the Velizh Jews shared with many other prisoners in diverse geographic and temporal contexts the different emotions—fear, loneliness, melancholia, futile rebellion, abject despair, boredom, and blind rage—that made prison life so painful.[11] For the prisoners and their families, long silences or interruptions in communication exacerbated the isolation. The Jews yearned for mundane details about the health and safety of friends and relatives, of wives and husbands, and especially of young children who were suddenly left without a parent. Predictably, not knowing how events were unfolding at home—while having little physical contact with their loved ones—wreaked emotional havoc on their psyches.

Although the evidence is sketchy, the individuals swept up in the investigation—jailers, guards, accusers, and inquisitors—suffered as well. Some fell ill for stretches of time; others were unable to confront their own demons. Given the proclivity for the inquisitors to omit or erase incriminating details from the official documentary record, we have only a few examples, though they are revealing in their own right. The domestic servant Maria Kovaleva, who allegedly assisted Jews in murdering two Christian boys, committed suicide after going through a particularly trying interrogation session. Perhaps her conscience got the better of her?[12] Ivan Cherniavskii, a security guard, had an affair with Melania Zhelnova (the eighteen-year-old peasant girl arrested in 1825). Although she did not play an important role in the case, Zhelnova had a baby and was forced to reside with the child in a small wooden cottage for the duration of the investigation. After several years of sneaking across the courtyard for nighttime visits, Cherniavskii was reprimanded and put in isolation. Eventually, the guard ended his life by slashing his throat with a razor. Shortly before he was found in his room in a pool of blood, another official overheard Cherniavskii complaining that "his life had become unbearable."[13]

Strakhov had much to gain by successfully completing his assignment. At the very least, the inspector-councilor would set himself up for a handsome promotion and a nice increase in monthly salary. Perhaps he would even receive an appointment to an administrative post that carried with it an impressive jump in civil service rank. To be sure, zealous service was an important measure of achievement in Russia's bureaucratic world. Nevertheless, it would be misleading to interpret Strakhov's obsessions solely in terms of his career aspirations. Belief in the efficacy of diabolical ritual practices retained much of its appeal to a broad spectrum of the population, including the judges, magistrates, and administrators who controlled the judicial machinery in the provincial world and beyond. In the Russian Empire, as in other times and places around the world, the distinction between enlightened skeptics and believers in supernatural, demonic forces was never rigid. What applied for the witch-hunts was also the case for the blood libel: judicial uncertainty could and often did coexist with the belief in the reality of the crime.[14]

The documentary evidence suggests that Strakhov was convinced that Jewish ritual murder was a fact of life. In the very first months of the investigation, the inspector-councilor outlined some of the reasons in a communication to Nikolai Nikolaevich Khovanskii. First, Strakhov dismissed the fact that not one blood libel accusation had stood the test of legal scrutiny, even though such cases were investigated "rather frequently." Strakhov was convinced that Jews were unusually resourceful at covering up their tracks and that they managed to find creative ways to mask their "evil deeds." That the accusations were made only in places where Jews enjoyed residential privileges served as the best indicator that they continued to practice demonic rituals. It was no coincidence that "in those provinces where residence was prohibited to Jews not one accusation had been made." Why would someone want to commit the offense? The most common explanations for any ordinary criminal act were enmity, hardship, and financial gain. But none of those potential motivations was helpful in solving this particular case. After a careful consideration of the facts, Strakhov concluded that Fedor's murder was no ordinary crime: "The boy was not in any position to harm anyone. Furthermore, what would someone gain from killing an innocent child? Even if we were to imagine that someone hoped to profit from the [murder], then wouldn't he have been killed by one blow [to the head], and not ritually murdered, as the forensic evidence demonstrates [so clearly]?"[15]

Taking a sweeping look at the fruit of the commission's labors, Strakhov could not have been more pleased with the progress. None of the extravagant claims made against him stood the test of legal scrutiny. By the fall of 1828, the inquisitorial commission amassed an impressive dossier: a forensic report, an assortment of confessions, one blood-stained cloth, two knives, a piece of foreskin, and reference works that clearly established the theological origins and historicity of ritual murder. As the investigation shifted to last, critical stage, all signs indicated that it was just a matter of time before the inquisitorial commission would resolve the contradictions and put the pieces together.

An impressive list of sophisticated accusatory works helped Strakhov and his team of inquisitors rationalize the murder. These learned treatises—based on a wealth of printed and oral expert testimonies—provided textual proof that ritual murder was real. By the end of the eighteenth century, no fewer than seventy-six books and pamphlets were printed in old Poland. Providing long descriptions of past cases, the published works played a significant role in the prosecution of Jews. Highly detailed quotations from the Talmud and other sacred writings—usually made by converts or renegade members of the Jewish community with knowledge of the Hebrew language—helped bolster the charge.[16]

The inquisitorial commission collected several different works, all of which justified the basic premise that Jews needed Christian blood for ritual purposes.[17] The most important of these was a partial translation of Bishop Kajetan Sołtyk's brochure Złość żydowska (Jewish Wrath). Sołtyk first gained notoriety in a ritual murder trial in Zhitomir.[18] In 1753, he accused thirty-one Jews of using Christian blood in religious rituals, twelve of whom were found guilty of the crime and sentenced to death by quartering. Sołtyk not only reprinted documents from the trial, but also referenced evidence supplied by an extremist Jewish sect known as the Frankists (followers of a man named Jacob Frank, a self-proclaimed prophet of Shabbetai Zvi). In highly publicized disputations with Polish rabbinical authorities, the Frankists, who at one point converted to Catholicism and attempted to conceal their Jewish identity, argued that all prophecies about the coming of the Messiah had already been fulfilled, that a person can achieve faith in the Messiah only through baptism, that the Talmud teaches that Jews need Christian blood, and that whoever believes in the Talmud is bound to use it. Manipulating a wide range of Jewish sacred works, usually by mistranslating or misrepresenting key passages, the Frankists taught that human sacrifice and the ritual use of Christian blood was an intrinsic part of Jewish religious practice.[19]

Borrowing freely from previously published almanacs and pamphlets, including Frankist popular teachings, Sołtyk explored ritual murder as both a religious and social phenomenon. First published in 1760 and subsequently reprinted several times, Złość żydowska demonstrated that holy books commanded Jews to use Christian blood in their rites and rituals and to defile Christian sacred objects. For Strakhov, Sołtyk's work was a crucial piece of expert evidence that connected the past with the present, because, as he explained to Khovanskii, it "described actual cases of superstitious acts and demonstrated convincingly that Jews required Christian blood for religious rituals."[20]

The Reverend Robert Walsh's 1827 travel narrative of the Ottoman Empire served as further proof that ritual murder could occur anytime and anywhere. Walsh described how one day, while passing through Galata, a suburb of Pera (in present-day Istanbul), he heard rumors that Jews had ritually murdered a Greek boy. "The child of a Greek merchant had disappeared," Walsh explained, "and no one could give any account of it." At first, the authorities thought that a Turk had taken the boy for a slave. But after the body was found, with the legs and arms bound tight and the wounds visible on the side, they assumed that the boy had died "in some extraordinary manner and for some extraordinary purpose." Everyone immediately suspected that Jews were responsible for the gruesome death. "As it was just after their paschal feast, suspicion, people said, was confirmed to certainty. Nothing could be discovered to give a clue to the perpetrators, but the story was universally talked of, and generally believed, all over Pera."[21]

Walsh bolstered the tale's credibility by referencing a pamphlet written by a Greek Orthodox monk, a convert from Judaism named Neophytos. Written in Romanian and originally printed in 1803, Neophytos's *A Mystery Hitherto Concealed and Now Published for the First Time* revealed how Jewish fanatical sects—influenced by ideas found in Jewish sacred writings—consumed Christian blood for ritual and medicinal purposes. The pamphlet circulated in East European Orthodox monasteries and was reissued several times.[22] In the Russian Empire, the production and consumption of accusatory literature on the blood libel lacked the vigor of those works produced in early modern Poland. Only a handful of books and pamphlets were published in the Russian language, nearly all of which were translations of Polish originals.[23] Nevertheless, this genre of literature—much like demonological materials on the practice of witchcraft—added religious and intellectual substance to the arguments made against Jews.[24] In Velizh, as well as in other criminal investigations of ritual murder, the works authored by Sołtyk, Walsh, and Neophytos, among others, were employed as scientific aids in prosecuting Jews for the crime of ritual murder.

After converting to Catholicism in August 1828, Anton Vikentiev Grudinskii disclosed to the inquisitorial commission that none other than the preeminent medieval Jewish philosopher and Torah scholar Moses Maimonides had allegedly authored a manuscript in which he described the cultural beliefs and practices that had historically motivated Jews to commit ritual murder. Grudinskii claimed that he had stumbled upon the work, *How Christian Children Should Be Murdered,* when he was browsing through a box of confiscated Jewish books in a synagogue in the provincial town of Mira. Grudinskii was not the only convert in the history of ritual murder trials who talked about the secret uses of Christian blood in Jewish religious rituals and ceremonies.[25] Most of the confessions came because of long torture sessions; some individuals claimed to have witnessed and participated firsthand in the blood libel rituals, but no one had bolstered the charge by referencing the authorial voice of one of the greatest minds of world civilization.[26]

Born in Andalusia, in the southern part of Spain, at the end of the golden age of Jewish culture, Maimonides (also known as Rambam, his Hebrew acronym) committed himself to revealing the inner meaning of Judaism and the hidden mysteries of the Torah. In his great work *Mishneh Torah,* Maimonides provided in clear and unambiguous language a guide to the *halakhic* (legal) world of Jewish civilization so that the entire Oral Law might become known to Jews.[27] What was once concealed and convoluted would now become accessible and comprehensible. In replies to legal queries, Maimonides provided a record of opinions on a wide range of subjects—on, among other things, marriage and divorce, ownership and rental of property, conversion to Judaism and apostasy, menstruation, and circumcision. With respect to the Israelite covenant of blood, Maimonides explained that human blood played no role whatsoever in the ritual drinking of blood or the baking of bread made with blood.[28]

In the ancient Near East, a sect by the name of the Sabians reportedly ate blood because they believed that it was the food of the devils and that whoever ate it fraternized with the *jinn* (prophesying demons). In response to these idolatrous practices, Maimonides explained that Jewish law prohibited not only the consumption of blood but also eating the flesh of slaughtered animals in the vicinity of its blood. Blood may have linked the Israelites with their God—as in the Passover sacrifice or the blood of sacrifices thrown against the altar—but it could not be used after the fashion of the idolaters.[29]

Most likely, Grudinskii had little or no expert knowledge of Maimonides' religious and philosophical writings. This did not stop him from using the great philosopher's name to his own advantage. Grudinskii explained that the first page of the alleged manuscript in his possession was illustrated with Rambam's portrait, two Christian boys, a wooden barrel, and an assortment of instruments Jews used to torture and kill Christian children. Jewish communities were required to keep a copy of the instruction manual, rolled up in a scroll, in the wooden cabinet of their synagogues. The wooden barrel, which was equipped with eight iron nails, was placed underneath the *bimah* (raised platform) of the synagogue, while the torture instruments—one iron coronet, two iron washtubs, a circumcision knife, and a chisel—were stored in either the communal synagogue or the school.

According to Grudinskii, Rambam instructed Jews to take an oath of secrecy. If anyone would begin to suspect Jews of the crime, they would be expected to make sure that no one would ever find out the truth. And if they were ever caught in the act, Jews should keep the rites and rituals associated with blood sacrifice of Christian children a well-guarded secret.[30] Grudinskii went on to say that, each year before the Passover holiday, exactly four executive board members of the Jewish community were responsible for abducting young Christian children. The Jewish communal government maintained power over Jewish religious institutions by way of a vast network of brotherhoods. To do this, it devised secret ceremonies and inculcated fanatical beliefs to maintain internal control over its members.[31]

Grudinskii claimed that Rambam's manuscript was hidden in an old synagogue, but he could not remember which one exactly. Convinced that Judaism was imbued with dark secrets, St. Petersburg instructed provincial governors to go door to door in search of religious works that helped expose fanatical beliefs and practices. In the fall of 1827 and winter of 1828, at the height of the panic, the Department of Spiritual Faiths of Foreign Confessions instructed provincial governors to search rabbis' homes for old Jewish books prescribing the use of Christian blood for religious rituals.[32] It is unclear how many Jewish communities were targeted or the number of books that were eventually confiscated. We do know that secret files were delivered to the inquisitors in Velizh, and that Catholic priests were summoned to summarize and translate key passages of books and pamphlets. Grudinskii took great care to translate an old manuscript, which he claimed was authored by the great philosopher. In due time, however, a linguistic expert, an apostate from Mstislavl, declared Grudinskii's translation "disingenuous." After a particularly intense interrogation session, Grudinskii eventually confessed that he had fabricated the story from start to finish.[33]

By the time the officials searched houses in search of Jewish religious texts, the scope of the investigation had expanded exponentially. Khovanskii was confident that the inquisitorial commission had gathered enough evidence to convict the Jews of a crime that resembled other disturbing episodes in a long chain of historical events. On October 13, 1829, Khovanskii reported to state councilor Count Aleksandr Ivanovich Chernyshev, "I have several archival files and various other types of documents in my possession that demonstrate how frequently [Jews] instruct their coreligionists, under the guise of religious law, to conceal the truth, make false statements, and violate sworn oaths."[34] The medical assessment of the body, as corroborated by the testimony of numerous witnesses, soundly established that this was no ordinary crime but the work of what the governor-general called "cruel and unusual forms of tyranny." The only thing left to do, he felt, was to assemble the dossier and transfer the interrogation records and supporting evidence to St. Petersburg.[35]

Peter the Great's judicial reforms of the early eighteenth century initiated substantive changes to record keeping. An important part of the bureaucratic process was the production of an orderly dossier. The Russian government created a formulaic template for assembling and signing paperwork. The commitment to systematic record keeping played an important role in the preparation of criminal files. Secretaries were charged with transcribing everything that was said in the interrogation room in special notebooks. All the letters, petitions, memos, transcripts, and material evidence needed to be catalogued and preserved.[36] Not only did imperial law spell out a commitment to order and ethics, it also required devotion to the bureaucratic ideals of form and procedure: for administrative files to be written, formatted, and preserved in an exact manner.[37] In October 1829, Khovanskii promised St. Petersburg that the clerical work would be completed in four months' time. When the deadline passed, the governor-general penned several memos in an impatient tone, urging Shkurin to "expedite the work to the best of your ability and bring the case to its long-awaited conclusion."[38]

Part of the problem was that the commission spent the better part of November in Vitebsk, investigating new developments in the case. It also did not help matters that Vasilii Ivanovich Strakhov—the man who worked so hard to assemble an airtight case against Jews—had fallen gravely ill. The first symptoms appeared on September 29, 1829, and for the better part of four weeks, the inspector-councilor spent his days in bed. By late October, Strakhov felt well enough to resume his duties, consisting largely of paperwork and last-minute interrogations and face-to-face confrontations. With the end finally in sight, Strakhov worked feverishly to complete the work he had started so long ago, but the illness returned before long. On February 19, 1830, Shkurin reported to the governor-general that the inspector-councilor lacked the strength to get out of bed. On May 12, doctors gave Strakhov only a few days to live, and exactly three days later, at 10:30 in the morning, he died of what the medical examiner categorized as "inflammation and suppuration of the brain."[39]

That spring, five scribes worked around the clock to format the documents according to the specifications of the law code. Eager to wrap up the investigation in a timely manner, Khovanskii was happy to send his most meticulous men to Velizh at a moment's notice. "If five scribes are not able to get the job done, then all [the commission] needs to do is request for more help." On May 16, the governor-general proclaimed that the investigation had run its course and that there was no reason for any members of the inquisitorial commission to remain in Velizh. The only thing left to do was to "itemize the files, fasten the pages together, and label the documents."[40]

It turned out that the formalities of record keeping and assembly of the files proved to be an extraordinarily consuming and demanding task. The scribes labored all summer, and only on August 27, 1830, was the dossier transferred to Vitebsk. As required by law, the original files remained with the governor-general's chancellery office for safekeeping; an identical copy was forwarded to St. Petersburg for official review. Khovanskii requested that all the prisoners' personal belongings purchased with official state funds to be itemized and handed over to the magistrate's office. Most important, the accused Jews were to remain locked up in Velizh until the Senate reached a decision, while the accusers were to be relocated to Smolensk. A caravan of twenty-six horses made the epic journey from Velizh to the provincial capital of Vitebsk, carrying dozens of sealed boxes filled with thousands of pages of documents: official reports, interrogations, depositions, forensic-medical evidence, transcripts of face-to-face confrontations, communiqués, lists, maps, translations of foreign-language books, knives, and an assortment of petitions, complaints, and letters.[41]

In addition to Fedor's death, Jews were charged with the murder conspiracy of nine other people—two boys, the noblewoman Dvorzhetskaia, two girls, and four peasant children—as well as the desecration of church property. Although nowhere near as severe as the charge of ritual murder, the interrogations also revealed that the Jews enticed the accusers to go "astray," a punishable criminal transgression. For centuries, the formal abandonment of Christianity was no small concern for church leaders. According to the Russian criminal law code, individuals who repudiated the Christian faith were categorized as apostates or heretics, subject to punitive measures for their transgressions, and sentenced to hard labor in Siberia for a period of eight to ten years.[42]

The Second Section of the Fifth Department of the Senate reviewed the Velizh dossier. Senators included eminent bureaucrats, officers, and a full complement of generals, all appointed by the tsar. In the first half of the nineteenth century, the Fifth Department reviewed an extensive dossier of cases dealing with peasant uprisings, runaway serfs, desertion and failure to fulfill military duties, contraband activities, sacrilege and blasphemy, deviation from religious norms, forgery and counterfeiting, contraband activities, the production of illegal goods, theft, and murder. The Senate possessed the authority to compel colleges and provincial governors and governors-general to carry out its orders. Although it functioned as a supreme court of appeals, the Senate was nevertheless subordinated to the tsar in judicial capacity. It could submit a recommendation to introduce, overturn, or amend a law, but the emperor always had final approval.[43]

It did not take long for the Senate to dismiss most of the charges for lack of supporting evidence. The court took much longer to deliberate over whether Jews murdered Fedor as a result of superstitious rites and convictions. As a separate but related question, it also considered if a sect of child murderers was secretly operating within the Jewish community—if, in other words, ritual murder was a fact of Jewish religious life. Although the principal suspects did not confess to the murder, the court had in its possession a wealth of incriminating facts: material and medical evidence; the confessions and partial confessions of Fratka Devirts, Itsko Nakhimovskii, and Nota Prudkov; and the testimonies of Terenteeva, Kozlovskaia, and Maksimova. The court also made note of several crucial details: that a small group of Jews gathered secretly in the middle of the night at the homes of Shmerka and Noson Berlin, that a Jewish watch guard was stationed outside Shmerka's home at precisely the time the boy disappeared, that the temperament and psychological disposition of the Jews changed dramatically during the interrogation sessions, and that an overwhelming majority of Christians in the town were convinced of Jews' guilt.[44]

Some of the evidence may have been ambiguous, inconclusive, or indirect, but when taken together, it was overwhelming. Senators I. F. Savrasov and K. G. Mikhailovskii were convinced that the Jews had ritually murdered Fedor, and there was no doubt in their mind that a special Jewish sect played a lead role in the conspiracy. On December 1, 1831, Savrasov and Mikhailovskii recommended the following punishment:

- Even though Maria Terenteeva, Avdotia Maksimova, and Praskoviia Kozlovskaia played a lead role in the murder and renounced their Christian faith, they voluntarily confessed to their crimes and named all the participants in the affair. For these reasons, their sentence would be reduced to exile to Siberia, where they would be expected to repent for their ways of life.
- Anna Eremeeva was expected to repent for her way of life.
- Khanna and Evzik Tsetlin, Slava, Hirsh, Noson, and Ryvka Berlin, Ruman Nakhimovskii, Iosel' Mirlas, Iosel' Glikman, Feiga Vul'fsonov, Orlik and Fratka Devirts, and Nota Prudkov would lose their civil liberties and be exiled to Siberia for hard labor. The men were to be punished by twenty blows of the knout and branded as criminals; the women would receive fifteen blows.
- Meir Berlin, Shmerka and Basia Aronson, and Itsko Vul'fson would lose their civil liberties and be exiled to Siberia for permanent residence. The men would be punished by twenty-five blows of the lash; the women would receive twenty blows.

- Rokhlia Feitel'son, Khasia Chernomordik, Leizer Zaretskii, Itsko Beliaev, and Abram Kisin would lose their civil liberties and be exiled to Siberia for permanent residence.
- Zelik Brusovanskii, Khaim Khrupin, Iankel' and Ester Chernomordik, Blium Nafanov, Malka Baradulina, Rokhlia Livensonov, Risa Mel'nikova, Abram Glushkov, Iosel' Turnovskii, Itsko Nakhimovskii, and Abram Katson would lose their civil liberties and be exiled to Siberia for permanent residence.
- Everyone else would be set free for lack of incriminating evidence.[45]

Consisting of a stiff thong of rawhide fastened by a bronze ring to a braided leather whip and attached to a wooden stick of two and a half feet in length, the knout was the harshest instrument of corporal punishment used in Russia. By the standards of the time, punishment of fifteen to twenty blows was not deemed particularly severe. Nevertheless, knouting was a highly symbolic public spectacle, traditionally carried out in the town square. As a penal instrument, the knout was reserved for the most serious crimes committed by the underprivileged masses. The flogger would strip the convict to the waist, bind their hands and feet with leather thongs and iron rings to posts, and apply the knout to the back with enough force to remove a layer of skin with every stroke.[46]

Exile also played a central role in judicial punishment. The journey to Tomsk, Ufa, and other provincial Siberian towns was especially arduous, and fewer than three-quarters of the exiles made it to the destination, where they lived their lives along military lines, lacking sufficient food, supplies, and other essential resources.[47] Senator A. N. Khovanskii was convinced that exile would prevent Jews from committing similar heretical acts, but he did not think that the knout or the lash was the appropriate form of punishment. As far as the question whether a sect of child murderers was operating within the Jewish community, he suggested that the Department of Spiritual Affairs of Foreign Confessions look into the matter. If it established that such a sect was in existence, the senator thought that it was important for the imperial government to create special institutions where all Jews, regardless of religious differences and beliefs, would be able to come together. Senator Khovanskii felt that public religious gatherings needed to take place only at fixed times in schools or synagogues, and always under the supervision of local police officers or trusted Jewish communal elders. Among other things, this would prevent Jews from carrying out "malicious ritual crimes." If Jews were caught in schools or homes at night or at other inappropriate times, the senator wanted them exiled immediately to Siberia.[48]

Senator V. I. Gechevich did not doubt the existence of Jewish ritual murder, and was concerned only by the pressing question of whether the alleged crime could be proved at law. He emphasized that none of the key Jewish witnesses in the case confessed to the murder, while the three primary accusers transgressed the law by renouncing their Christian faith. Furthermore, the interrogations and face-to-face confrontations revealed several unresolved discrepancies; he did not think, for instance, that the inquisitorial commission had gathered sufficient evidence to convict the Jews. For all these reasons, Gechevich was skeptical that they were guilty as charged and proposed instead that their actions and behavior be closely monitored, especially during the ritually charged time of the calendar season, when suspicious acts could result in more troublesome accusations.[49]

When the Senate failed to reach agreement, the criminal case, as required by law, was forwarded to the Department of Civil and Ecclesiastical Affairs of the State Council. Standing between the tsar and the Senate, the council deliberated over cases not covered by existing law or involving a textual interpretation.[50] It met five times in 1834 (on May 23, 25, 30, June 6, and October 19) to discuss whether the inquisitorial commission compiled enough solid evidence to prove that Jewish child murderers had killed the little boy. Admiral Count Nicholai S. Mordvinov reviewed the Velizh files for the State Council. Born into a distinguished noble family, Mordvinov spent the early years of his life in England. There, he served on English naval and merchant vessels and took an extended tour of France, Germany, and Portugal. Upon his return to Russia, Mordvinov socialized with the highest circles of Petersburg aristocracy. His career was filled with rapid promotions, scandals, and intrigues.[51] Tsar Alexander I nominated Mordvinov vice-chairman of the Admiralty College, where he participated in reorganizing the Senate and emerged as a dedicated follower of economic liberalism and a most passionate defender of property rights.[52]

In July 1821, Alexander appointed Mordvinov head of the Department of Civil and Ecclesiastical Affairs, a position he held until his retirement from service in 1838. This post, which in fact was a demotion in retribution for his long-standing feud with the finance minister, gave Mordvinov an opportunity to voice his views on a broad range of topics concerning law and human rights. Inspired by the classical penal reformers Cesare Beccaria and Jeremy Bentham, Mordinov insisted on careful handling of evidence and the abolition of unnecessarily harsh punishment.[53] In cases adjudicated at the State Council, he repeatedly questioned evidence presented by secret inquisitorial commissions as unequivocal truth. He opposed the practice of holding a person under suspicion if the court could not come to a rapid decision as to his or her guilt or innocence. "The purport of the law," Mordvinov explained, "was to protect the innocent, not to punish the guilty."[54] The spectacle and the instrument of torture were cruel forms of punishment. "The knout," he observed, "is a monstrous instrument that rips the flesh of the human body from the bone, sprays bloody droplets through the air, and spills blood over the body of the man. This [instrument of] torture is more powerful than all other known instruments. . . . It takes an entire hour to administer twenty lashes of the knout, and it is well known that when a tormented criminal receives a large number of lashes, sometimes when he is not even guilty, this beating can take from sunup to sundown."[55]

Borrowing freely from Beccaria, Mordvinov posited that the certainty required to declare a person guilty of crime was life's most important undertaking. The judge had only one task before him and that was to use common sense when assessing the facts. Leafing through the voluminous paperwork, the elderly statesman quickly realized that the Velizh case was no ordinary occult crime, but concerned the timeless question of whether Jews practice the ritual of blood sacrifice of young Christian children. In a lengthy legal opinion, Mordvinov noted that spiritual and secular authorities had taken up the question for hundreds of years and always arrived at the same result. In the thirteenth century, Pope Innocent IV issued papal bulls condemning blood accusations. Three centuries later, Polish rulers made similar pronouncements on several different occasions. In the eighteenth century, after a lengthy investigation of ritual crimes in Poland, the Vatican characterized the charges against the Jews as baseless. Even the Russian government instructed provincial officials, as late as 1817, to rely on strict documentary evidence when prosecuting the alleged crime of ritual murder.[56]

To the average observer, the inquisitorial commission had compiled a solid case against the Jews based on a wealth of evidence.[57] Mordvinov, however, belonged to a select group of men in the imperial establishment who were well educated, adored firm precision in the law, and insisted that official matters be dealt with quickly and accurately.[58] Having rejected archaic creeds in favor of science and civilization, he showed no tolerance, either in his personal or professional life, for anything that smacked of mysticism or irrationalism. Mordvinov believed that Governor-General Khovanskii "paid no attention to past juridical opinions, and did everything in his power to make the case that the Jews, having spilled Christ's blood, are enemies of Christendom." Furthermore, the statesman had a hard time comprehending how "in this day and age a blood libel charge could make its way up the juridical ladder to the supreme institution of the empire." But with more than forty Jews under arrest, and many more feeling the inquisitors' assault on their community, the head of the Department of Civil and Ecclesiastical Affairs saw no choice but to give his complete and devout attention to the complexities of the case.[59]

Under the inquisitorial system, to convict a suspect required two issues to be proven: that the crime was in fact committed (*corpus delicti*, or, in Russian legal terminology, *sostav prestupleniia*), and that the accused in question was the perpetrator. In Nicholaevan Russia, as in continental Europe, forensic-medical testimony took on an influential role in the decision-making process. Although the physician's conclusions did not always bind the judge, expert testimony could and often did influence the outcome. To establish a firm case against the Jews, the inquisitors would need to have perfect proof: a complete and sound voluntary confession from the perpetrators, and a medical report that unequivocally corroborated the fact of the crime. In cases of crime involving the human body such as ritual murder, medical testimony took on an especially important role, standing second only to the confession.[60]

Mordvinov first took issue with the veracity of the confessions. Terenteeva and Maksimova had every opportunity to explain the most important circumstances of the case, but Mordvinov felt there were too many gaps, contradictions, and inaccuracies in their stories. They had a hard time remembering or agreeing upon, for example, where the murder allegedly took place or where exactly the boy's body was buried. At one point, they blamed the murder on one Jewish man, but then changed their minds and called out the entire Jewish community. How was it possible, Mordvinov asked, "after twelve long months of interrogations, for both women to remember so many intimate details of the crime—at a time, no less, when they were supposed to have been intoxicated?" And why did no other Jews, outside of Fratka Devirts and Nota Prudkov (two of the more problematic Jewish suspects in the case), voluntarily confess to the crime? For Mordvinov, one of the more troubling aspects of the investigation was that so many Jews continued to deny their role in the murder conspiracy, while emphasizing, under the most trying circumstances, that Jewish religious law explicitly forbade the consumption of human blood.[61]

Medical Report	Witnesses' Testimony
In various places on the body, the skin turned a burnt yellow or red color from a strong fricative force; and then hardened, as usually happens when the body is rubbed too harshly for too long.	The soldier's son was swung from side to side in a barrel. The naked body was completely red, as if it was burned.
On the hands, back of the legs, the back, the head, the torso, and behind the ears are small circular sores, no more than one-third of an inch in depth, as though the boy was shot with a rifle.	The entire body and head were stabbed with a sharp iron nail. After the body was washed, little pea-sized wounds remained.
On both legs, below the knee, the skin turned a dark blue, almost black, color. A strong rope was used to stop the circulation of the blood.	Before the boy was stabbed, both of his legs were tied together with a belt.
The lips were pressed firmly against the teeth, while the nose was smashed in violently; the dark crimson bruise on the back of the neck signified that rope encircled the neck.	When transferred to the Jewish school, the boy's mouth was tied shut with a kerchief, so that he would not be able to cry out; and his nose was smashed in.
The internal organs, both the stomach and intestines, were completely empty, filled only with air.	While hidden in Khanna Tsetlina's home, it appears that the boy was not fed.

Source: RGIA, f. 1345, op. 235, d. 65, chast' 20, ll. 305–3050b

In the hierarchies of official proofs weighed by the inquisitorial system, medical testimony was accorded the prized status of complete proof, "when it, having been conducted on legal grounds, contains clear and positive confirmation about the examined subject and does not contradict the reliable circumstances of the case."[62] Mordvinov observed that there were three main discrepancies between the medical report and the statements provided by the three primary accusers. First, the women claimed that the boy was pierced "cleanly and effortlessly with an iron nail," but the forensic-medical report detailed that all fourteen wounds on the boy's body were made with a dull instrument, which would have required "time and effort." Second, the accusers claimed that more than forty individuals took turns stabbing the boy, but the medical examiner determined that there were no more than fourteen small bodily wounds. And finally, they claimed that the body had turned completely white after it was washed, but the medical report stated that the body had turned a burnt yellow or red color, as though someone had vigorously scrubbed it with a coarse cloth or brush.[63]

There were other troubling aspects of the case as well. Chief among them was the timing of the murder. If the boy's mouth and nose were wrapped firmly, as Terenteeva had asserted, then he would not have been able to breathe for very long, and he certainly would not have been alive when the police searched Aronson's home on May 4. Among other things, Mordvinov also could not understand how so much blood (more than three full bottles) could be collected from such a small body. But even if it was possible that so much blood could flow from the boy's veins, then it was beyond the realm of possibility for it not to have spoiled in over twelve months' time, especially during the summer months, when the blood was allegedly distributed to Vitebsk, Liozno, and other neighboring towns. The inquisitorial commission was obligated to explain the truth of the events, to defend the innocent from libelous claims, but the inquisitors, he wrote, had "intentionally overlooked crucial facts and testimony." For Mordvinov, the most troubling aspect of the case was that dozens of innocent people were imprisoned for so long based on flawed evidence.[64]

And so on January 18, 1835, nearly twelve years after little Fedor's lifeless body was found in the thick woods on the outskirts of Velizh, the longest investigation of ritual murder in the modern world was finally concluded. Nicholas's regime may have been preoccupied with rooting out savage zealotry and doctrinal deviation, but it nevertheless coordinated its operations in a spirit of juridical rationalism. In the final analysis, Mordvinov did not establish *corpus delicti* or find substantial proof that linked Jews with the ritual crime. The most damaging evidence of all—the statements provided by Terenteeva, Maksimova, and Kozlovskaia—did not stand the test of legal scrutiny. Furthermore, although according to the rules of inquisitorial procedure, medical testimony carried decisive weight in judicial proceedings, Mordvinov felt that there was nothing in the forensic report that linked the Jews with the murder conspiracy. Based on a thorough examination of the evidence, Mordvinov recommended that the government dismiss the ritual murder accusations, open all sealed synagogues and schools, and free the Velizh Jews from further judgment and inquiry. For uttering unsubstantiated libels against Jews, the three primary accusers would be exiled to Siberia, and Anna Eremeeva was to be turned over to a priest for admonition for masquerading as a fortune-teller.[65]

EPILOGUE

AFTER CAREFULLY CONSIDERING THE FACTS of the case, Nicholas I concurred with the State Council that the claims against the Jews of Velizh could not be proved at law. "Owing to the vagueness of the legal deductions," he wrote, "no other decision than the one embodied in the ruling could have been reached." Yet however powerful the evidence may have been in the Jews' favor, Nicholas was wary of dismissing the charge outright. "I do not have and indeed cannot have the inner conviction," he continued, "that the murder has not been committed by Jews." Numerous examples from different times and places around the world revealed that "among Jews there probably exist fanatics or sectarians who consider Christian blood necessary for their rites." In the tsar's eyes, Jews were as capable of committing ritual child murder as the Skoptsy, the most despised religious sect of all, were of performing ritual castration. Without suggesting that this custom was common to all Jews, Nicholas did not discount the idea that "there may be among them fanatics just as horrible as among us Christians." Leaving open the possibility of ritual intent, the opinion cast a lingering shadow over all future blood accusations in the Russian Empire.[1]

The reluctance of the judicial apparatus to prohibit ritual murder trials meant that further accusations would need to be settled in the courtroom. In fact, less than twelve months after the State Council's ruling, the matter reached St. Petersburg once again. This case concerned Fekla

Selezneva, a twenty-three-year-old serf from the village of Borisovo in Minsk province. Selezneva ran away from her husband on November 10, 1833, and took on the journey her twelve-year-old cousin. In due time, Selezneva's landlord managed to track her down. When he inquired about the girl's whereabouts, Selezneva first declared that she was hiding out in "a trusted place" but eventually revealed that the Jew Orko Sabun had strangled her to death so that "he could rub [the blood] on his child's eyes and lips." The girl's naked body was found in a barn hidden under a pile of straw. The documentary evidence suggests that Selezneva and Sabun had a history together, perhaps even had engaged in intimate relations. The peasant woman testified, at one point, that they "fornicated all night long" after Sabun strangled the girl to death in the middle of the night. Sabun, for his part, could not keep his story straight. None of his alibis vouched for him; some went so far as to claim that "he might have killed her himself."

The case was heard first by two courts at the provincial level and then by the Senate before it reached the State Council. On January 13, 1836, the council convicted Selezneva of murdering the girl but did not implicate Sabun directly in the crime—though it did punish him for lying and taking in a runaway serf, for which he received forty blows of the knout and permanent exile to Siberia. One question that the court decided not to address at the time was whether Jews needed Christian blood for their religious rites and rituals.[2]

That Nicholas's regime was actively unmasking radical Christian sects for their savage heresies only heightened suspicion against Jewish perversion. In the 1830s, the most powerful judicial and administrative bodies in the empire considered two more sensational cases. The events in Tel'shi, Kovno province, began in 1827, at the height of the mass suspicions in Velizh, and ended officially only in 1838, when the Senate exonerated twenty-eight Jews charged with ritual murder.[3] The second case concerned three Jews who were accused of severing a peasant's tongue in Zaslav, Volynia province. Prokop Kazan testified that he was "overtaken" by the Jews the moment he came out of the woods:

> First one Jew came over and started to talk with me as I was walking along the road and then another one and finally a third one. I didn't suspect that they would do anything malicious to me, so I answered

their questions. Then, all of a sudden one Jew pounced on me from behind and threw me down on the ground, at which point the other two Jews joined in. They crushed my chest and choked me so fiercely that I must have stuck my tongue out when I lost conscience. When I finally came around, I found myself on my knees, with my head facing the ground. One of the Jews was holding my head up with his hands, while another one placed a cup underneath my mouth to collect the blood, which was flowing in a heavy stream.[4]

As soon as the Jews had finished their deed, they took off in a spring britzka with the blood and twelve silver rubles. Kazan explained that he stumbled upon the silver rubles in the marketplace at the town fair and that the Jews stole the money from him. The Senate characterized Kazan's explanation as "wildly fantastic." The medical assessment of the body confirmed that the tongue had been cut off by a sharp object but failed to establish that it was forcibly severed when the incident had allegedly occurred.

Tsar Nicholas I was well known for his fears of hidden plots and conspiracies. To achieve dominance over his expansive realm, the regime defended against pernicious forces of revolution. In the aftermath of the Decembrist uprising of 1825, the judicial system carried out harsh investigations of social disorders that threatened to undermine the emperor's absolute power. Most alleged state criminals were tried swiftly in military tribunals. Nicholas's militarized regime used the knout (a three-tailed whip with metal talons), the lash (a three-tailed whip with braided leather knots), and birch rods as the chief instruments to punish criminals. The average yearly number of exiles and penal laborers sent to Siberia increased nearly twofold, from 4,570 from 1819 to 1823 to 7,719 from 1823 to 1860. In addition to rebels, political dissidents, and vagabonds, the regime targeted for relocation petty thieves, violent drunks, "barbarous Asiatics," hardened criminals, and a host of schismatic sects.[5]

The intense preoccupation with socially dangerous elements—including Jewish ritual murder—occurred in a climate of concern with heresy and fanaticism. The Ministry of the Interior kept meticulous records of schismatic sects. The most viciously prosecuted sect—the Skoptsy—was punished for crimes against faith, systematically deported to Siberia, and kept under close police watch.[6] For hundreds of years,

Russia's courts grouped heresy, along with witchcraft and treason, as the highest crime. They believed that heretics and witches possessed an element of evil power and so were often sentenced to death by execution. Russian officials continued to prosecute dissenting sects with extreme ferocity, but the second quarter of the nineteenth century witnessed a dramatic shift in judicial thinking. Judges began to voice increasing reluctance to hear cases concerning witchcraft. What accounted for this change? Why did criminal courts refuse to prosecute people accused of controlling the supernatural by magical means as witches or sorcerers and punish sectarians for heresies? What specific evidence helped establish the facts of the crime?

One of the most important reasons for the shift had to do with the cultural authority of scientific observation. Beginning in the 1830s, medical inspections of the human body acquired privileged status within the system of criminal proofs. Under the rules of evidence, the physician's testimony carried decisive weight in determining the character of the crime. Medical experts provided a wealth of clinical details that helped unmask the invisible threats lurking within. Doctors' expert testimony played a decisive role in the types of crimes the state deemed especially pernicious. The Skoptsy's "savage zealotry," for example, could be easily recognized by scars, shrunken genitals, removal of testicles, excised nipples, and sparse body hair. By contrast, the possession of herbs, incantations, recipes for herbal potions, or magical powders no longer sufficed to establish the phenomenon of witchcraft. By offering medical diagnosis such as hysteria or melancholia for aberrant or irrational behavior, doctors helped challenge the notion that witchcraft was real.[7]

Significantly, the power afforded to forensic science, statistics, and ethnographic observation played an important role in perpetuating the ritual murder charge. The stab wounds on a corpse established Jews' demonic blood rituals in much the same way that bodily signs documented the Skoptsy's ritual perversions. In all the instances that Jews were charged with ritual murder, social-scientific observation structured the terms of the criminal investigation. Scientific knowledge was employed in the service of empire not only to direct a new positive course for Russia but also to carve out a better, purer world—to weed out harmful or unreliable elements from public view.[8] Nicholas's policing tactics coincided with an ambitious program of surveying Russia's social and economic conditions to resolve the empire's problems and deficiencies. A new generation of men, enrolled in elite schools and anxious to build successful careers in the civil service, strove to understand the complexities of Russian life. Lev A. Perovskii, the minister of internal affairs under Nicholas I, looked to the social sciences as a gateway to formulating imperial policy. In an effort to expand his expertise of non-Russian populations, Perovskii commissioned ethnographic studies of heresy in all its savage forms and deviations, including its Jewish component. In 1841, Perovskii appointed Vladimir Dal' and Nikolai Nadezhdin as officials of the special order of his personal chancellery. Both men worked on a variety of different projects reserved for the minister's personal attention, including serving on a committee that was charged with investigating dangerous schismatic sects.[9]

In this capacity, Dal' produced two reports, both issued in tiny print runs in 1844, dedicated to exposing the fanatical secrets of blood rituals. One was on the Skoptsy (the authorship was eventually attributed to Nadezhdin after Nicholas refused to accept it for publication because of Dal's Lutheran origins).[10] The other work, entitled *An Inquiry into the Killing of Christian Children and the Use of Their Blood*, was devoted to Jewish ritual murder. The text incorporated materials from the Ministry of the Interior archive and some well-known accusatory works printed in eighteenth-century Poland, with much space devoted to the Velizh case. Dal' left no doubt that blood sacrifice was a fact of Jewish life. In every place where Jews are tolerated, he wrote, "corpses of babies have been found from time to time, always in the same mutilated condition or at least with similar signs of violence and death. Just as true is that these signs have attested to a premeditated and deliberate atrocity—the painful murder of Christian children."[11] A great deal of legal and medical evidence helped substantiate this reality, not least of which, Dal' noted, were the external marks on the dead bodies, confirming in each instance that the killings were the result of cruel and unusual premeditated Jewish savagery.

In the 1860s and 1870s, when the issue of Jewish criminality first became a topic of public discussion, conservative journalists and expert witnesses turned to Dal's work to substantiate the charge.[12] The defrocked Catholic priest Ippolit Liutostanskii, for instance, was one of a number of hacks who took the dangers of blood sacrifice to another level. In the highly sensational book *The Question of the Use by Jewish Sectarians of Christian Blood for Religious Purposes*, published in 1876, Liutostanskii recycled Dal's language to single out a small group of fanatics for engaging in anti-Christian acts of sacrilege and desecration. "Jews who acquire only the external trappings of European—and, consequently, of Christian—civilization, sitting down at the table of humane enlightenment, not only are blameless of this custom, but don't even know about it."[13] It did not take long for a committed group of publicists, commentators, and politicians to link sectarian fanaticism directly with the Hasidic movement. "It is certain," the influential Polish ethnographer Oscar Kolberg explained, "that there exists among [Jews] a fanatical sect that craves such wild sacrifices," an accusation that would play out in the mass circulation press, with forces lining up on all sides of the political divide.[14]

The Velizh case had the makings of sensational, deeply divisive drama and might have erupted into a cause célèbre, along the lines of the ritual murder case in Damascus (1840), the Dreyfus affair in France (1894–1906), or the sensational trial of Mendel Beilis in 1913 for the murder of a Gentile youth in Kiev two years earlier. But before Tsar Alexander II and his advisers redesigned the legal system, the secret workings of the chancellery concealed every stage of the judicial process.[15] During the reign of Nicholas I, the publication of transcripts, legal commentaries, and speeches was forbidden, nor was the courtroom the site of social spectacle to a thrill-seeking public. The inquisitorial chamber—the principal site of the investigative drama—was shut to public scrutiny. As a result, news was not able to spread to well-placed emissaries who enjoyed political influence in the international arena and could mobilize a vast network of resources and political connections in the face of crisis.[16] The closed nature of the judicial process meant that the Velizh case was decided locally, firmly outside the apprehensive gaze of public opinion.

A product of the Great Reform era, the open, adversarial courtroom made a new social spectacle of the Jewish ritual murder charge. The indictment of nine Georgian Jews in the 1878 ghastly murder of Sara Iosifova Modebadze in Kutaisi resulted in the first blood libel accusation tried before a jury of peers, where all aspects of the case were made public, from written testimony to cross-examinations and the verdict itself. In the end, two of Russia's leading defense attorneys debunked the evidence, and the trial ended with the full acquittal of the Jewish defendants on March 13, 1879.[17] Kutaisi turned out to be the first of six sensational ritual murder cases in Europe, the last of which was the Beilis case of 1911–1913, tried in the open courtroom. The dramatic courtroom scenes were structured by powerful rules of expert knowledge.[18] Supported by scientific evidence and medical observation, the legal prosecution of Jews generated mass publicity, even as shared assumptions in popular magic and mysticism, to say nothing of conspiratorial fears, continued to influence conceptions of Jewish criminality. For the mass of populations in the Russian Empire, it was entirely within the realm of perceived wisdom that Jews could commit the crime at any time and place.

APPENDIX
Jewish Prisoners Held in the Town of Velizh

Name	Approximate Age	Date Arrested
Slava Berlina	52	April 8, 1826
Khanna Tsetlina	47	April 8, 1826
Itsko Nakhimovskii	32	April 15, 1826
Abram Glushkov	30	April 15, 1826
Iosel' Turnovskii	64	April 15, 1826
Shmerka Berlin	50s	June 20, 1826
Evzik Tsetlin	49	June 20, 1826
Hirsh Berlin	28	February 28, 1827
Orlik Devirts	53	February 28, 1827
Iankel' Hirsh Aronson	19	February 28, 1827
Iosel'-Zavel' Mirlas	50	June 28, 1827
Shmerka Aronson	48	July 11, 1827
Basia Aronson	37	July 11, 1827
Noson Berlin	38	July 11, 1827
Meir Berlin	46	July 11, 1827
Fratka Devirts	46	July 11, 1827
Ruman Nakhimovskii	46	July 11, 1827
Rokhlia Feitsel'sonova	43	November 9, 1827
Rokhlia Livenson	37	November 9, 1827

Name	Approximate Age	Date Arrested
Iankel' Chernomordik	59	November 11, 1827
Ester Chernomordika	57	November 11, 1827
Abram Katson	52	November 17, 1827
Abram Kisin	35	November 29, 1827
Risa Mel'nikova	45	November 30, 1827
Khasia Shubinskaia	36	December 22, 1827
Khaim Khrupin	39	December 22, 1827
Leia Rudniakova	36	December 23, 1827
Itsko Vul'fson	34	January 5, 1828
Iosel' Glikman	56	January 5, 1828
Ryvka Berlina	74	January 6, 1828
Genemiklia Iankeleva	19	January 6, 1828
Itsko Tsetlin	19	January 7, 1828
Bliuma Nafonova	37	January 9, 1828
Zusia Rudniakov	31	January 17, 1828
Khaika Chernomordika	30	January 27, 1828
Malka Baradudina	61	February 3, 1828
Leizar' Zaretskii	57	February 4, 1828
Nota Prudkov	36	February 4, 1828
Feiga Vul'fson	34	March 9, 1828
Movsha Belenitskii	35	August 9, 1828
Nokhon Perepletchikov	54	November 7, 1828
Zelik Brusovanskii	57	November 9, 1828
Iankel' Korshakov	44	February 5, 1829

Source: *Spravka k dokladu po evreiskomu voprosu*, part 5 (St. Petersburg: Kantseliariia Soveta ob"edinennykh dvorianskikh obshchestv, 1912), 52–61

NOTES

Abbreviations

CAHJP	Central Archives for the History of the Jewish People
GARF	Gosudarstvennyi arkhiv rossiiskoi federatsii
KAA	Kauno Apskrities Archyve
NIAB	Natsional'nyi istoricheskii arkhiv Belarusi
RGIA	Rossiiskii gosudarstvennyi istoricheskii arkhiv
RNB	Rossiiskaia natsional'naia biblioteka
YIVO	Institute for Jewish Research

Preface

1. On the blood libel commission, see Viktor E. Kel'ner, *Missioner istorii: Zhizn' i trudy Semena Markovicha Dubnova* (St. Petersburg: Mir, 2008), 512–546; and Sergei Kan, *Lev Shternberg: Anthropologist, Russian Socialist, Jewish Activist* (Lincoln: University of Nebraska Press, 2009), 289–290.

2. Mary McAuley, *Bread and Justice: State and Society in Petrograd, 1917–1922* (Oxford: Clarendon Press, 1991), 47–69, 261–304.

3. On the Jewish cultural renaissance in Revolutionary Russia, see Kenneth B. Moss, *Jewish Renaissance in the Russian Revolution* (Cambridge, MA: Harvard University Press, 2009).

4. Simon M. Dubnov and Grigorii Ia. Krasnyi-Admoni, eds., *Materialy dlia istorii anti-evreiskikh pogromov v Rossii*, vol. 1 (Petrograd: Istoriko-Etnograficheskoe obshchestvo, 1919), v. For a brief description of the activities of the archival commissions, see

Alfred Greenbaum, *Jewish Scholarship and Scholarly Institutions in Soviet Russia, 1918–1953* (Jerusalem: Centre for Research and Documentation of East European Jewry, 1978), 8–9.

5. The Velizh affair archive is preserved at the RGIA, f. 1345, op. 235, d. 65, ch. 1–25; and the NIAB, f. 1297, op. 1.

6. As quoted in Kel'ner, *Missioner istorii*, 516.

7. YIVO, RG 80, Box 100, Folder 945, pp. 73904–73905 (letter from L. N. Etingen to Simon Dubnov, April 19, 1893).

8. YIVO, RG 80, Box 100, Folder 945, pp. 73906–73908 (letters from L. N. Etingen to Simon Dubnov, May 26 and June 29, 1893).

9. YIVO, RG 80, Box 100, Folder 945, pp. 73912–73913 (letter from M. D. Ryvkin to Simon Dubnov, November 21, 1893).

10. Simon Dubnov, "Alitat dam be'ir Bobovne: ve-yihusah li-gezerat Velizsh," *Luah Ahi'asaf*, vol. 2 (1894): 282–298; vol. 3 (1895): 303–306.

11. Simon Dubnov, *Kniga zhizni: Vospominaniia i razmyshleniia*, ed. Viktor E. Kel'ner (St. Petersburg: Peterburgskoe vostokovedenie, 1998), 183.

12. YIVO, RG 80, Box 100, Folder 945, pp. 77156–77157 (letter from M. D. Ryvkin to Simon Dubnov, February 5, 1901). Ryvkin's publications on the Velizh case include "Velizhskoe delo v osveshchenii mestnykh predanii i pamiatnikov," *Perezhitoe* 3 (1911): 60–102; and the historical novel *Navet: Roman iz epokhi Aleksandra I—Nikolaia I* (St. Petersburg: Dvigatel', 1912), which was translated into the Yiddish in 1913 and into the Hebrew in 1933.

13. YIVO, RG 80, Box 100, Folder 945, pp. 77158–77159 (letter from Iulii Gessen to Simon Dubnov, February 5, 1901).

14. YIVO, RG 80, Box 100, Folder 945, p. 77163 (letter from Iulii Gessen to Simon Dubnov, April 15, 1901).

15. Iulii Gessen, *Velizhskaia drama: Iz istorii obvineniia evreev v ritual'nykh prestupleniiakh* (St. Petersburg: Tipografiia A. G. Rozena, 1904). For the earliest analysis of the case, see Robert Lippert, *Anklagen der Juden in Russland wegen Kindermords, Gebrauchs von Christenblut und Gotteslästerung: Ein Beitrag zur Geschichte der Juden in Russland im letzten Jahrzehend und früherer Zeit* (Leipzig: W. Engelmann, 1846). For a recent treatment that relies heavily on Gessen's original research, see I. M. Shkliazh, *Velizhskoe delo: Iz istorii antisemitizma v Rossii* (Odessa: [n.p.], 1998).

16. Dubnov, *Kniga zhizni*, 437.

17. Paul L. Horecky, "The Slavic and East European Resources and Facilities of the Library of Congress," *Slavic Review* 23, no. 2 (1964): 311.

Introduction

1. See, for example, Helmut Walser Smith, *The Butcher's Tale: Murder and Anti-Semitism in a German Town* (New York: W. W. Norton, 2002); Alan Dundes, ed., *The Blood Libel Legend: A Casebook in Anti-Semitic Folklore* (Madison: University

of Wisconsin Press, 1991); Jonathan Frankel, *The Damascus Affair: "Ritual Murder," Politics, and the Jews in 1840* (Cambridge: Cambridge University Press, 1997); Pierre Birnbaum, *A Tale of Ritual Murder in the Age of Louis XIV: The Trial of Raphael Levy, 1669*, trans. Arthur Goldhammer (Stanford: Stanford University Press, 2012); and Hannah Johnson, *Blood Libel: The Ritual Murder Accusation at the Limit of Jewish History* (Ann Arbor: University of Michigan Press, 2012). An important exception is R. Po-chia Hsia's *The Myth of Ritual Murder: Jews and Magic in Reformation Germany* (New Haven: Yale University Press, 1988).

2. On ancient sacrifice legends, see Jan N. Bremmer, "Human Sacrifice: A Brief Introduction," in *The Strange World of Human Sacrifice*, ed. Bremmer (Leuven: Peeters Publishers, 2007), 3–4; Norman Cohn, *Europe's Inner Demons: The Demonization of Christians in Medieval Christendom*, rev. ed. (London: Pimlico, 1993), 5–7, 35–37; and Hermann L. Strack, *The Jew and Human Sacrifice*, trans. Henry Blanchamp (New York: The Bloch Publishing Company, 1909).

3. Thomas of Monmouth, *The Life and Miracles of St. William of Norwich*, trans. and ed. Augustus Jessopp and Montague Rhodes James (Cambridge: Cambridge University Press, 1896), 21, 36, 51–53. On William of Norwich, see E. M. Rose, *The Murder of William of Norwich: The Origins of the Blood Libel in Medieval Europe* (New York: Oxford University Press, 2015); Gavin I. Langmuir, *Toward a Definition of Antisemitism* (Berkeley: University of California Press, 1990), 209–236; and Miri Rubin, "Making of a Martyr: William of Norwich and the Jews," *History Today* 60 (2010): 48–54.

4. Smith, *The Butcher's Tale*, 91–103.

5. Hsia, *The Myth of Ritual Murder*, 3.

6. Caroline Walker Bynum, *Wonderful Blood: Theology and Practice in Late Medieval Northern Europe and Beyond* (Philadelphia: University of Pennsylvania Press, 2007), 5–6.

7. On the ritual calendar, see Edward Muir, *Ritual in Early Modern Europe*, 2nd ed. (Cambridge: Cambridge University Press, 2005), 70–72, 233–238; and Elisheva Carlebach, *Palaces of Time: Jewish Calendar and Culture in Early Modern Europe* (Cambridge, MA: Harvard University Press, 2011), 146–148.

8. Stuart Clark, "Witchcraft and Magic in Early Modern Culture," in *Witchcraft and Magic in Europe: The Period of the Witch Trials*, ed. Bengt Ankarloo and Stuart Clark (Philadelphia: University of Pennsylvania Press, 2002), 108; and Richard Godbear, *The Devil's Dominion: Magic and Religion in Early New England* (Cambridge: Cambridge University Press, 1992), 13.

9. Lyndal Roper, *Witch Craze: Terror and Fantasy in Baroque Germany* (New Haven: Yale University Press, 2004), 10.

10. Quoted in Cecil Roth, ed., *The Ritual Murder Libel and the Jew: The Report by Cardinal Lorenzo Ganganelli (Pope Clement XIV)* (London: Woburn Press, 1934), 97–98. Pope Innocent IV issued the pronouncement to the archbishops and bishops of Germany and France on July 5, 1247.

11. Brian P. Levack, "The Decline and End of Witchcraft Prosecutions," in *Witchcraft and Magic in Europe: The Eighteenth and Nineteenth Centuries*, ed. Bengt Ankarloo and Stuart Clark (Philadelphia: University of Pennsylvania Press, 1999), 3–93.

12. Keith Thomas, *Religion and the Decline of Magic* (London: Penguin Books, 1971), 538–539.

13. Hsia, *The Myth of Ritual Murder*.

14. Zenon Guldon and Jacek Wijacka, "The Accusation of Ritual Murder in Poland, 1500–1800," *Polin* 10 (1997): 139–140; and Jacek Wijacka, "Ritual Murder Accusations in Poland throughout the 16th to 18th Centuries," in *Ritual Murder: Legend in European History*, ed. Susanna Buttaroni and Stanislaw Musial (Krakow: Association for Cultural Initiatives, 2003), 195–210.

15. Magda Teter, *Jews and Heretics in Catholic Poland: A Beleaguered Church in the Post-Reformation Era* (Cambridge: Cambridge University Press, 2006), 113–121; and Pawel Maciejko, *The Mixed Multitude: Jacob Frank and the Frankist Movement, 1755–1816* (Philadelphia: University of Pennsylvania Press, 2011), 94. For the Grand Duchy of Lithuania, see Jurgita Šiaučiunaitė-Verbickienė, "Blood Libel in a Multi-Confessional Society: The Case of the Grand Duchy of Lithuania," *East European Jewish Affairs* 38, no. 2 (2008): 201–209.

16. For a bold rethinking of the formation of the Jewish community in Eastern Europe, see Shaul Stampfer, "Violence and the Migration of Ashkenazi Jews to Eastern Europe," in *Jews in the East European Borderlands: Essays in Honor of John D. Klier*, ed. Eugene M. Avrutin and Harriet Murav (Boston: Academic Studies Press, 2012), 127–146.

17. Arlette Farge and Jacques Revel, *The Vanishing Children of Paris: Rumor and Politics before the French Revolution*, trans. Claudia Mieville (Cambridge, MA: Harvard University Press, 1993), 112; and Michael Specter, "Comment: The Fear Question," *The New Yorker*, October 20, 2014, 29. See also Luise White, *Speaking with Vampires: Rumor and History in Colonial Africa* (Berkeley: University of California Press, 2000), 56–86. For studies that largely stress the significance of print culture for the dissemination of ritual murder discourse, see John D. Klier, *Imperial Russia's Jewish Question, 1855–1881* (Cambridge: Cambridge University Press, 1995), 418–436; and Hillel J. Kieval, "Death and the Nation: Ritual Murder as Political Discourse in the Czech Lands," in his *Languages of Community: The Jewish Experience in the Czech Lands* (Berkeley: University of California Press, 2000), 181–97. For an influential statement on the importance of oral culture, see Robert Darton, *The Great Cat Massacre and Other Episodes in French Cultural History* (New York: Penguin Books, 1984), esp. 75–106.

18. John D. Klier, "The Origins of the 'Blood Libel' in Russia," *Newsletter of the Study Group on Eighteenth Century Russia* 14 (1986): 12–22; Klier, "Krovavyi navet v russkoi pravoslavnyi traditsii," in *Evrei i khristiane v pravoslavnykh obshchestvakh Vostochnoi Evropy*, ed. M. V. Dmitrieva (Moscow: Indrik, 2011): 181–205; and Marcin Wodzinski, "Blood and the Hasidim: On the History of Ritual Murder

Accusations in Nineteenth-Century Poland," *Polin* 22 (2010): 273–290. For two recent explorations, see Robert Weinberg, *Blood Libel in Late Imperial Russia: The Ritual Murder Trial of Mendel Beilis* (Bloomington: Indiana University Press, 2014); and the essays collected in Eugene M. Avrutin, Jonathan Dekel-Chen, and Robert Weinberg, eds., *Ritual Murder in Russia, Eastern Europe, and Beyond: New Histories of an Old Accusation* (Bloomington: Indiana University Press, 2017).

19. On the modern revival argument, see David Biale, *Blood and Belief: The Circulation of a Symbol between Jews and Christians* (Berkeley: University of California Press, 2007), 126–129.

20. Yohanan Petrovsky-Shtern, *The Golden Age Shtetl: A New History of Jewish Life in East Europe* (Princeton: Princeton University Press, 2014), 164–171. Jolanta Żyndul provides a wonderful (but by no means exhaustive) map of blood libel accusations in the Russian Empire, *Kłamstwo krwi: Legenda mordu rytualnego na ziemiach polskich w XIX i XX wieku* (Warsaw: Wydawnictwo Cyklady, 2011), map insert between 116–117.

21. V. I. Dal', *Zapiska o ritual'nykh ubiistvakh* (Moscow: "Vitiaz'," 1995), 48–54. The booklet was first published as *Rozyskanie o ubienii evreiami khristianskikh mladentsev i upotreblenii krovi ikh. Napechatano po prikazaniiu g. ministra vnutrennikh del, L. A. Perovskii* (St. Petersburg, 1844), and is preserved at the RGIA, f. 1282, op. 2, d. 2138, ll. 1–118ob. The identity of the author has aroused considerable debate over the years, and it is not my intention to revisit the question here. Most likely, the celebrated lexicographer and folklorist Vladimir Ivanovich Dal', who was serving at the Ministry of the Interior at the time, authored the report. For a succinct overview of the controversy, see Klier, *Imperial Russia's Jewish Question*, 418–419; and Anne J. Frederickson, "The Dual Faces of Modernity: The Russian Intelligentsia's Pursuit of Knowledge and the Publication History of 'Note on Ritual Murder,'" MA thesis, Arizona State University, 2004. For an argument that opposes this view, see Semen Reznik, *Zapiatnannyi Dal': Mog li sozdatel' "Tolkovogo slovaria zhivogo velikorusskogo iazyka" byt' avtorom "Zapiski o ritual'nykh ubiistvakh"?* (St. Petersburg: Filologicheskii fakul'tet Sankt-Peterburgskogo gosudarstvennogo universiteta, 2010).

22. "Gavriil," in *Pravoslavnaia entsiklopediia*, vol. 10 (Moscow: Tserkovno-nauchnyi tsentr, 2005), 200–201; and *Sviatoi muchenik Gavriil Belostokskii: Nebesnyi pokrovitel' detei i podrostkov* (Minsk: Belorusskaia Pravoslavnaia Tserkov', 2009). Believers connected to their patron saints a great range of powers to work miracles on all aspects of the human condition. See Robert H. Greene, *Bodies like Bright Stars: Saints and Relics in Orthodox Russia* (DeKalb: Northern Illinois Press, 2010), 60.

23. Sarah Maza, *Private Lives and Public Affairs: The Causes Célèbres of Prerevolutionary France* (Berkeley: University of California Press, 1993); and Joy Wiltenburg, *Crime and Culture in Early Modern Germany* (Charlottesville: University of Virginia Press, 2012).

24. On the deeply divisive nature of affairs, with forces lining up with the villain, victim, or forces of authority, see Sarah Maza, *Violette Nozière: A Story of Murder in 1930s Paris* (Berkeley: University of California Press, 2011), 142.

25. Quoted in Sidney Monas, *The Third Section: Police and Society in Russia under Nicholas I* (Cambridge, MA: Harvard University Press, 1961), 141.

26. W. Bruce Lincoln, *Nicholas I: Emperor and Autocrat of All the Russias* (DeKalb: Northern Illinois Press, 1989), 236; and Richard S. Wortman, *Scenarios of Power: Myth and Ceremony in Russian Monarchy*, vol. 1 (Princeton: Princeton University Press, 1995), 303. See also A. I. Stan'ko, *Russkie gazety pervoi poloviny XIX veka* (Rostov-on-Don: Izdatel'stvo Rostovskogo universiteta, 1969).

27. Edward Morton, *Travels in Russia, and a Residence in St. Petersburg and Odessa in the Years 1827–1829* (London: Longman, Rees, Orme, Brown, and Green, 1830), 71–72.

28. On the inquisitorial system, see Edward Peters, *Torture*, expanded ed. (Philadelphia: University of Pennsylvania Press, 1999), 40–73; and Adhémar Esmein, *A History of Continental Criminal Procedure: With Special Reference to France*, trans. John Simson (Boston: Little, Brown, and Company, 1913), 78–144. For Russia, see Nancy Shields Kollmann, *Crime and Punishment in Early Modern Russia* (Cambridge: Cambridge University Press, 2012), 114–121. For Poland, see Michael Ostling, *Between the Devil and the Host: Imagining Witchcraft in Early Modern Poland* (Oxford: Oxford University Press, 2011), 90–92.

29. Brian P. Levack, "Witchcraft and the Law," in *The Oxford Handbook of Witchcraft in Early Modern Europe and Colonial America*, ed. Brian Levack (Oxford: Oxford University Press, 2013), 473.

30. Not all the jurisdictions that had adopted the inquisitorial mode convicted large numbers of suspects. Those regimes such as the Spanish, Portuguese, and Roman inquisitions that had adhered to strict procedural rules processed much smaller numbers of convictions. On inquisitorial techniques, see James B. Given, *Inquisition and Medieval Society: Power, Discipline, and Resistance in Languedoc* (Ithaca: Cornell University Press, 1997), 23–51.

31. Richard S. Wortman, *The Development of a Russian Legal Consciousness* (Chicago: University of Chicago Press, 1976), 15. See also Claudia Verhoeven, *The Odd Man Karakozov: Imperial Russia, Modernity, and the Birth of Terrorism* (Ithaca: Cornell University Press, 2009), 13–14.

32. John P. LeDonne, "Criminal Investigations before the Great Reforms," *Russian History* 1, no. 2 (1974): 112.

33. My own views on ritual murder and small-town life have been influenced by outstanding histories of witchcraft and magic. One of my personal favorites is Robin Briggs's *Witches and Neighbors: The Social and Cultural Context of European Witchcraft* (London: Penguin Books, 1996). For a succinct exploration of the term "popular belief," see Robert W. Scribner, "Elements of Popular Belief," in *Handbook of European History, 1400–1600: Late Middle Ages, Renaissance, and*

Reformation, ed. Thomas A. Brady Jr., Heiko A. Oberman, and James D. Tracy (Grand Rapids, MI: William B. Eerdsmans Publishing Company, 1994), 1: 231–262.

34. Gershon D. Hundert, *Jews in Poland-Lithuania in the Eighteenth Century: A Genealogy of Modernity* (Berkeley: University of California Press, 2004).

35. On the fluidity of boundaries, see Adam Teller and Magda Teter, "Introduction: Borders and Boundaries in the Historiography of the Jews in the Polish-Lithuanian Commonwealth," *Polin* 22 (2010): 3–46. On the problem of coexistence in the borderlands, see Omer Bartov and Eric D. Weitz, eds., *Shatterzone of Empires: Coexistence and Violence in the German, Habsburg, Russian, and Ottoman Borderlands* (Bloomington: Indiana University Press, 2013); and David Frick, *Kith, Kin, and Neighbors: Communities and Confessions in Seventeenth-Century Wilno* (Ithaca: Cornell University Press, 2013).

36. For an excellent study of neighborly relations and legal culture, see Bruce H. Mann, *Neighbors and Strangers: Law and Community in Early Connecticut* (Chapel Hill: University of North Carolina Press, 1987).

37. Historians working on a wide range of geographic regions and across vast chronological time frames have heatedly debated the popular beliefs of populations who left few written records of their everyday prejudices, fears, and preoccupations. For the Russian Empire, see, for example, Simon Dixon, "Superstition in Imperial Russia," in *Past and Present*, supplement 3 (2008): 207–228; Christine D. Worobec, *Possessed: Women, Witches, and Demons in Imperial Russia* (DeKalb: Northern Illinois Press, 2003), 20–63; and Greene, *Bodies like Bright Stars*, 17–102.

38. W. F. Ryan, *The Bathhouse at Midnight: Magic in Russia* (University Park: Pennsylvania State University Press, 1999), 79.

39. On the relationship between microhistory and crime, see Edward Muir and Guido Ruggiero, eds., *History from Crime* (Baltimore: Johns Hopkins University Press, 1994).

40. Barbara H. Rosenwein, *Emotional Communities in the Early Middle Ages* (Ithaca: Cornell University Press, 2006). See also Ute Frevert, *Emotions in History: Lost and Found* (Budapest: Central European University Press, 2011); and Daniel Lord Smail, *The Consumption of Justice: Emotions, Publicity, and Legal Culture in Marseille, 1264–1423* (Ithaca: Cornell University Press, 2003).

41. On the ability of clerks of the courts for capturing oral culture of the interrogation chamber, see Lisa Silverman, *Tortured Subjects: Pain, Truth, and the Body in Early Modern France* (Chicago: University of Chicago Press, 2001), 12.

Chapter 1

1. NIAB, f. 1297, op. 1, d. 190, ll. 30b–8 (testimony by Agafia Prokof'eva and Emel'ian Ivanov, May 1823); and RGIA, f. 1345, op. 235, d. 65, chast' 1, ll. 17–240b (testimony by Emel'ian Ivanov, November 1825).

2. Elise Kimerling Wirtschafter, *From Serf to Russian Soldier* (Princeton: Princeton University Press, 1990), 34; and John L. H. Keep, *Soldiers of the Tsar: Army and Society in Russia, 1462–1874* (Oxford: Clarendon Press, 1985), 197–199.

3. RGIA, f. 1345, op. 235, d. 65, chast' 25, ll. 3–5.

4. NIAB, f. 1297, op. 1, d. 190, ll. 30b–8; and RGIA, f. 1345, op. 235, d. 65, chast' 1, ll. 17–240b.

5. NIAB, f. 1297, op. 1, d. 190, ll. 4–70b.

6. NIAB, f. 1297, op. 1, d. 190, l. 9; and RGIA, f. 1345, op. 235, d. 65, chast' 25, l. 4.

7. NIAB, f. 1297, op. 1, d. 190, ll. 13–150b; and RGIA, f. 1345, op. 235, d. 65, chast' 25, l. 6.

8. NIAB, f. 1297, op. 1, d. 190, l. 9; and RGIA, f. 1345, op. 235, d. 65, chast' 25, l. 4.

9. NIAB, f. 1297, op. 1, d. 190, ll. 20–220b; and RGIA, f. 1345, op. 235, d. 65, chast' 25, l. 7.

10. See the discussion in Yohanan Petrovsky-Shtern, *The Golden Age Shtetl: A New History of Jewish Life in East Europe* (Princeton: Princeton University Press, 2014), 243–255.

11. Miron Ryvkin, "Velizhskoe delo v osveshchenii mestnykh predanii i pamiatnikov," *Perezhitoe* 3 (1911): 69–81.

12. Glenn Dynner, *Yankel's Tavern: Jews, Liquor, and Life in the Kingdom of Poland* (New York: Oxford University Press, 2014), 17–20; and Petrovsky-Shtern, *The Golden Age Shtetl*, 129–135.

13. Ryvkin, "Velizhskoe delo," 79.

14. This is a point made most eloquently by Robin Briggs, *Witches and Neighbors: The Social and Cultural Context of European Witchcraft* (London: Penguin Books, 1988), 146.

15. NIAB, f. 1297, op. 1, d. 190, ll. 18–19, 29–30; and RGIA, f. 1345, op. 235, d. 65, chast' 25, ll. 6–7, 9.

16. NIAB, f. 1297, op. 1, d. 190, ll. 62–650b; and RGIA, f. 1345, op. 235, d. 65, chast' 25, l. 12.

17. RGIA, f. 1345, op. 235, d. 65, chast' 25, l. 116.

18. NIAB, f. 1297, op. 1, d. 190, l. 234.

19. NIAB, f. 1297, op. 1, d. 190, ll. 240b–33, 46, 51, 74–81, 112–1130b; and RGIA, f. 1345, op. 235, d. 65, chast' 25, ll. 5, 11, 13, 18, 23.

20. NIAB, f. 1297, op. 1, d. 190, ll. 215–2160b.

21. NIAB, f. 1297, op. 1, d. 190, ll. 100–102; and RGIA, f. 1345, op. 235, d. 65, chast' 25, ll. 15–16.

22. NIAB, f. 1297, op. 1, d. 190, ll. 2170b–2190b (Khanna Tsetlina's complaint to the magistrate, January 8, 1824).

23. NIAB, f. 1297, op. 1, d. 190, ll. 93–98.

24. NIAB, f. 1297, op. 1, d. 190, ll. 39–41, 144, 181, 1870b–189.

25. Abby M. Schrader, *Languages of the Lash: Corporal Punishment and Identity in Imperial Russia* (DeKalb: Northern Illinois University Press, 2002). See

also Nancy Shields Kollmann, *Crime and Punishment in Early Modern Russia* (Cambridge: Cambridge University Press, 2012), 303–413.

26. RGIA, f. 821, op. 8, d. 296, ll. 1–2; and Simon M. Dubnov, *History of the Jews in Russia and Poland: From the Earliest Times until the Present Day*, trans. I. Friedlander, 3 vols. (Philadelphia: Jewish Publication Society of America, 1916–1920), 2: 74–75. A detailed summary of the Grodno case is preserved at the RGIA, f. 1151, op. 2, d. 169, ll. 2–52. See also Iulii Gessen, "Ritual'nye protsessy 1816 goda," *Evreiskaia Starina* 4, no. 2 (1912): 144–163.

27. RGIA, f. 1345, op. 235, d. 65, chast' 25, ll. 24–26.

28. Brian P. Levack, "The Decline and End of Witchcraft Prosecutions," in *Witchcraft and Magic in Europe: The Eighteenth and Nineteenth Centuries*, ed. Bengt Ankarloo and Stuart Clark (Philadelphia: University Pennsylvania Press, 1999), 86–87.

29. RGIA, f. 1345, op. 235, d. 65, chast' 25, l. 27.

30. On charity and mutual aid, see Adele Lindenmeyr, *Poverty Is Not a Vice: Charity, Society, and the State in Imperial Russia* (Princeton: Princeton University Press, 1996); and Mordechai Zalkin, "Charity," in *The YIVO Encyclopedia of Jews in Eastern Europe*, 2 vols. (New Haven: Yale University Press, 2008), 1: 306–309.

31. Keith Thomas, *Religion and the Decline of Magic* (London: Penguin Books, 1972), 660–669; and Briggs, *Witches and Neighbors*, 137–146.

Chapter 2

1. "Gibel' detei ot nedostatka prismotra," *Zhurnal ministerstva vnutrennikh del*, pt. 9 (1845): 133–134, 138–139; pt. 10 (1845): 123; pt. 11 (1845): 214–215.

2. "Detoubiistvo," *Zhurnal ministerstva vnutrennikh del*, pt. 12 (1845): 139–140.

3. David L. Ransel, *Mothers of Misery: Child Abandonment in Russia* (Princeton: Princeton University Press, 1998), 8–30, 150–175. For a wide-ranging exploration of infanticide accusations and trials in France, Germany, and other places, see Mark Jackson, ed., *Infanticide: Historical Perspectives on Child Murder and Concealment, 1550–2000* (Aldershot: Ashgate, 2002).

4. Viktor Lindenberg, "Materialy k voprosu detoubiistve i plodoizgnanii v Vitebskoi gubernii" (PhD diss., Iur'ev University, 1910).

5. Robert Johnson, *Travels through Parts of the Russian Empire and the Country of Poland, along the Southern Shores of the Baltic* (London: J. J. Stockdale, 1815), 372.

6. Edward Morton, *Travels in Russia, and a Residence in St. Petersburg and Odessa in the Years 1827–1829* (London: Longman, Rees, Orme, Brown, and Green, 1830), 128, 129.

7. *Voenno-statisticheskoe obozrenie Rossiiskoi imperii: Vitebskaia guberniia*, vol. 8, pt. 1 (St. Petersburg: Tipografiia departmenta general'nago shtaba, 1852), 15.

8. Johnson, *Travels through Parts of the Russian Empire and the Country of Poland*, 373.

9. David L. Ransel, "Mothering, Medicine, and Infant Mortality in Russia: Some Comparisons," *Occasional Paper, Kennan Institute for Advanced Russian Studies*, no. 236 (1990): 3–4, 24–30; Gershon D. Hundert, "The Importance of Demography

and Patterns of Settlement for an Understanding of the Jewish Experience in East-Central Europe," in *The Shtetl: New Evaluations*, ed. Steven T. Katz (New York: New York University Press, 2007), 32–33; and Boris Mironov, *A Social History of Imperial Russia, 1700–1917* (Boulder, CO: Westview, 2000), 107. See also Ransel's *Village Mothers: Three Generations of Change in Russia and Tataria* (Bloomington: Indiana University Press, 2000), 20–42; and Shaul Stampfer, "Love and Family," in his *Families, Rabbis, and Education: Traditional Jewish Society in Nineteenth-Century Eastern Europe* (Oxford: The Littman Library of Jewish Civilization, 2010), 30–31. For examples of child murder cases in Vitebsk province, see NIAB, f. 3309, op. 1, d. 1848 (1827); d. 1849 (1827); and d. 2052 (1829).

10. Langston Hughes, *The Ways of White Folks* (New York: Vintage Classics, 1990), 3. For histories of Velizh, see O. M. Kiselev, comp., *Velizh* (Vitebsk: Gubernskaia tipografiia, 1895); and *Iz istorii Velizha i raiona* (Smolensk: Smolenskaia gorodskaia tipografiia, 2002). Much useful information on Vitebsk province is included in the wide-ranging books by Mikhail Dolbilov and Alexei Miller, eds., *Zapadnye okrainy Rossiiskoi imperii* (Moscow: Novoe literaturnoe obozrenie, 2007); and Ina Sorkina, *Miastechki Belarusi w kantsy XVIII-pershai palove XIX st.* (Vilnius: Evropeiskii gumanitarnyi universitet, 2010). See also Sachar Schybeka, "Die Nordwestprovinzen im Russischen Reich (1795–1917)," in *Handbuch der Geschichte Weissrusslands*, ed. Dietrich Beyrau and Rainer Lindau (Göttingen: Vandenhoeck & Ruprecht, 2001), 119–134; and Yakov Leshtinski, "Yidn in Vitebsk un Vitebsker gubernye," in *Vitebsk amol: geshichte, zikhroynes, khurbn*, ed. Grigori Aronson, Yakov Leshtinski, and Avraham Kihn (New York: Waldon Press, 1956), 57–92.

11. John D. Klier, *Rossiia sobiraet svoikh evreev: Proiskhozhdenie evreiskogo voprosa v Rossii, 1772–1825*, expanded edition (Moscow: Mosty kul'tury, 2000), 102; and Barbara Skinner, *The Western Front of the Eastern Church: Uniate and Orthodox Conflict in 18th-Century Poland, Ukraine, Belarus, and Russia* (DeKalb: Northern Illinois University Press, 2009), 145–146.

12. For suggestive treatments of borderlands, see Omer Bartov and Eric D. Weitz, "Introduction," in *Shatterzone of Empires: Coexistence and Violence in the German, Habsburg, Russian, and Ottoman Borderlands*, ed. Bartov and Weitz (Bloomington: Indiana University Press, 2013), 1–20; and Kate Brown, *A Biography of No Place: From Ethnic Borderland to Soviet Heartland* (Cambridge, MA: Harvard University Press, 2004).

13. Antony Polonsky, *The Jews in Poland and Russia*, 3 vols. (Oxford: The Littman Library of Jewish Civilization, 2010–2012), 1: 68–90; and Gershon D. Hundert, *The Jews in a Polish Private Town: The Case of Opatów in the Eighteenth Century* (Baltimore: Johns Hopkins University Press, 1992), 3–10. See also Glenn Dynner, "Jewish Quarters: The Economics of Segregation in the Kingdom of Poland," in *Purchasing Power: The Economics of Modern Jewish History*, ed. Rebecca Kobrin and Adam Teller (Philadelphia: University of Pennsylvania Press, 2015), 91–111.

14. In the second half of the nineteenth century, Jews continued to face restrictions on their residence in cities such as Vil'na, Kovno, and Zhitomir. See Benjamin Nathans, *Beyond the Pale: The Jewish Encounter with Late Imperial Russia* (Berkeley: University of California Press, 2002), 113–114.

15. Klier, *Rossiia sobiraet svoikh evreev*, 98 (the first edition of Klier's book listed thirty thousand Jews); Skinner, *The Western Front of the Eastern Church*, 147; "Velizh," in *Evreiskaia entsiklopediia: Svod znanii o evreistve i ego kul'ture v proshlom i nastoiashchem*, 16 vols. (Moscow: Terra, 1991), 5: 406.

16. The numbers for Velizh and the province of Vitebsk can be found in RGIA, f. 1281, op. 11, d. 21, ll. 18–19 (1829). For comparable data, listing Velizh with 6,791 inhabitants, see RGIA, f. 1290, op. 1, d. 16, l. 40b (1828).

17. Skinner, *The Western Front of the Eastern Church*, 43, 63–64. See also Mikhail Dolbilov, *Russkii krai, chuzhaia vera: Etnokonfessional'naia politika v Litve i Belorussii pri Alexandre II* (Moscow: Novoe literaturnoe obozrenie, 2010), 68–108.

18. My analysis of Velizh's topography is based on "Plan g. Velizha," RGIA, f. 1293, op. 166, d. 19; and "Geometricheskii plan g. Velizha," RGIA, f. 1293, op. 166, d. 18. See also the map in Miron Ryvkin, "Velizhskoe delo v osveshchenii mestnykh predanii i pamiatnikov," *Perezhitoe* 3 (1911): 67 (which is probably based on RGIA, f. 1293, op. 166, d. 18). For an exceptionally detailed analysis of seventeenth-century Wilno's (Vil'na's) physical topography, an inspiration to my own work, see David Frick, *Kith, Kin, and Neighbors: Communities and Confessions in Seventeenth-Century Wilno* (Ithaca: Cornell University Press, 2013), 20–58.

19. Shaul Stampfer, "Heder Study, Knowledge of Torah, and the Maintenance of Stratification," in his *Families, Rabbis, and Education*, 145–166.

20. On the *shtibl*, see Shaul Stampfer, "How and Why Did Hasidism Spread?" *Jewish History* 27, no. 2 (2013): 201–219; Glenn Dynner, *Yankel's Tavern: Jews, Liquor, and Life in the Kingdom of Poland* (New York: Oxford University Press, 2014), 38–39; and Louis Jacobs, *Hasidic Prayer* (New York: Schocken Books, 1973), 43–44.

21. Gershon D. Hundert, *Jews in Poland-Lithuania: A Genealogy of Modernity* (Berkeley: University of California Press, 2004), 53; and Leshtinski, "Yidn in Vitebsk un Vitebsker gubernye," in *Vitebsk amol*, 64–71.

22. Johnson, *Travels through Parts of the Russian Empire and the Country of Poland*, 374–376.

23. E. R. Romanov, *Materialy po istoricheskoi topografii Vitebskoi gubernii, uezd Velizhskii* (Mogilev: [n. p.], 1898), 32–33, 39. See also the discussion about poverty in *Voenno-statisticheskoe obozrenie Rossiiskoi imperii*, 147–148.

24. Gavriil R. Derzhavin, "Mnenie ob otvrashchenii v Belorussii goloda i ustroistva byta evreev," in *Sochineniia Derzhavina*, ed. Ia. Grota (St. Petersburg: Tipografiia Imperatorskoi akademii nauk, 1872), 230.

25. Klier, *Rossiia sobiraet svoikh evreev*, 171–173; and ChaeRan Y. Freeze and Jay M. Harris, "Introduction: The Imperial Context," in *Everyday Jewish Life in Imperial*

Russia: Select Documents, ed. Freeze and Harris (Waltham: Brandeis University Press, 2013), 11.

26. Dominic Lieven, *Russia against Napoleon: The True Story of the Campaigns of War and Peace* (London: Penguin Books, 2009), 124, 129, 146, 170, 269.

27. Morton, *Travels in Russia*, 129.

28. Johnson, *Travels through Parts of the Russian Empire and the Country of Poland*, 368.

29. Jakob Walter, *The Diary of a Napoleonic Foot Soldier*, ed. Marc Raeff (New York: Doubleday, 1991), 44.

30. S. M. Ginzburg, *Otechestvennaia voina 1812 goda i russkie evrei* (St. Petersburg: Razum, 1912), 109–110.

31. Vladimir Medvedev, "Velizh: Otechestvennaia voina 1812 goda," *Krai Smolenskii: Istoriia Velizhskogo kraia*, no. 3 (2013): 29.

32. RGIA, f. 1287, op. 12, d. 86, ll. 1–10b, 3–30b, 13, 42, 46–490b.

33. Concerning reports of the high number of illnesses and deaths in Vitebsk and Mogilev provinces, see RGIA, f. 1263, op. 1, d. 418, ll. 754–755 (1825). On D. O. Baranov, see Klier, *Rossiia sobiraet svoikh evreev*, 288.

34. Ginzburg, *Otechestvennaia voina 1812 goda*, 136; Klier, *Rossiia sobiraet svoikh evreev*, 288–289; and Dynner, *Yankel's Tavern*, 55–56.

35. NIAB, f. 1297, op. 1, d. 7858, ll. 1–20b, 12–13 (accessed at the CAHJP).

36. Yohanan Petrovsky-Shtern, *Jews in the Russian Army: Drafted into Modernity* (Cambridge: Cambridge University Press, 2009); and Michael Stanislawski, *Tsar Nicholas I and the Jews: The Transformation of Jewish Society in Russia, 1825–1855* (Philadelphia: Jewish Publication Society of America, 1983), 13–34.

37. Eugene M. Avrutin, *Jews and the Imperial State: Identification Politics in Tsarist Russia* (Ithaca: Cornell University Press, 2010), 21–52.

38. On the Habad movement, see Immanuel Etkes, *Rabbi Shneur Zalman of Liady: The Origins of Chabad Hasidism*, trans. Jeffrey M. Green (Waltham: Brandeis University Press, 2015); Naftali Lowenthal, *Communicating the Infinite: The Emergence of the Habad School* (Chicago: University of Chicago Press, 1990); and Ilia Lurie, *The Habad Movement in Tsarist Russia, 1828–1882* [Hebrew] (Jerusalem: Magnes Press, 2006). For an excellent overview, see Lowenthal's "Lubavitch Hasidism," in *The YIVO Encyclopedia of Jews in Eastern Europe*, 2 vols. (New Haven: Yale University Press, 2008), 1: 1094–1097.

39. David Assaf and Gadi Sagiv, "Hasidism in Tsarist Russia: Historical and Social Aspects," *Jewish History* 27, no. 2 (2013): 241–269.

40. "Evreiskie religioznye sekty v Rossii," *Zhurnal ministerstva vnutrennikh del*, part 16 (1846): 574–575.

41. Derzhavin, "Mnenie ob otvrashchenii v Belorussii goloda i ustroistva byta evreev," in *Sochineniia Derzhavina*, 254. See also Klier, *Rossiia sobiraet svoikh evreev*, 178; and Etkes, *Rabbi Shneur Zalman of Liady*, 188.

42. As quoted in Moshe Rosman, *Founder of Hasidism: A Quest for the Historical Ba'al Shem Tov*, 2nd ed. (Oxford: The Littman Library of Jewish Civilization, 2013), 36.

43. Etkes, *Rabbi Shneur Zalman of Liady*, 28–30, 50, 54, 69–70.

44. "O razvitii torgovli i promyshlennosti v Vitebskoi gubernii," RGIA, f. 560, op. 4, d. 1413, l. 17 (1851); and RGIA, f. 1281, op. 11, d. 20, ll. 64–64ob.

45. "O merakh dlia ustroistva Vitebskoi i Mogilevskoi gubernii," RGIA, f. 1287, op. 3, d. 85, ll. 99ob–100 (1853); and *Voenno-statisticheskoe obozrenie Rossiiskoi imperii: Vitebskaia guberniia*, 148.

46. "Po otchetu Vitebskoi gubernii," RGIA, f. 1281, op. 4, d. 82, ll. 60b, 90b (1841).

47. RGIA, f. 1281, op. 11, d. 20, ll. 69–69ob.

48. Hans Rogger, "Jews after the Liberation of the Serfs," in his *Jewish Policies and Right-Wing Politics in Imperial Russia* (Berkeley: University of California Press, 1986), 116–117.

49. RGIA, f. 560, op. 4, d. 1413, l. 170b. For a general overview of pre-industrialized market towns, see Boris Mironov, *A Social History of Imperial Russia, 1700–1917* (Boulder: Westview, 2000), 443–461.

50. RGIA, f. 1281, op. 4, d. 82, l. 15. For an overview of the economy before the Great Reforms, see M. F. Bolbas, *Razvitie promyshlennosti v Belorussii (1795–1861 gg.)* (Minsk: Akademiia nauk BSSR, 1966).

51. For a classic statement, see Jan DeVries, *The Economy of Europe in an Age of Crisis, 1600–1750* (Cambridge: Cambridge University Press, 1976), esp. 32–33. On mobility and innovation in the medieval and early modern economies, see Robert S. Duplessis, *Transitions to Capitalism in Early Modern Europe* (Cambridge: Cambridge University Press, 1997). The flow of goods from Vitebsk province established wider connections with Riga, Moscow, and St. Petersburg, where linen, bread, and spring wheat were shipped (RGIA, f. 1281, op. 4, d. 82, ll. 14–140b). For an exploration of the wider economic context, see Sorkina, *Miastechki Belarusi*, 141–169.

52. Yohanan Petrovsky-Shtern, *The Golden Age Shtetl: A New History of Jewish Life in East Europe* (Princeton: Princeton University Press, 2014), 97.

53. Catherine Evtukhov, *Portrait of a Russian Province: Economy, Society, and Civilization in Nineteenth-Century Nizhnii Novgorod* (Pittsburgh: University of Pittsburgh Press, 2011), 9–10.

54. RGIA, f. 1281, op. 4, d. 89A, ll. 42–420b (1849); and Albert Kaganovitch, *The Long Life and Swift Death of Jewish Rechitsa: A Community in Belarus, 1625–2000* (Madison: University of Wisconsin, 2013), 98–99.

55. Avrutin, *Jews and the Imperial State*, 89–90; and Arcadius Kahan, "The Impact of Industrialization in Tsarist Russia on Socioeconomic Conditions of the Jewish Population," in his *Essays in Jewish Social and Economic History*, ed. Roger Weiss (Chicago: University of Chicago Press, 1986), 1–69. For an excellent overview of Russia's great transformation, see Mustafa Tuna, *Imperial Russia's Muslims: Islam, Empire, and European Modernity, 1788–1914* (Cambridge: Cambridge University Press, 2015), 109–116.

56. *Iz istorii Velizha*, 157.

57. N. A. Troinitskii, ed., *Pervaia vseobshchaia perepis' naseleniia Rossiiskoi impe-rii, 1897 g.*, 120 vols. (St. Petersburg: Izdatel'stva Tsentral'nago statisticheskago komiteta Ministerstva vnutrennikh del, 1899–1905), vol. 5, part 2: 54. On the cultural life of Vitebsk, see Aleksandra Shatskikh, *Vitebsk: The Life of Art*, trans. Katherine Foshko Tsan (New Haven: Yale University Press, 2007), 2–3.

58. For a judicious discussion of Jewish social life and education in Minsk province, paralleling in many respects the story of Velizh, see Kaganovitch, *The Long Life and Swift Death of Jewish Rechitsa*, 169–170.

59. Abraham Cahan, *Bleter fun mein leben*, vol. 1 (New York: Forverts Asosieyshon, 1926), 453.

60. A. M. Sementovskii, ed., *Pamiatnaia knizhka Vitebskoi gubernii na 1864 god* (St. Petersburg: Tipografiia K. Vul'fa, 1864), 235, 239; and *Pervaia vseobshchaia perepis' naseleniia Rossiiskoi imperii, 1897 g.*, vol. 5, part 3: 198–201. See also the discus-sion in Arkadii Zel'tser, *Evrei sovetskoi provintsii: Vitebsk i mestechki, 1917–1941* (Moscow: ROSSPEN, 2006), 9–10.

61. Magda Teter, *Jews and Heretics in Catholic Poland: A Beleaguered Church in the Post-Reformation Era* (Cambridge: Cambridge University Press, 2006), 21–40; and Hundert, *Jews in Poland-Lithuania in the Eighteenth Century*, 38–44.

62. On neighborly contact in the early modern period, see, for example, David Frick, "Jews and Others in Seventeenth-Century Wilno: Life in the Neighborhood," *Jewish Studies Quarterly* 12, no. 1 (2005): 10–20; and David Fram, *Ideals Face Reality: Jewish Law and Life in Poland, 1550–1655* (Cincinnati: Hebrew Union College Press, 1997), 30–31.

63. Adam Teller, "The Shtetl as an Arena for Polish-Jewish Integration in the Eighteenth Century," *Polin* 17 (2004): 37; and Jacob Katz, *Exclusiveness and Tolerance: Studies in Jewish-Gentile Relations in Medieval and Modern Times* (Springfield, NJ: Behrman House, 1961), 9.

64. On popular uses of the court system in the Russian Empire, see Jane Burbank, *Russian Peasants Go to Court: Legal Culture in the Countryside, 1905–1917* (Bloomington: Indiana University Press, 2004).

65. For an extensive analysis of the court cases, see Eugene M. Avrutin, "Jewish Neighborly Relations and Imperial Russian Legal Culture," *Journal of Modern Jewish Studies* 9, no. 1 (2010): 1–16.

66. Michael J. Broyde and Michael Ausubel, "Legal Institutions," in *The YIVO Encyclopedia of Jews in Eastern Europe*, 2 vols. (New Haven: Yale University Press, 2008), 1: 1008.

67. See, for example, Burbank, *Russian Peasants Go to Court*, 84, n. 5.

68. Daniel Jütte, "Interfaith Encounters between Jews and Christians in the Early Modern Period and Beyond: Toward a Framework," *American Historical Review* 118, no. 2 (2013): 398. See also Jütte's " 'They Shall Not Keep Their Doors or Windows Open': Urban Space and the Dynamics of Conflict and Contact in Premodern Jewish-Christian Relations," *European History Quarterly* 46, no. 2

(2016): 209–237; and Benjamin J. Kaplan, *Divided by Faith: Religious Conflict and the Practice of Toleration in Early Modern Europe* (Cambridge, MA: Harvard University Press, 2007), 237–265. For a perceptive analysis of social relations in a small community, see John Putnam Demos, *Entertaining Satan: Witchcraft and the Culture of Early New England*, updated ed. (New York: Oxford University Press, 2004), 275–312.

69. This point is based on a survey of roughly two hundred criminal cases from 1833 to 1869 in Kovno province (KAA, f. 76, op. 1). I would like to thank Aušra Paulauskienė for research assistance with these files.

70. Mary Lindemann, *Medicine and Society in Early Modern Europe*, 2nd ed. (Cambridge: Cambridge University Press, 2010), 38–39; and Roy Porter, *The Greatest Benefit to Mankind: A Medical History of Humanity* (New York: W. W. Norton & Company, 1997), 18–19.

71. Quoted in Alla Sokolova, "In Search of the Exotic: 'Jewish Houses' and Synagogues in Russian Travel Notes," in *Writing Jewish Culture: Paradoxes in Ethnography*, ed. Andreas Kilchner and Gabriella Safran (Bloomington: Indiana University Press, 2016), 299–301.

72. Cahan, *Bleter fun mein leben*, 450.

73. Moisei Berlin, *Ocherk etnografii evreiskago narodonaseleniia v Rossii* (St. Petersburg: Tipografiia V. Bezobrazova, 1861), 3–5.

74. Yekhezkel Kotik, *Journey to a Nineteenth-Century Shtetl: The Memoirs of Yekhezkel Kotik*, ed. David Assaf (Detroit: Wayne State University Press, 2002), 152.

75. *Vitebskie gubernskie vedomosti*, no. 35 (1839), 2; no. 9 (1841), 1–2.

76. NIAB, f. 1297, op. 1, d. 2477 (1827); and d. 2473, l. 6 (1827).

77. RGIA, f. 1281, op. 4, d. 71A (1846), ll. 21–21ob, 23ob–24.

78. "O dostavlenii vrachami svedenii v Vitebskuiu vrachebnuiu upravu o bol'nykh i ospoprivivanii," *Vitebskie gubernskie vedomosti*, no. 9 (1841), 1–2. See also "Postanovlenii i predpisaniia gubernskago nachal'stva," *Vitebskie gubernskie vedomosti*, no. 38 (1842), 1–2.

79. "O bezporiadkakh po obozreniiu Vitebskoi gubernii," RGIA, f. 1287, op. 31, d. 821, l. 4 (1844).

80. "Narodnoe zdravie i obshchestvennoe prizrenie," in *Obzor Vitebskoi gubernii za 1910 god* (Vitebsk: Gubernskaia tipografiia, 1911), 47–53. For a fascinating examination of medical practices in early modern Poland, see Yohanan Petrovsky-Shtern, "'You Will Find It in the Pharmacy': Practical Kabbalah and Natural Medicine in the Polish-Lithuanian Commonwealth, 1690–1750," in *Holy Dissent: Jewish and Christian Mystics in Eastern Europe*, ed. Glenn Dynner (Detroit: Wayne State University Press, 2011), 13–54.

81. This paragraph draws on Petrovsky-Shtern's "'You Will Find It in the Pharmacy'," 13–54.

82. R. Pinchas Kaztenelbogen's remedy for fever is translated in the collection of primary sources, Freeze and Harris, eds., *Everyday Jewish Life in Imperial Russia*, 265.

83. *Vitebskie gubernskie vedomosti*, pt. 2, no. 3, (1857), 1–3; pt. 2, no. 9 (1857), 1–4; pt. 2, no. 23 (1857), 1–2. On traditional healing and folk medicine in Vitebsk and Mogilev provinces, see L. I. Min'ko, *Narodnaia meditsina Belorussii: Kratkii istoricheskii ocherk* (Minsk: Izdatel'stvo "Nauka i tekhnika," 1969).

84. W. F. Ryan, *The Bathhouse at Midnight: Magic in Russia* (University Park: Pennsylvania State University Press, 1999), 46–57, 94–114; and Robert H. Greene, *Bodies like Bright Stars: Saints and Relics in Orthodox Russia* (DeKalb: Northern Illinois University Press, 2010), 39–72.

85. Pauline Wengeroff, *Memoirs of a Grandmother: Scenes from the Cultural History of the Jews of Russia in the Nineteenth Century*, vol. 1, trans. Shulamit S. Magnus (Stanford: Stanford University Press, 2010), 146, 170.

86. Kotik, *Journey to a Nineteenth-Century Shtetl*, 150.

87. On spirit possession, see, for example, Matt Goldish, ed., *Spirit Possession in Judaism: Cases and Contexts from the Middle Ages to the Present* (Detroit: Wayne State University Press, 2003).

88. Gedalyah Nigal, *The Hasidic Tale*, trans. Edward Levin (Oxford: The Littman Library of Jewish Civilization, 2008), 195–233.

89. Kotik, *Journey to a Nineteenth-Century Shtetl*, 157.

90. For a classic statement, see Joshua Trachtenberg, *Jewish Magic and Superstition: A Study in Folk Religion* (New York: Atheneum, 1970). For a succinct exploration, see Avriel Bar-Levav, "Magic," *The YIVO Encyclopedia of Jews in Eastern Europe*, vol. 1: 1113–1114. See also Dean Phillip Bell, "Jews, Magic, and Community in Seventeenth-Century Worms," in *Werewolves, Witches, and Wandering Spirits: Traditional Belief and Folklore in Early Modern Europe*, ed. Kathryn A. Edwards (Kirksville, MO: Truman State University, 2002), 93–118.

91. Michael Ostling, "Imagined Crimes, Real Victims: Hermeneutical Witches and Jews in Early Modern Poland," in *Ritual Murder in Russia, Eastern Europe, and Beyond: New Histories of an Old Accusation*, ed. Eugene M. Avrutin, Jonathan Dekel-Chen, and Robert Weinberg (Bloomington: Indiana University Press, 2017), 18–38. For a perceptive analysis of the significance of popular medical knowledge and the blood libel, see Khanna Vengzhinek, "Meditsinskie znaniia i istochniki 'krovavykh navetov' v staroi Pol'she," in *Narodnaia meditsina i magiia v slavianskoi i evreiskoi kul'turnoi traditsii*, ed. O. V. Belova (Moscow: Sefer, 2007), 81–88. For an analysis of contemporary understandings, see Aleksandr L'vov, "Mezhetnicheskie otnoshenie ugoshchenie i 'krovavyi navet,'" in *Shtetl XXI vek: Polevye issledovaniia*, ed. V. A. Dymshits, A. L. L'vov, and A. V. Sokolova (St. Petersburg: Evropeiskii universitet v Sankt-Peterburge, 2008), 65–82. See also R. Po-chia Hsia's *The Myth of Ritual Murder: Jews and Magic in Reformation Germany* (New Haven: Yale University Press, 1988), 6–9; and Joshua Trachtenberg, *The Devil and the Jews: The Medieval Conception of the Jew and Its Relation to Modern Anti-Semitism* (Philadelphia: The Jewish Publication Society, 1983).

Chapter 3

1. Alan Palmer, *Alexander I: Tsar of War and Peace* (New York: Harper & Row, 1974), 397–401, quote on 401. See also Richard S. Wortman, *Scenarios of Power: Myth and Ceremony in Russian Monarchy*, vol. 1 (Princeton: Princeton University Press, 1995), 238–243.

2. RGIA, f. 1345, op. 235, d. 65, chast' 1, ll. 5–50b. Based on the emperor's private correspondence and his official itinerary, scholars have established that Alexander spent the month of July in and around St. Petersburg. Although July 15, 1825, is the date printed on the complaint, most likely Alexander read it on September 4, the same day he dispatched a short note from Velizh to St. Petersburg. See Nikolai Mikhailovich, *Imperator Aleksandr I: Opyt istoricheskago izsledovaniia*, 2nd ed. (Petrograd: Ekspeditsiia zagotovleniia gosudarstvennykh bumag, 1914), 679, 737.

3. John P. LeDonne, "Russian Governors General, 1775–1825," *Cahiers du monde russe* 42, no. 1 (2001): 5–30; and LeDonne, "Administrative Regionalization in the Russian Empire, 1802–1826," *Cahiers du monde russe* 43, no. 1 (2002): 5–34. For a short biography of Khovanskii, see *Slovar' russkikh generalov, uchastnikov boevykh deistvii protiv armii Napoleona Bonaparta v 1812–1815* (Moscow: Studiia "TRITE" N. Mikhalkova, 1996), 599–600.

4. Wortman, *Scenarios of Power*, vol. 1, 264–269, 297–332; and Daniel Beer, *The House of the Dead: Siberian Exile under the Tsars* (New York: Alfred A. Knopf, 2017), 54–55.

5. On Russian sectarianism, see Nikolai Varadinov, *Istoriia Ministerstva vnutrennikh del*, vol. 8 (St. Petersburg: Tipografiia Ministerstva vnutrennikh del, 1863), 188–193. For recent studies, see Laura Engelstein, *Castration and the Heavenly Kingdom: A Russian Folktale* (Ithaca: Cornell University Press, 1999), 49–51; J. Eugene Clay, "Orthodox Missionaries and 'Orthodox Heretics' in Russia, 1886–1917," in *Of Religion and Empire: Missions, Conversion, and Tolerance in Tsarist Russia*, ed. Robert Geraci and Michael Khodarkovsky (Ithaca: Cornell University Press, 2001), 38–69; Sergei I. Zhuk, *Russia's Lost Reformation: Peasants, Millennialism, and Radical Sects in Southern Russia and Ukraine, 1830–1917* (Baltimore: Johns Hopkins University Press, 2004); Nicholas Breyfogle, *Heretics and Colonizers: Forging Russia's Empire in the South Caucasus* (Ithaca: Cornell University Press, 2005); and Nicholas Breyfogle, "The Religious World of Russian Sabbatarians (Subbotniks)," in *Holy Dissent: Jewish and Christian Mystics in Eastern Europe*, ed. Glenn Dynner (Detroit: Wayne State University Press, 2011), 359–392.

6. RGIA, f. 1345, op. 235, d. 65, chast' 1, ll. 17–240b, 45–470b, 49–520b, 63–700b.

7. RGIA, f. 1345, op. 235, d. 65, chast' 1, ll. 25–260b (November 22, 1825).

8. RGIA, f. 1345, op. 235, d. 65, chast' 1, l. 27.

9. RGIA, f. 1345, op. 235, d. 65, chast' 1, ll. 28–280b.

10. RGIA, f. 1345, op. 235, d. 65, chast' 1, l. 29.

11. RGIA, f. 1345, op. 235, d. 65, chast' 1, ll. 30–31.

12. RGIA, f. 1345, op. 235, d. 65, chast' 1, ll. 37–370b.
13. RGIA, f. 1345, op. 235, d. 65, chast' 1, ll. 380b–39.
14. RGIA, f. 1345, op. 235, d. 65, chast' 1, ll. 39–41.
15. For a firsthand account, see Pauline Wengeroff, *Memoirs of a Grandmother: Scenes from the Cultural History of the Jews of Russia in the Nineteenth Century*, vol. 1, trans. Shulamit S. Magnus (Stanford: Stanford University Press, 2010), 207.
16. Judith Kalik, "Christian Servants Employed by Jews in the Polish-Lithuanian Commonwealth in the Seventeenth and Eighteenth Centuries," *Polin* 14 (2001): 267; and Magda Teter, *Jews and Heretics in Catholic Poland: A Beleaguered Church in the Post-Reformation Era* (Cambridge: Cambridge University Press, 2006), 63–69. On questions regarding halakhic teachings and everyday life, see Jacob Katz, *The "Shabbes" Goy: A Study in Halakhic Flexibility*, trans. Yoel Lerner (Philadelphia: Jewish Publication Society, 1989), 49–67, 80–81, 87–105.
17. Judith Kalik, "Fusion versus Alienation—Erotic Attraction, Sex, and Love between Jews and Christians in the Polish-Lithuanian Commonwealth," in *Kommunikation durch symbolische Akte: Religiöse Heterogenität und politische Herrschaft in Polen-Litauen*, ed. Yvonne Kleinmann (Stuttgart: Steiner, 2010), 159–160.
18. Gershon D. Hundert, *Jews in Poland-Lithuania in the Eighteenth Century: A Genealogy of Modernity* (Berkeley: University of California Press, 2004), 38.
19. Iulii Gessen, "Naem lichnyi (usluzhenie khristian) po russkomu zakonodatel'stvu," *Evreiskaia entsiklopediia: Svod znanii o evreistve i ego kul'ture v proshlom i nastoiashchem*, 16 vols. (Moscow: "Terra," 1991), 11: 492–496.
20. Ellie R. Schainker, *Confessions of the Shtetl: Converts from Judaism in Imperial Russia, 1817–1906* (Stanford: Stanford University Press, 2016), 147–148.
21. Gessen, "Naem lichnyi," *Evreiskaia entsiklopediia*, 11: 492–496; and Eugene M. Avrutin, "Returning to Judaism after the 1905 Law on Religious Freedom in Tsarist Russia," *Slavic Review* 65, no. 1 (2006): 94.
22. This paragraph draws on Breyfogle, "The Religious World of Russian Sabbatarians (Subbotniks)," in Dynner, *Holy Dissent*, 359–392.
23. Kalik, "Christian Servants Employed by Jews in the Polish-Lithuanian Commonwealth in the Seventeenth and Eighteenth Centuries," 266.
24. RGIA, f. 1345, op. 235, d. 65, chast' 1, ll. 91–92 (December 4, 1825).
25. RGIA, f. 1345, op. 235, d. 65, chast' 1, ll. 96–960b (December 5, 1825).
26. RGIA, f. 1345, op. 235, d. 65, chast' 1, ll. 98–99.
27. RGIA, f. 1345, op. 235, d. 65, chast' 1, ll. 127–128, 132 (December 15, 1825).
28. RGIA, f. 1345, op. 235, d. 65, chast' 1, ll. 1280b–130.
29. John P. LeDonne, "Criminal Investigations before the Great Reforms," *Russian History* 1, no. 2 (1974): 102.
30. RGIA, f. 1345, op. 235, d. 65, chast' 1, l. 2130b.

31. RGIA, f. 1345, op. 235, d. 65, chast' 25, l. 151, 155. Strakhov interrogated Anna Eremeeva on December 28, 1825 (RGIA, f. 1345, op. 235, d. 65, chast' 25, ll. 145–162).

32. Peter Brooks, *Troubling Confessions: Speaking Guilt in Law and Literature* (Chicago: University of Chicago Press, 2000), 40; and Richard A. Leo, *Police Interrogation and American Justice* (Cambridge, MA: Harvard University Press, 2008), 38–39.

33. On systems of proofs, see Elisa M. Becker, *Medicine, Law, and the State in Imperial Russia* (Budapest: Central European Press, 2011), 28–39; and Kollmann, *Crime and Punishment in Early Modern Russia*, 114–118. For a broader prospective, see John H. Langbein, *Torture and the Law of Proof: Europe and England in the Ancien Regime* (Chicago: University of Chicago Press, 2006).

34. Brooks, *Troubling Confessions*, 35.

35. RGIA, f. 1345, op. 235, d. 65, chast' 3, ll. 2157–2158, 2162–2171ob; and RGIA, f. 1345, op. 235, d. 65, chast' 25, ll. 171, 174.

36. RGIA, f. 1345, op. 235, d. 65, chast' 1, ll. 167–178ob (Terenteeva, January 12, 1826); ll. 401–416 (Terenteeva, June 3, 1826); ll. 455–458ob (Kozlovskaia, June 14, 1826); ll. 589–606ob (Terenteeva, September 23, 1826); ll. 615–617, 620–632ob (Maksimova, October 17, 1826). A succinct summary is included in RGIA, f. 1345, op. 235, d. 65, chast' 25, ll. 30–39.

37. RGIA, f. 1345, op. 235, d. 65, chast' 1, l. 615 (October 8, 1826).

38. On the emergence of the Christian servant as a character in the blood libel tale, see E. M. Rose, *The Murder of William of Norwich: The Origins of the Blood Libel in Medieval Europe* (New York: Oxford University Press, 2015).

39. RGIA, f. 1345, op. 235, d. 65, chast' 25, ll. 38–39. See also RGIA, f. 1345, op. 235, d. 65, chast' 1, 167–178ob.

40. RGIA, f. 1345, op. 235, d. 65, chast' 25, ll. 40–41.

41. RGIA, f. 1345, op. 235, d. 65, chast' 25, ll. 42–43. See also RGIA, f. 1345, op. 235, d. 65, chast' 1, ll. 401–416.

42. RGIA, f. 1345, op. 235, d. 65, chast' 25, ll. 43–44.

43. RGIA, f. 1345, op. 235, d. 65, chast' 25, ll. 44, 50. See also RGIA, f. 1345, op. 235, d. 65, chast' 1, ll. 615–617.

44. RGIA, f. 1345, op. 235, d. 65, chast' 25, l. 50.

45. RGIA, f. 1345, op. 235, d. 65, chast' 25, l. 51.

46. RGIA, f. 1345, op. 235, d. 65, chast' 25, l. 51.

47. RGIA, f. 1345, op. 235, d. 65, chast' 25, l. 52. See also RGIA, f. 1345, op. 235, d. 65, chast' 1, ll. 620–632ob.

48. Barbara Skinner, *The Western Front of the Eastern Church: Uniate and Orthodox Conflict in 18th-Century Poland, Ukraine, Belarus, and Russia* (DeKalb: Northern Illinois University Press, 2009), 60–61.

49. RGIA, f. 1345, op. 235, d. 65, chast' 25, l. 44. See also RGIA, f. 1345, op. 235, d. 65, chast' 1, ll. 589–606ob.

50. RGIA, f. 1345, op. 235, d. 65, chast' 25, l. 45, 48–49.

51. RGIA, f. 1345, op. 235, d. 65, chast' 25, l. 37.

52. For an enlightening discussion of the challenges of convicting witches in early modern Germany, see Thomas Robisheaux, *The Last Witch of Langenburg: Murder in a German Village* (New York: W. W. Norton, 2009).

Chapter 4

1. RGIA, f. 1345, op. 235, d. 65, chast' 2, ll. 13370b–1338 (oral interrogation of Itsko Nakhimovskii, May 25, 1827).

2. RGIA, f. 1345, op. 235, d. 65, chast' 1, l. 4640b (Strakhov described the conditions of the local prison in a memo to Khovanskii).

3. On Russian prisons, see Nancy Shields Kollmann, *Crime and Punishment in Early Modern Russia* (Cambridge: Cambridge University Press, 2012), 83–93; Evgenii Anisimov, *Dyba i knut: Politicheskii sysk i russkoe obshchestvo v XVIII veke* (Moscow: Novoe literaturnoe obozrenie, 1999), 589–614; and Daniel Beer, *The House of the Dead: Siberian Exile under the Tsars* (New York: Alfred A. Knopf, 2017). For a recent analysis of the exile system, see Andrew A. Gentes, *Exile to Siberia, 1590–1822* (New York: Palgrave Macmillan, 2008); and Gentes, *Exile, Murder, and Madness in Siberia, 1823–1861* (New York: Palgrave Macmillan, 2010).

4. Bruce F. Adams, *The Politics of Punishment: Prison Reform in Russia, 1863–1917* (DeKalb: Northern Illinois University Press, 1996), 9. For a comparative perspective on the limits of using local prisons for incarceration, see Randall McGowen, "The Well-Ordered Prison: England, 1780–1865," in *The Oxford History of the Prison: The Practice of Punishment in Western Society*, ed. Norval Morris and David J. Rothman (New York: Oxford University Press, 1995), 91.

5. Ritual murder was not specifically a feminine crime, and gender did not seem to play a factor in who was formally accused. On gender and witchcraft accusations, see Alison Rowlands, "Witchcraft and Gender in Early Modern Europe," in *The Oxford Handbook of Witchcraft in Early Modern Europe and Colonial America*, ed. Brian P. Levack (Oxford: Oxford University Press, 2013), 449–467; Robin Briggs, *Witches and Neighbors: The Social and Cultural Context of European Witchcraft* (New York: Penguin Books, 1998), 259–286; and Valerie Kivelson, *Desperate Magic: The Moral Economy of Witchcraft in Seventeenth-Century Russia* (Ithaca: Cornell University Press, 2013), 127–167.

6. For an exhaustive treatment of face-to-face confrontations in Russian criminal practice, see Anisimov, *Dyba i knut*, 313–390.

7. Thomas Robisheaux, *The Last Witch of Langenburg: Murder in a German Village* (New York: W. W. Norton, 2009), 193–212. This technique was used in the Soviet Union. See, for example, Hiroaki Kuromiya, *Conscience on Trial: The Fate of Fourteen Pacifists in Stalin's Ukraine, 1952–1953* (Toronto: University of Toronto Press, 2012).

8. RGIA, f. 1345, op. 235, d. 65, chast' 2, ll. 1484–14900b; and RGIA, f. 1345, op. 235, d. 65, chast' 25, l. 71 (oral interrogation of Shmerka Berlin, June 15, 1827).

9. RGIA, f. 1345, op. 235, d. 65, chast' 2, ll. 1484–14900b; RGIA, f. 1345, op. 235, d. 65, chast' 3, ll. 1735–17360b; RGIA, f. 1345, op. 235, d. 65, chast' 3, l. 1954; and RGIA, f. 1345, op. 235, d. 65, chast' 25, l. 72.

10. RGIA, f. 1345, op. 235, d. 65, chast' 2, ll. 1462–1463, 1465–1466 (oral interrogation of Slava Berlina, June 9, 1827).

11. RGIA, f. 1345, op. 235, d. 65, chast' 3, ll. 1699–1703 (ochnaia stavka, July 7, 1827).

12. RGIA, f. 1345, op. 235, d. 65, chast' 2, ll. 1465–1466, 1467–14720b; and RGIA, f. 1345, op. 235, d. 65, chast' 25, ll. 69–70.

13. RGIA, f. 1345, op. 235, d. 65, chast' 2, ll. 1620–1628 (oral interrogation of Hirsh Berlin, June 30, 1827).

14. RGIA, f. 1345, op. 235, d. 65, chast' 25, ll. 74–75.

15. RGIA, f. 1345, op. 235, d. 65, chast' 3, ll. 1784–17860b, 1789–1790 (oral interrogation of Noson Berlin, July 13, 1827); and RGIA, f. 1345, op. 235, d. 65, chast' 3, ll. 1792–17930b, 1795–17970b (oral interrogation of Meir Berlin, July 13, 1827); and RGIA, f. 1345, op. 235, d. 65, chast' 25, ll. 76–79.

16. RGIA, f. 1345, op. 235, d. 65, chast' 3, ll. 1922–1923, 1930–19380b (oral interrogation of Evzik Tsetlin, August 3–4, 1827); and RGIA, f. 1345, op. 235, d. 65, chast' 25, ll. 59–62.

17. RGIA, f. 1345, op. 235, d. 65, chast' 25, l. 59.

18. RGIA, f. 1345, op. 235, d. 65, chast' 25, l. 60.

19. RGIA, f. 1345, op. 235, d. 65, chast' 25, ll. 159–160.

20. RGIA, f. 1345, op. 235, d. 65, chast' 2, ll. 1449–14490b (June 7, 1827).

21. RGIA, f. 1345, op. 235, d. 65, chast' 25, l. 57.

22. RGIA, f. 1345, op. 235, d. 65, chast' 25, l. 63.

23. RGIA, f. 1345, op. 235, d. 65, chast' 25, l. 95.

24. RGIA, f. 1345, op. 235, d. 65, chast' 25, l. 109.

25. RGIA, f. 1345, op. 235, d. 65, chast' 25, l. 117.

26. RGIA, f. 1345, op. 235, d. 65, chast' 4, ll. 2651–26510b; RGIA, f. 1345, op. 235, d. 65, chast' 3, ll. 1773–1774; and RGIA, f. 1345, op. 235, d. 65, chast' 25, l. 87 (oral interrogation of Basia Aronson, July 13 and October 31, 1827).

27. RGIA, f. 1345, op. 235, d. 65, chast' 25, ll. 88–89.

28. RGIA, f. 1345, op. 235, d. 65, chast' 25, ll. 98–99.

29. RGIA, f. 1345, op. 235, d. 65, chast' 25, ll. 98–99.

30. RGIA, f. 1345, op. 235, d. 65, chast' 25, ll. 109–110.

31. RGIA, f. 1345, op. 235, d. 65, chast' 25, l. 111.

32. RGIA, f. 1345, op. 235, d. 65, chast' 25, l. 101.

33. Guy Geltner, *The Medieval Prison: A Social History* (Princeton: Princeton University Press, 2008), 72. On the practice of keeping captives in private homes in medieval Europe, see Jean Dunbabin, *Captivity and Imprisonment in Medieval Europe, 1000–1300* (New York: Palgrave Macmillan, 2002), 62–79.

34. RGIA, f. 1345, op. 235, d. 65, chast' 10, l. 4160b.

35. RGIA, f. 1345, op. 235, d. 65, chast' 10, l. 336.

36. RGIA, f. 1345, op. 235, d. 65, chast' 10, l. 413. For an insightful analysis of sign language and other forms of communication in prisons, see Patricia O'Brien, *The Promise of Punishment: Prisons in Nineteenth-Century France* (Princeton: Princeton University Press, 1982), 77–79, 88.

37. RGIA, f. 1345, op. 235, d. 65, chast' 3, ll. 1833–1834, 1892–1897, 1925–19250b.

38. RGIA, f. 1345, op. 235, d. 65, chast' 10, l. 3340b.

39. RGIA, f. 1345, op. 235, d. 65, chast' 10, l. 4180b.

40. RGIA, f. 1345, op. 235, d. 65, chast' 25, l. 188; and RGIA, f. 1345, op. 235, d. 65, chast' 2, l. 1236.

41. RGIA, f. 1345, op. 235, d. 65, chast' 10, l. 4180b.

42. RGIA, f. 1345, op. 235, d. 65, chast' 10, l. 415.

43. RGIA, f. 1345, op. 235, d. 65, chast' 10, l. 414.

44. RGIA, f. 1345, op. 235, d. 65, chast' 10, l. 489.

45. RGIA, f. 1345, op. 235, d. 65, chast' 10, ll. 489–490.

46. RGIA, f. 1345, op. 235, d. 65, chast' 10, ll. 585–5850b.

47. RGIA, f. 1345, op. 235, d. 65, chast' 10, l. 3340b.

48. RGIA, f. 1345, op. 235, d. 65, chast' 10, ll. 335–3350b.

49. RGIA, f. 1345, op. 235, d. 65, chast' 10, l. 489.

50. RGIA, f. 1345, op. 235, d. 65, chast' 10, ll. 857–8570b.

51. RGIA, f. 1345, op. 235, d. 65, chast' 10, l. 858.

52. RGIA, f. 1345, op. 235, d. 65, chast' 10, ll. 590–5900b.

53. RGIA, f. 1345, op. 235, d. 65, chast' 25, l. 182.

54. For a perceptive analysis of concealment practices, see Frank Rosengarten, "Introduction," *Letters from Prison: Antonio Gramsci*, vol. 1, ed. Frank Rosengarten, trans. Raymond Rosenthal (New York: Columbia University Press, 1994), 13.

55. RGIA, f. 1345, op. 235, d. 65, chast' 10, ll. 858–8580b.

56. RGIA, f. 1345, op. 235, d. 65, chast' 25, l. 187.

57. RGIA, f. 1345, op. 235, d. 65, chast' 10, l. 4850b; and RGIA, f. 1345, op. 235, d. 65, chast' 25, l. 187.

58. RGIA, f. 1345, op. 235, d. 65, chast' 10, l. 379.

59. RGIA, f. 1345, op. 235, d. 65, chast' 25, l. 188.

60. RGIA, f. 1345, op. 235, d. 65, chast' 25, l. 188.

61. RGIA, f. 1345, op. 235, d. 65, chast' 25, ll.188–192, quotes on ll. 190, 192.

62. RGIA, f. 1345, op. 235, d. 65, chast' 25, ll. 102–106; and RGIA, f. 1345, op. 235, d. 65, chast' 2, ll. 1337–13370b, 13390b (oral interrogation of Itsko Nakhimovskii, May 25, 1827).

63. RGIA, f. 1345, op. 235, d. 65, chast' 25, ll. 134–149; and RGIA, f. 1345, op. 235, d. 65, chast' 6, ll. 4767–47670b.

64. RGIA, f. 1345, op. 235, d. 65, chast' 7, ll. 5371–53710b, 5380–53810b, 5932–59330b (discussion of failed attempt to escape and desire to convert).

65. RGIA, f. 1345, op. 235, d. 65, chast' 3, ll. 1781–1783ob (oral interrogation of Fratka Devirts, July 13, 1827).

66. RGIA, f. 1345, op. 235, d. 65, chast' 3, ll. 2135–2136 (petition by Rieva Kateonov, August 29, 1827).

67. RGIA, f. 1345, op. 235, d. 65, chast' 3, ll. 2103–2112.

68. RGIA, f. 1345, op. 235, d. 65, chast' 3, ll. 2103–2112; and RGIA, f. 1345, op. 235, d. 65, chast' 25, ll. 134–149.

69. RGIA, f. 1345, op. 235, d. 65, chast' 3, l. 2347; and RGIA, f. 1345, op. 235, d. 65, chast' 25, ll. 134–149.

70. RGIA, f. 1345, op. 235, d. 65, chast' 25, ll. 134–149.

71. RGIA, f. 1345, op. 235, d. 65, chast' 7, ll. 5839–5839ob (on Fratka's attempt to commit suicide). When the case was finally closed, all the items, including the alleged piece of foreskin, were forwarded to St. Petersburg. The knives eventually ended up at the Russian State Historical Archive, as did the foreskin, which, according to a medical examiner, was the intestines of a fish and not a piece of human flesh. The same official determined that at least one of the knives was in such bad shape, bent and rusty in places, that he did not think it was "capable of cutting very much." (The archival inventory does list an envelope with a "piece of dried leather" [kusok sukhoi kozhitsy], but the archivist refused to show it to me.) For a discussion of the knives and alleged foreskin, see RGIA, f. 1345, op. 235, d. 65, chast' 7, ll. 6048–6048ob, 6051–6052ob, 6073ob; and chast' 8, ll. 6130, 6131–6132.

Chapter 5

1. RGIA, f. 1345, op. 235, d. 65, chast' 1, ll. 418–421ob (complaint by Shmerka Berlin and Evzik Tsetlin to N. N. Khovanskii, May 25, 1826).

2. RGIA, f. 1345, op. 235, d. 65, chast' 1, ll. 418–421ob.

3. Eli Lederhendler, *The Road to Modern Jewish Politics: Political Tradition and Political Reconstruction in the Jewish Community of Tsarist Russia* (New York: Oxford University Press, 1989), 33–35.

4. On the emergence of the new Jewish networks in global perspective, see Abigail Green, "Old Networks, New Connections: The Emergence of the Jewish International," in *Religious Internationals in the Modern World: Globalization and Faith Communities since 1750*, ed. Abigail Greene and Vincent Viaene (New York: Palgrave Macmillan, 2012), 53–81. See also Green's "Intervening in the Jewish Question, 1840–1878," in *Humanitarian Intervention: A History*, ed. Brendan Simms and D. J. B. Trim (Cambridge: Cambridge University Press, 2011), 139–158; and "Nationalism and the 'Jewish International': Religious Internationalism in Europe and the Middle East c. 1840–c. 1880," *Comparative Studies in Society and History* 50, no. 2 (2008): 535–558.

5. RGIA, f. 1345, op. 235, d. 65, chast' 1, ll. 461–465 (memorandum from Strakhov to Khovanskii, June 27, 1826).

6. RGIA, f. 1345, op. 235, d. 65, chast' 1, ll. 465ob–468ob.

7. RGIA, f. 1345, op. 235, d. 65, chast' 1, ll. 636–643 (complaint by Sheftel Tsetlin and Berka Nakhimovskii, August, 27, 1826).

8. John D. Klier, *Russia Gathers Her Jews: The Origins of the "Jewish Question" in Russia, 1772–1825* (DeKalb: Northern Illinois University Press, 1986), 104. See also Marcin Wodzinski, "Blood and Hasidim: On the History of Ritual Murder Accusations in Nineteenth-Century Poland," *Polin* 22 (2010): 273–290.

9. RGIA, f. 1345, op. 235, d. 65, chast' 1, ll. 464, 466.

10. RGIA, f. 1345, op. 235, d. 65, chast' 1, ll. 767ob, 772ob, 782ob, 785ob (memorandum from Strakhov to Khovanskii, November 17, 1826).

11. RGIA, f. 1345, op. 235, d. 65, chast' 1, ll. 777–780ob.

12. RGIA, f. 1345, op. 235, d. 65, chast' 1, ll. 781–781ob.

13. RGIA, f. 1345, op. 235, d. 65, chast' 1, l. 781ob.

14. Quoted in Lederhendler, *The Road to Modern Jewish Politics*, 53.

15. On the politics of intercession, see Lederhendler, *The Road to Modern Jewish Politics*, 30–33; and Israel Bartal, *The Jews of Eastern Europe, 1772–1881*, trans. Chaya Naor (Philadelphia: University of Pennsylvania Press, 2002), 24–26.

16. On Jewish deputies, see Ol'ga Minkina, *"Syny Rakhili": Evreiskie deputaty v Rossiiskoi imperii, 1772–1825* (Moscow: Novoe literaturnoe obozrenie, 2011); Lederhendler, *The Road to Modern Jewish Politics*, 52–57; Iulii Gessen, " 'Deputaty evreiskogo naroda' pri Aleksandre I," *Evreiskaia starina*, nos. 3–4 (1909): 17–28, 196–206; and Vassili Schedrin, *Jewish Souls, Bureaucratic Minds: Jewish Bureaucracy and Policymaking in Late Imperial Russia, 1850–1917* (Detroit: Wayne State University Press, 2016), 31–36.

17. Ol'ga Minkina, "Rumors in Early 19th Century Jewish Society and Their Perception in Administrative Documents," *Pinkas: Annual of the Culture and History of East European Jewry* 1 (2006): 41–56. For a wide-ranging analysis of Jews and secrecy in early modern Europe, see Daniel Jütte, *The Age of Secrecy: Jews, Christians, and the Economy of Secrets, 1400–1800*, trans. Jeremiah Riemer (New Haven: Yale University Press, 2015).

18. Minkina, *"Syny Rakhili,"* 153–156.

19. Lederhendler, *The Road to Modern Jewish Politics*, 57.

20. On the pre–Great Reform Jewish community in St. Petersburg, see Iulii Gessen, "Sankt-Peterburg," *Evreiskaia entsiklopediia: Svod znanii o evreistve i ego kul'ture v proshlom i nastoiashchem* (St. Petersburg: "Terra," 1991), 941–942; and Minkina, *"Syny Rakhili,"* 132–141.

21. RGIA, f. 1345, op. 235, d. 65, chast' 19, ll. 8–130ob, 65–680ob, 69–690ob, 76–810ob, 109–116, 234–2370b (petitions from Hirsh Berkovich Brouda to the Senate).

22. RGIA, f. 1345, op. 235, d. 65, chast' 19, ll. 100b, 120b (petition from Brouda to the Senate)

23. D. J. B. Trim, " 'If a prince use tyrannie towards his people': Interventions in Early Modern Europe," in Simms and Trim, *Humanitarian Intervention*, 41.

24. RGIA, f. 1345, op. 235, d. 65, chast' 19, ll. 65–68ob (petition from Brouda to the Senate).

25. RGIA, f. 1345, op. 235, d. 65, chast' 19, l, iii (petition from Brouda to the Senate).

26. RGIA, f. 1345, op. 235, d. 65, chast' 19, ll. 110–110ob (petition from Brouda to the Senate).

27. RGIA, f. 1345, op. 235, d. 65, chast' 1, ll. 385–386 (complaint from the Velizh *kahal* to the police, May 12, 1826).

28. RGIA, f. 1345, op. 235, d. 65, chast' 19, l. 114 (petition from Brouda to the Senate).

29. Quoted in Trim, "'If a prince use tyrannie towards his people': Interventions in Early Modern Europe," in Simms and Trim, *Humanitarian Intervention*, 35.

30. Green, "Old Networks, New Connections: The Emergence of the Jewish International," in *Religious Internationals in the Modern World*, 53–81; and Trim, "'If a prince use tyrannie towards his people': Interventions in Early Modern Europe," in Simms and Trim, *Humanitarian Intervention*, 65. For a sweeping examination of "humanity before human rights," see Samuel Moyn, *The Last Utopia: Human Rights in History* (Cambridge, MA: Harvard University Press, 2010), 12–43.

31. Jonathan Frankel, *The Damascus Affair: "Ritual Murder," Politics, and the Jews in 1840* (Cambridge: Cambridge University Press, 1997), 9.

32. Abigail Green, *Moses Montefiore: Jewish Liberator, Imperial Hero* (Cambridge, MA: Harvard University Press, 2010), 180.

33. Quoted in Green, *Moses Montefiore*, 179, 181.

34. On the correspondence between Montefiore and Kiselev, see Iulii Gessen, "Iz sorokovykh godov: Graf P. Kiselev i Moisei Montefiore," *Perezhitoe* 4 (1913): 149–180; and Louis Loewe, ed., *Diaries of Sir Moses and Lady Montefiore*, 2 vols. (London: Jewish Historical Society of England, 1983), 2: 359–384. For a recent treatment, see Lara Lempertiene, "Sir Moses Montefiore's 1846 Visit to Vilna and Its Reflection in Local Maskilic Literature," *East European Jewish Affairs* 41, no. 3 (2011): 181–188.

35. RGIA, f. 1345, op. 235, d. 65, chast' 25, l. 37; and RGIA, f. 1345, op. 235, d. 65, chast' 2, l. 1392.

36. Simon Dubnow, *History of the Jews in Russia and Poland: From the Earliest Times until the Present Day*, 3 vols. (Philadelphia: Jewish Publication Society of America, 1916–1920), 2: 13–45.

37. Richard S. Wortman, *The Development of a Russian Legal Consciousness* (Chicago: University of Chicago Press, 1976), 237.

38. Valerie Kivelson, "Muscovite 'Citizenship': Rights without Freedom," *The Journal of Modern History* 74, no. 3 (2002): 481.

39. RGIA, f. 1345, op. 235, d. 65, chast' 2, ll. 1229–1230ob (April 27, 1827).

40. Kivelson, "Muscovite 'Citizenship'," 481.

41. For a perceptive analysis of the workings of Russian legal culture, see Valerie Kivelson, *Cartographies of Tsardom: The Land and Its Meanings in Seventeenth-Century Russia*

(Ithaca: Cornell University Press, 2006), 50–55; and Jane Burbank, "An Imperial Rights Regime: Law and Citizenship in the Russian Empire," *Kritika: Explorations in Russian and Eurasian History* 7, no. 3 (2006): 397–431. On the Chancellery for Receipt of Petitions, see Eugene M. Avrutin, *Jews and the Imperial State: Identification Politics in Tsarist Russia* (Ithaca: Cornell University Press, 2010), 16–17; and Barbara Alpern Engel, *Breaking the Ties That Bound: The Politics of Marital Strife in Late Imperial Russia* (Ithaca: Cornell University Press, 2011), 18–29.

42. RGIA, f. 1345, op. 235, d. 65, chast' 2, ll. 1235–1236.

43. RGIA, f. 1345, op. 235, d. 65, chast' 19, ll. 6–70b (communication from Khovanskii to the Senate, January 12, 1827). Khovanskii filed a similar report on September 22, 1827 (RGIA, f. 1345, op. 235, d. 65, chast' 19, ll. 233–2330b).

44. RGIA, f. 1345, op. 235, d. 65, chast' 2, ll. 1236–1239.

45. RGIA, f. 1345, op. 235, d. 65, chast' 2, l. 1240.

Chapter 6

1. RGIA, f. 1345, op. 235, d. 65, chast' 3, ll. 1644–1645, 16470b.

2. RGIA, f. 1345, op. 235, d. 65, chast' 3, ll. 1702–1703; and NIAB, op. 1297, op. 1, d. 1253, l. 14.

3. RGIA, f. 1345, op. 235, d. 65, chast' 4, ll. 2855–28550b.

4. Lyndal Roper, *Witch Craze: Terror and Fantasy in Baroque Germany* (New Haven: Yale University Press, 2004), 49–51.

5. My thinking on the power of conspiracies draws on the work of Jean Comaroff and John Comaroff, "Transparent Fictions; or, The Conspiracies of a Liberal Imagination: An Afterword," in *Transparency and Conspiracy: Ethnographies of Suspicion in the New World Order*, ed. Harry G. West and Todd Sanders (Durham, NC: Duke University Press, 2003), 290.

6. John P. LeDonne, "Russian Governors General, 1775–1825: Territorial or Functional Administration?" *Cahiers du monde russe* 42, no. 1 (2001): 8–9.

7. Nancy Shields Kollmann, *Crime and Punishment in Early Modern Russia* (Cambridge: Cambridge University Press, 2012); and LeDonne, "Russian Governors General, 1775–1825," 8–9.

8. RGIA, f. 1345, op. 235, d. 65, ll. 2142–2145 (a list of detailed questions the Senate asked the governor-general).

9. On July 5, 1827, in a communication to Governor-General Khovanskii, Strakhov explained that it was nearly impossible to come up with an exact date when the commission hoped to wrap up its work (RGIA, f. 1345, op. 235, d. 65, chast' 3, ll. 1644–1645, 16470b).

10. Iulii Gessen, *Velizhskaia drama: Iz istorii obvineniia evreev v ritual'nykh prestuple-niiakh* (St. Petersburg: Tipografiia A. G. Rozena, 1904), 64.

11. RGIA, f. 1345, op. 235, d. 65, chast' 3, ll. 2291–2306; RGIA, f. 1345, op. 235, d. 65, chast' 4, ll. 2876–2877; and RGIA, f. 1345, op. 235, d. 65, chast' 12, ll. 698–744.

12. RGIA, f. 1345, op. 235, d. 65, chast' 25, l. 212–214.
13. RGIA, f. 1345, op. 235, d. 65, chast' 25, l. 215.
14. RGIA, f. 1345, op. 235, d. 65, chast' 25, ll. 217–218.
15. RGIA, f. 1345, op. 235, d. 65, chast' 25, l. 218; and NIAB, f. 1297, op. 1, d. 3717, ll. 79–104.
16. RGIA, f. 1345, op. 235, d. 65, chast' 25, l. 219.
17. RGIA, f. 1345, op. 235, d. 65, chast' 25, ll. 220–226, 235–236.
18. RGIA, f. 1345, op. 235, d. 65, chast' 12, ll. 293–308.
19. RGIA, f. 1345, op. 235, d. 65, chast' 25, ll. 237–238.
20. RGIA, f. 1345, op. 235, d. 65, chast' 25, l. 239.
21. RGIA, f. 1345, op. 235, d. 65, chast' 25, ll. 240–241.
22. RGIA, f. 1345, op. 235, d. 65, chast' 25, ll. 242–243.
23. RGIA, f. 1345, op. 235, d. 65, chast' 15, ll. 3420b–410.
24. RGIA, f. 1345, op. 235, d. 65, chast' 25, ll. 247–249.
25. RGIA, f. 1345, op. 235, d. 65, chast' 25, ll. 251–252.
26. RGIA, f. 1345, op. 235, d. 65, chast' 25, ll. 253–257.
27. RGIA, f. 1345, op. 235, d. 65, chast' 25, ll. 258–260.
28. RGIA, f. 1345, op. 235, d. 65, chast' 14, ll. 231–2650b.
29. RGIA, f. 1345, op. 235, d. 65, chast' 25, ll. 264–265.
30. RGIA, f. 1345, op. 235, d. 65, chast' 25, l. 266.
31. RGIA, f. 1345, op. 235, d. 65, chast' 25, ll. 269–270.
32. RGIA, f. 1345, op. 235, d. 65, chast' 25, l. 272.
33. RGIA, f. 1345, op. 235, d. 65, chast' 25, ll. 280–281.
34. On the symbolic role of the host, see Miri Rubin, *Gentile Tales: The Narrative Assault on Late Medieval Jews* (Philadelphia: University of Pennsylvania Press, 1999), 194.
35. Michael Ostling, "Imagined Crimes, Real Victims: Hermeneutical Witches and Jews in Early Modern Poland," in *Ritual Murder in Russia, Eastern Europe, and Beyond: New Histories of an Old Accusation*, ed. Eugene M. Avrutin, Jonathan Dekel-Chen, and Robert Weinberg (Bloomington: Indiana University Press, 2017), 18–38. For the broader context, see Luise White, *Speaking with Vampires: Rumor and History in Colonial Africa* (Berkeley: University of California Press, 2000), 23, 30.
36. R. Po-chia Hsia, *The Myth of Ritual Murder: Jews and Magic in Reformation Germany* (New Haven: Yale University Press, 1988), 12; and David Biale, *Blood and Belief: The Circulation of a Symbol Between Jews and Christians* (Berkeley: University of California Press, 2007), 112–113.
37. RGIA, f. 1345, op. 235, d. 65, chast' 25, ll. 281–285.
38. RGIA, f. 1345, op. 235, d. 65, chast' 25, ll. 286–289, 295.
39. RGIA, f. 1345, op. 235, d. 65, chast' 25, ll. 289, 293.
40. RGIA, f. 1345, op. 235, d. 65, chast' 16, ll. 229–254; and RGIA, f. 1345, op. 235, d. 65, chast' 17, ll. 353–414.

41. This paragraph draws on Magda Teter's excellent analysis of theft and defilement of sacred property in early modern Poland. See *Sinners on Trial: Jews and Sacrilege after the Reformation* (Cambridge, MA: Harvard University Press, 2011), 40–62.

42. RGIA, f. 1345, op. 235, d. 65, chast' 25, ll. 299–304.

43. RGIA, f. 1345, op. 235, d. 65, chast' 25, l. 300.

44. RGIA, f. 1345, op. 235, d. 65, chast' 25, ll. 303–304.

45. RGIA, f. 1345, op. 235, d. 65, chast' 25, ll. 309–311.

46. RGIA, f. 1345, op. 235, d. 65, chast' 25, ll. 312–313.

47. RGIA, f. 1345, op. 235, d. 65, chast' 25, ll. 316–317, 321, 327.

48. Gessen, *Velizhskaia drama,* 97–98. The Tel'shi case eventually reached the Senate and was officially resolved in 1838 in Jews' favor. See Darius Staliunas, *Enemies for a Day: Antisemitism and Anti-Jewish Violence in Lithuania under the Tsars* (Budapest: Central European University Press, 2015), 28–32.

49. See, for example, the collection of essays edited by West and Sanders, *Transparency and Conspiracy.*

50. Thomas Robisheaux, *The Last Witch of Langenburg: Murder in a German Village* (New York: W. W. Norton & Company, 2009), 156–159.

51. Brian P. Levack, *The Witch-Hunt in Early Modern Europe,* 2nd ed. (London: Longman, 1995), 21–22.

52. Paul Boyer and Stephen Nissenbaum, *Salem Possessed: The Social Origins of Witchcraft* (Cambridge: Harvard University Press, 1974), 52, 146–147, 188.

Chapter 7

1. Edward Peters, *Torture,* expanded edition (Philadelphia: University of Pennsylvania Press, 1999), 68.

2. Timothy Brook, Jérôme Bourgon, and Gregory Blue, *Death by a Thousand Cuts* (Cambridge, MA: Harvard University Press, 2008), 9, 46–48.

3. Valerie Kivelson, *Desperate Magic: The Moral Economy of Witchcraft in Seventeenth-Century Russia* (Ithaca: Cornell University Press, 2013), 206–208.

4. Nancy Shields Kollmann, *Crime and Punishment in Early Modern Russia* (Cambridge: Cambridge University Press, 2012), 134–135.

5. Kollmann, *Crime and Punishment in Early Modern Russia,* 258–279, 421–423. See also Jonathan W. Daly, "Criminal Punishment and Europeanization in Late Imperial Russia," *Jahrbücher für Geschichte Osteuropas* 47, no. 3 (2000): 341–362; and Abby M. Schrader, "Containing the Spectacle of Punishment: The Russian Autocracy and the Abolition of the Knout, 1817–1845," *Slavic Review* 56, no. 4 (1997): 613–644.

6. Quoted in Peters, *Torture,* 96.

7. John P. LeDonne, "Criminal Investigations before the Great Reforms." *Russian History* 1, no. 2 (1974): 111.

8. On sadism and demonstration of power in the interrogation chamber, see Kivelson, *Desperate Magic,* 204–205; William Schulz, ed., *The Phenomenon of Torture: Readings*

and Commentary (Philadelphia: University of Pennsylvania Press, 2007), 155–191; and Richard A. Leo, *Police Interrogation and American Justice* (Cambridge, MA: Harvard University Press, 2008).

9. For a description of contemporary psychological torture practices, which are eerily similar to those conducted in the eighteenth and nineteenth centuries, see Almerindo E. Ojeda, ed., *The Trauma of Psychological Torture* (Westport, CT: Praeger, 2008); and William Schulz, ed., *The Phenomenon of Torture.*

10. RGIA, f. 1345, op. 235, d. 65, chast' 1, l. 7810b.

11. On prison writings, see Elizabeth Foyster, "Prisoners Writing Home: The Functions of Their Letters c. 1680–1800," *Journal of Social History* 47, no. 4 (2014): 943–967; and Philip Priestley, *Victorian Prison Lives: English Prison Biography, 1830–1914* (London: Methuen, 1985).

12. On Maria Kovaleva's suicide, see NIAB, f. 1297, op. 1, d. 3717, ll. 79–104 (November 20, 1829).

13. On Ivan Cherniavskii's suicide, see RGIA, f. 1345, op. 235, d. 65, chast' 6, ll. 4563–4572; and GARF, f. 109, 4 ekspeditsiia, op. 221, d. 11, kn. 6, ll. 16–18 (accessed at CAHJP).

14. Brian P. Levack, "The Decline and End of Witchcraft Prosecutions," in *Witchcraft and Magic in Europe: The Eighteenth and Nineteenth Centuries,* ed. Bengt Ankarloo and Stuart Clark (Philadelphia: University of Pennsylvania Press, 1999), 7.

15. RGIA, f. 1345, op. 235, d. 65, chast' 1, l. 615.

16. Pawel Maciejko, *The Mixed Multitude: Jacob Frank and the Frankist Movement, 1755–1816* (Philadelphia: University of Pennsylvania Press, 2011), 94, 96.

17. The inquisitorial commission commissioned translations of passages from select books and pamphlets (RGIA, op. 235, d. 65, chast' 20, ll. 278–288, 317–318; and chast' 21, ll. 403, 405–411, 414–415, 494–495). Some of these texts were published by the Senate and are currently preserved at the Russian National Library, St. Petersburg. See "Zakliuchenie po proizvodstvu v Velizhe sledstviiu deistvitel'no li soldatskii syn Emel'ianov umershchvlen Evreiami," parts B–E (n.d., n.p.).

18. This paragraph draws on Maciejko, *The Mixed Multitude,* 103–126. On Bishop Kajetan Sołtyk, see Richard Butterwick, *The Polish Revolution and the Catholic Church, 1788–1792* (New York: Oxford University Press, 2012), 28–30.

19. Maciejko, *The Mixed Multitude,* 103–126.

20. RGIA, f. 1345, op. 235, d. 65, chast' 1, ll. 7830b–7840b (memorandum, Strakhov to Khovanskii, November 17, 1826).

21. Robert Walsh, *Narrative of a Journey from Constantinople to England* (London: Frederick Westley and A. H. Davis, 1828), 12–13. For the Russian translation, see RGIA, op. 235, d. 65, chast' 20, ll. 317–318; and "Zakliuchenie po proizvodstvu v Velizhe sledstviiu," part G.

22. On the publication history of Neophytos's pamphlet, see Jonathan Frankel, *The Damascus Affair: "Ritual Murder," Politics, and the Jews in 1840* (Cambridge: Cambridge University Press, 1997), 264.

23. John D. Klier, "The Origins of the 'Blood Libel' in Russia," *Newsletter of the Study Group on Eighteenth-Century Russia: Newsletter* 14 (1986): 17–19.

24. On demonologies, see the classic work by Stuart Clark, *Thinking with Demons: The Idea of Witchcraft in Early Modern Europe* (Oxford: Oxford University Press, 1997). A useful summary is provided by Gerhild Scholz Williams, "Demonologies," in *The Oxford Handbook of Witchcraft in Early Modern Europe and Colonial America*, ed. Brian P. Levack (Oxford: Oxford University Press, 2013), 69–83.

25. Daniil A. Khvol'son, a convert to Russian Orthodoxy and a leading authority on the Jewish question, went to great lengths to document the baptized Jews who stood in defense of blood libel accusations. See Khvol'son's *O nekotorykh sredneve-kovykh obvineniiakh protiv evreev: Istoricheskoe izsledovanie po istochnikam* (St. Petersburg: Tipografiia Tsederbauma i Goldenbliuma, 1880), 300–322.

26. Maciejko, *The Mixed Multitude*, 99–102; and R. Po-Chia Hsia, *Trent 1475: Stories of a Ritual Murder Trial* (New Haven: Yale University Press, 1992), 95–104. In his influential work on the Jewish uses of Christian blood, which was first published in 1876, the defrocked Catholic priest, Ippolit Liutostanskii, attempted to bolster his claim with fraudulent citations from Maimonides as well. See John D. Klier, *Imperial Russia's Jewish Question* (Cambridge: Cambridge University Press, 1995), 425.

27. Moshe Halbertal, *Maimonides: Life and Thought*, trans. Joel Linsider (Princeton: Princeton University Press, 2014), 11. See also Joel L. Kraemer, *Maimonides: The Life and World of One of Civilization's Greatest Minds* (New York: Doubleday, 2008).

28. David Biale, *Blood and Belief: The Circulation of a Symbol between Jews and Christians* (Berkeley: University of California Press, 2007), 21.

29. Biale, *Blood and Belief*, 42.

30. RGIA, f. 1345, op. 235, d. 65, chast' 25, ll. 373–381.

31. Grudinskii's fantasies anticipated the conspiratorial theories of Iakov Brafman, author of the notorious *Book of the Kahal*, and various other publicists, journalists, and writers writing on the topic in the second half of the nineteenth century. For a balanced reading of Brafman, see Klier, *Imperial Russia's Jewish Question, 1855–1881*, 262–283.

32. Marcin Wodzinski, "Blood and the Hasidim: On the History of Ritual Murder Accusations in Nineteenth-Century Poland," *Polin* 22 (2009): 281; and Victoria Khiterer, "The Social and Economic History of Jews in Kiev before 1917" (PhD diss., Brandeis University, 2008), 84–85.

33. RGIA, f. 1345, op. 235, d. 65, chast' 8, ll. 6074–6077; and RGIA, f. 1345, op. 235, d. 65, chast' 21, ll. 405–411.

34. RGIA, f. 1345, op. 235, d. 65, chast' 20, l. 2810b.

35. RGIA, f. 1345, op. 235, d. 65, chast' 20, ll. 282–2840b, 3040b; "Gavriil," in *Pravoslavnaia entsiklopediia*, vol. 10 (Moscow: Tserkovno-nauchnyi tsentr, 2005), 200–201; and *Sviatoi muchenik Gavriil Belostokskii: Nebesnyi pokrovitel' detei i*

podrostkov (Minsk: Belorusskaia Pravoslavnaia Tserkov', 2009). On the genealogy of ritual murder, see Hsia, *Trent 1475*, 92–94.

36. Kollman, *Crime and Punishment in Early Modern Russia*, 54–58, 186–187. For a thoughtful study of paperwork, see Ben Kafka, *The Demon of Writing: Powers and Failures of Paperwork* (New York: Zone Books, 2012).

37. Kollmann, *Crime and Punishment in Early Modern Russia*, 183–191; and W. Bruce Lincoln, *In the Vanguard of Reform: Russia's Enlightened Bureaucrats 1825–1861* (DeKalb: Northern Illinois University Press, 1982), 1–40.

38. RGIA, f. 1345, op. 235, d. 65, chast' 20, l. 2800b.

39. RGIA, f. 1345, op. 235, d. 65, chast' 8, ll. 6515–65150b, 6533, 6978, 7034, 7039–7040.

40. RGIA, f. 1345, op. 235, d. 65, chast' 8, ll. 6988–69890b, 7042–70450b.

41. RGIA, f. 1345, op. 235, d. 65, chast' 8, ll. 7086–7088.

42. Eugene M. Avrutin, "Returning to Judaism after the 1905 Law on Religious Freedom," *Slavic Review* 65, no. 1 (2006): 93–95. For a comparative perspective, see Paul W. Werth, *The Tsar's Foreign Faiths: Toleration and the Fate of Religious Freedom in Imperial Russia* (New York: Oxford University Press, 2014), 83–85.

43. John P. LeDonne, *Absolutism and Ruling Class: The Formation of the Russian Political Order, 1700–1825* (Oxford: Oxford University Press, 1991), 88–89, 109–112; and Richard S. Wortman, *The Development of a Russian Legal Consciousness* (Chicago: University of Chicago Press, 1976), 54–69.

44. RGIA, f. 1345, op. 235, d. 65, chast' 25, ll. 386–387.

45. RGIA, f. 1345, op. 235, d. 65, chast' 25, ll. 390–391.

46. This paragraph draws on Abby M. Schrader's "Containing the Spectacle of Punishment: The Russian Autocracy and the Abolition of the Knout, 1817–1845," *Slavic Review* 56, no. 4 (1997): 613–614.

47. Kollmann, *Crime and Punishment in Early Modern Russia*, 248; and Andrew A. Gentes, *Exile to Siberia, 1590–1822* (New York: Palgrave Macmillan, 2008), 150.

48. RGIA, f. 1345, op. 235, d. 65, chast' 25, ll. 391–392.

49. RGIA, f. 1345, op. 235, d. 65, chast' 25, ll. 393–394.

50. Established on January 1, 1810, the State Council presided over the government as a legislative body and, on occasion, as with the Velizh case, Supreme Court. See George L. Yaney, *The Systematization of Russian Government: Social Evolution in the Domestic Administration of Imperial Russia, 1711–1905* (Urbana: University of Illinois Press, 1973), 194–195.

51. Helma Repczuk, "Nicholas Mordvinov (1754–1845): Russia's Would-Be Reformer," (PhD diss., Columbia University, 1962), 4.

52. On Mordvinov and the debates over property, see Ekaterina Pravilova, *A Public Empire: Property and the Quest for the Common Good in Imperial Russia* (Princeton: Princeton University Press, 2014), 21–22, 39–40.

53. On the importance of Beccaria and other classical reformers of Russian judicial thought, see, for example, T. Cizova, "Beccaria in Russia," *Slavonic and East European Review* 40, no. 95 (1962): 384–408; and Sergii Zarudnii, *Bekkariia o*

prestupleniiakh i nakazaniiakh i russkoe zakonodatel'stvo (St. Petersburg: Tipografiia
E. I. V. Kantseliariia, 1879).

54. Repczuk, "Nicholas Mordvinov," 32.

55. Schrader, "Containing the Spectacle of Punishment," 631–632.

56. Nikolai S. Mordvinov, "Delo o velizhskikh evreev," *Arkhiv grafov Mordvinovykh*, ed.
V. A. Bil'basova, vol. 8 (St. Petersburg: Tipografiia Skorohodovykh, 1903), 120–122.

57. Wortman, *The Development of a Russian Legal Consciousness*, 60; and Lincoln, *In
the Vanguard of Reform*, 12.

58. Repczuk, "Nicholas Mordvinov," 21; and Lincoln, *In the Vanguard of Reform*, 1–40.

59. Mordvinov, "Delo o velizhskikh evreev," 125.

60. Elisa M. Becker, *Medicine, Law, and the State in Imperial Russia* (Budapest: Central
European University Press, 2011), 31–33.

61. Mordvinov, "Delo o velizhskikh evreev," 131.

62. Quoted in Becker, *Medicine, Law, and the State in Imperial Russia*, 33.

63. Mordvinov, "Delo o velizhskikh evreev," 133–134.

64. Mordvinov, "Delo o velizhskikh evreev," 134–136.

65. "Mnenie Gosudarstvennago Soveta," in *Velizhskoe delo: Dokumenty* (Orange,
CT: Antiquary, 1988), 113.

Epilogue

1. *Spravka k dokladu po evreiskomu* voprosu, part 5 (St. Petersburg: Kantseliariia
Soveta ob"edinennykh dvorianskikh obshchestv, 1912), 173–174; *Velizhskoe delo:
Dokumenty* (Orange, CT: Antiquary, 1988), 113; and Simon Dubnow, *History of
the Jews in Russia and Poland: From the Earliest Times until the Present Day*, 3
vols., trans. I. Friedlander (Philadelphia: Jewish Publication Society of America,
1916–1920), 2: 83.

2. On the Borisovo case, see *Spravka k dokladu po evreiskomu voprosu*, 5: 176–207,
quote on pp. 201, 205, 206; and GARF, f. 109, 4 ekspeditsiia, d. 68, ll. 100–103ob
(accessed at CAHJP).

3. Darius Staliunas, *Enemies for a Day: Antisemitism and Anti-Jewish Violence in
Lithuania under the Tsars* (Budapest: Central European University Press, 2015),
28–32. See also GARF, f. 109, 4 ekspeditsiia, d. 164, ll. 150–151ob, 164–167
(accessed at CAHJP).

4. V. I. Dal', *Zapiska o ritual'nykh ubiistvakh* (Moscow: "Vitiaz'," 1995), 57–60,
quote on p. 57 (first published in 1844 as *Rozyskanie o ubienii evreiami khristianskikh mladentsev i upotreblenii krovi ikh*); and "Delo o trekh evreiakh, obviniae-
mykh v urezanii u krest'ianina iazyka," RGIA, f. 1151, op. 2–1837, d. 81, ll. 2–18.
See also M. D. Ryvkin, *Iz istorii ritual'nykh del* (Smolensk: Tipografiia gazeta
Smolenskii vestnik, 1914), 2–3.

5. Andrew A. Gentes, *Exile, Murder and Madness in Siberia, 1823–1861* (New York:
Palgrave Macmillan, 2010), 21–49; and Daniel Beer, "Decembrists, Rebels, and

Martyrs in Siberian Exile: The 'Zerentui Conspiracy' of 1828 and the Fashioning of a Revolutionary Genealogy," *Slavic Review* 72, no. 3 (2013): 528–551. On military-judicial procedure, see John P. LeDonne, "The Administration of Military Justice under Nicholas I," *Cahiers du monde russe et soviétique* 13, no. 2 (1972): 180–191.

6. See, for example, Nikolai Vorodinov, ed., *Istoriia Ministerstva vnutrennikh del*, part 8 (St. Petersburg: Tipografiia vtorago otdeleniia sobstvennoi E. I. V. kantseliarii, 1861); Gentes, *Exile, Murder, and Madness in Siberia*, 38–46; and Nancy Shields Kollmann, *Crime and Punishment in Early Modern Russia* (Cambridge: Cambridge University Press, 2012), 332–355.

7. Christine D. Worobec, "Decriminalizing Witchcraft in Pre-Emancipation Russia," in *Späte Hexenprozesse: Der Umgang der Aufklärung mit dem Irrationalen*, ed. Wolfgang Behringer, Sönke Lorenz, and Dieter R. Bauer (Gütersloh: Verlag für Regionalgeschichte, 2016), 281–307. See also Worobec's *Possessed: Women, Witches, and Demons in Imperial Russia* (DeKalb: Northern Illinois University Press, 2003), 40. On medical observation, see Laura Engelstein, *Castration and the Heavenly Kingdom: A Russian Folktale* (Ithaca: Cornell University Press, 1999), 61.

8. Statisticians were called on to categorize the population by estate, occupation, religion, and nationality. Geographers and ethnographers assembled information about diverse cultures, customs, and resources, while forensic-medical experts assessed human bodies. On the rise of the discipline of statistics, see Peter Holquist, "To Count, to Extract, to Exterminate: Population Statistics and Population Politics in Late Imperial and Soviet Russia," in *A State of Nations: Empire and Nation-Making in the Age of Lenin and Stalin*, ed. Ronald Grigor Suny and Terry Martin (New York: Oxford University Press, 2001), 111–144. On ethnography, see Nathaniel Knight, "Science, Empire, and Nationality: Ethnography in the Russian Geographical Society, 1845–1855," in *Imperial Russia: New Histories for the Empire*, ed. Jane Burbank and David L. Ransel (Bloomington: Indiana University Press, 1998), 108–141. For a broader perspective on accusations of ritual murder and other forms of criminality, see Hillel Kieval, "The Rules of the Game: Forensic Medicine and the Language of Science in the Structuring of Modern Ritual Murder Trials," *Jewish History* 26, no. 3–4 (2012): 287–307; and Scott Spector, *Violent Sensations: Sex, Crime, and Utopia in Vienna and Berlin, 1860–1914* (Chicago: University of Chicago Press, 2016).

9. W. Bruce Lincoln, *In the Vanguard of Reform: Russia's Enlightened Bureaucrats, 1825–1861* (DeKalb: Northern Illinois University Press, 1982), 36, 69; and Alexander Etkind, "Whirling with the Other: Russian Populism and Religious Sects," *Russian Review* 62, no. 4 (2003): 570–571. See also Anne J. Frederickson, "The Dual Faces of Modernity: The Russian Intelligentsia's Pursuit of Knowledge and the Publication History of 'Note on Ritual Murder,'" MA thesis, Arizona State University, 2004. For an example of an ethnography devoted to Jewish

"sectarian" communities, see Vasilii Vasil'evich Grigor'ev, *Evreiskie religioznye sekty v Rossii* (St. Petersburg: Tipografiia Ministerstva vnutrennikh del, 1847).

10. V. I. Dal', "Issledovanie o skopcheskoi eresi," in *Neizvestnyi Vladimir Dal'* (Noginsk: Rossiiskii Osteon-fond, 2006), 13–104. For a perceptive analysis of the report, see Engelstein, *Castration and the Heavenly Kingdom*, 58–60.

11. Dal', *Zapiska o ritual'nykh ubiistvakh*, 105.

12. Dal's work went through numerous editions and enjoyed a long afterlife. The most exhaustive discussion can be found in Frederickson, "The Dual Faces of Modernity."

13. Ippolit Liutostanskii, *Vopros ob upotreblenii evreiami-sektatorami khristianskoi krovi dlia religioznykh tselei, v sviazi s voprosami ob otnosheniiakh evreistva k khristianstvu voobshche* (Moscow, 1876), quoted in John D. Klier, *Imperial Russia's Jewish Question, 1855–1881* (Cambridge: Cambridge University Press, 1995), 426.

14. Quoted in Marcin Wodzinski, "Blood and Hasidim: On the History of Ritual Murder Accusations in Nineteenth-Century Poland," *Polin* 22 (2009): 285.

15. Richard S. Wortman, *The Development of a Russian Legal Consciousness* (Chicago: University of Chicago Press, 1976), 238.

16. On the internationalization of the Damascus case, see Jonathan Frankel, *The Damascus Affair: "Ritual Murder," Politics, and the Jews in 1840* (Cambridge: Cambridge University Press, 1997).

17. On the Kutaisi case, see Klier, *Imperial Russia's Jewish Question*, 427–430. On sensational crime in the Russian imperial context, see Louise McReynolds, *Murder Most Russian: True Crime and Punishment in Late Imperial Russia* (Ithaca: Cornell University Press, 2013).

18. Kieval, "The Rules of the Game," 306. See also Spector, *Violent Sensations*, 202–243; and Marina Mogilner, "Human Sacrifice in the Name of a Nation: The Religion of Common Blood," *Ritual Murder in Russia, Eastern Europe, and Beyond: New Histories of an Old Accusation*, ed. Eugene M. Avrutin, Jonathan Dekel-Chen, and Robert Weinberg (Bloomington: Indiana University Press, 2017), 130–150.

SELECTED BIBLIOGRAPHY

Archival Collections

Central Archives for the History of the Jewish People (CAHJP), Jerusalem, Israel

Gosudarstvennyi arkhiv rossiiskoi federatsii (GARF), Moscow, Russia
- Fond 109, Tret'e otdelenie

Institute for Jewish Research Archives (YIVO), New York
- RG 80, Mizrakh Yidisher Historisher Arkhiv

Kauno Apskrities Archyve (KAA), Kovno, Lithuania
- Fond 76, Kovenskaia palata ugolovnovo suda, 1840–1872

Natsional'nyi istoricheskii arkhiv Belarusi (NIAB), Minsk, Belarus
- Fond 1297, Kantseliariia general-gubernatora vitebskogo, mogilevskogo i smolenskogo
- Fond 1430, Kantseliariia vitebskogo grazhdanskogo gubernatora
- Fond 3309, Vitebskii povetovyi sud

Rossiiskaia natsional'naia biblioteka (RNB), St. Petersburg, Russia
- Fond 731, Mikhail Speranskii

Rossiiskii gosudarstvennyi istoricheskii arkhiv (RGIA), St. Petersburg, Russia
- Fond 560, Obshchaia kantseliariia ministerstva Finansov
- Fond 821, Departament dukhovnykh del inostrannykh ispovedanii

- Fond 1151, Departament grazhdanskikh i dukhovnykh del Gosudarstvennogo soveta
- Fond 1263, Komitet ministrov
- Fond 1281, Sovet ministra vnutrennikh del
- Fond 1287, Khoziaistvennyi departament MVD
- Fond 1290, Tsentral'nyi statisticheskii komitet MVD
- Fond 1293, Tekhniko-stroitel'nyi komitet MVD
- Fond 1345, Piatyi (ugolovnyi) departament Senata

Periodicals

Evreiskaia starina
Perezhitoe
Vitebskie gubernskie vedomosti
Zhurnal ministerstva vnutrennikh del

Books and Articles

Adams, Bruce F. *The Politics of Punishment: Prison Reform in Russia, 1863–1917.* DeKalb: Northern Illinois University Press, 1996.

Anisimov, Evgenii. *Dyba i knut: Politicheskii sysk i russkoe obshchestvo v XVIII veke.* Moscow: Novoe literaturnoe obozrenie, 1999.

Ankarloo, Bengt, and Stuart Clark, eds. *Witchcraft and Magic in Europe: The Eighteenth and Nineteenth Centuries.* Philadelphia: University of Pennsylvania Press, 1999.

Assaf, David, and Gadi Sagiv. "Hasidism in Tsarist Russia: Historical and Social Aspects." *Jewish History* 27, no. 2 (2013): 241–269.

Avrutin, Eugene M. "Jewish Neighborly Relations and Imperial Russian Legal Culture." *Journal of Modern Jewish Studies* 9, no. 1 (2010): 1–16.

———. *Jews and the Imperial State: Identification Politics in Tsarist Russia.* Ithaca: Cornell University Press, 2010.

———. "Returning to Judaism after the 1905 Law on Religious Freedom in Tsarist Russia." *Slavic Review* 65, no. 1 (2006): 90–110.

Avrutin, Eugene M., Jonathan Dekel-Chen, and Robert Weinberg, eds. *Ritual Murder in Russia, Eastern Europe, and Beyond: New Histories of an Old Accusation.* Bloomington: Indiana University Press, 2017.

Bartal, Israel. *The Jews of Eastern Europe, 1772–1881.* Translated by Chaya Naor. Philadelphia: University of Pennsylvania Press, 2002.

Bartov, Omer, and Eric D. Weitz, eds. *Shatterzone of Empires: Coexistence and Violence in the German, Habsburg, Russian, and Ottoman Borderlands.* Bloomington: Indiana University Press, 2013.

Becker, Elisa M. *Medicine, Law, and the State in Imperial Russia.* Budapest: Central European Press, 2011.

Beer, Daniel. "Decembrists, Rebels, and Martyrs in Siberian Exile: The 'Zerentui Conspiracy' of 1828 and the Fashioning of a Revolutionary Genealogy." *Slavic Review* 72, no. 3 (2013): 528–551.

———. *The House of the Dead: Siberian Exile under the Tsars*. New York: Knopf, 2017.

Bell, Dean Phillip. "Jews, Magic, and Community in Seventeenth-Century Worms." In *Werewolves, Witches, and Wandering Spirits: Traditional Belief and Folklore in Early Modern Europe*. Edited by Kathryn A. Edwards, 93–118. Kirksville, MO: Truman State University, 2002.

Berlin, Moisei. *Ocherk etnografii evreiskago narodonaseleniia v Rossii*. St. Petersburg: Tipografiia V. Bezobrazova, 1861.

Biale, David. *Blood and Belief: The Circulation of a Symbol between Jews and Christians*. Berkeley: University of California Press, 2007.

Birnbaum, Pierre. *A Tale of Ritual Murder in the Age of Louis XIV: The Trial of Raphael Levy, 1669*. Translated by Arthur Goldhammer. Stanford: Stanford University Press, 2012.

Bolbas, M. F. *Razvitie promyshlennosti v Belorussii (1795–1861 gg.)*. Minsk: Akedemiia nauk BSSR, 1966.

Boyer, Paul, and Stephen Nissenbaum. *Salem Possessed: The Social Origins of Witchcraft*. Cambridge: Harvard University Press, 1974.

Bremmer, Jan N., ed. *The Strange World of Human Sacrifice*. Leuven: Peeters Publishers, 2007.

Breyfogle, Nicholas. *Heretics and Colonizers: Forging Russia's Empire in the South Caucasus*. Ithaca: Cornell University Press, 2005.

———. "The Religious World of Russian Sabbatarians (Subbotniks)." In *Holy Dissent: Jewish and Christian Mystics in Eastern Europe*. Edited by Glenn Dynner, 359–392. Detroit: Wayne State University Press, 2011.

Briggs, Robin. *Witches and Neighbors: The Social and Cultural Context of European Witchcraft*. London: Penguin, 1996.

Brook, Timothy, Jérôme Bourgon, and Gregory Blue. *Death by a Thousand Cuts*. Cambridge, MA: Harvard University Press, 2008.

Brooks, Peter. *Troubling Confessions: Speaking Guilt in Law and Literature*. Chicago: University of Chicago Press, 2000.

Brown, Kate. *A Biography of No Place: From Ethnic Borderland to Soviet Heartland*. Cambridge, MA: Harvard University Press, 2004.

Burbank, Jane. "An Imperial Rights Regime: Law and Citizenship in the Russian Empire." *Kritika: Explorations in Russian and Eurasian History* 7, no. 3 (2006): 397–431.

———. *Russian Peasants Go to Court: Legal Culture in the Countryside, 1905–1917*. Bloomington: Indiana University Press, 2004.

Buttaroni, Susanna, and Stanislaw Musial, eds. *Ritual Murder: Legend in European History*. Krakow: Association for Cultural Initiatives, 2003.

Butterwick, Richard. *The Polish Revolution and the Catholic Church, 1788–1792*. New York: Oxford University Press, 2012.

Bynum, Caroline Walker. *Wonderful Blood: Theology and Practice in Late Medieval Northern Europe and Beyond*. Philadelphia: University of Pennsylvania Press, 2007.

Cahan, Abraham. *Bleter fun mein leben*. Volume 1. New York: Forverts Asosieyshon, 1926.

Carlebach, Elisheva. *Palaces of Time: Jewish Calendar and Culture in Early Modern Europe*. Cambridge, MA: Harvard University Press, 2011.

Cizova, T. "Beccaria in Russia." *Slavonic and East European Review* 40, no. 95 (1962): 384–408.

Clark, Stuart. *Thinking with Demons: The Idea of Witchcraft in Early Modern Europe*. Oxford: Oxford University Press, 1997.

Clay, J. Eugene. "Orthodox Missionaries and 'Orthodox Heretics' in Russia, 1886–1917." In *Of Religion and Empire: Missions, Conversion, and Tolerance in Tsarist Russia*. Edited by Robert Geraci and Michael Khodarkovsky, 38–69. Ithaca: Cornell University Press, 2001.

Cohn, Norman. *Europe's Inner Demons: The Demonization of Christians in Medieval Christendom*. Revised edition. London: Pimlico, 1993.

Comaroff, Jean, and John Comaroff. "Transparent Fictions; or, The Conspiracies of a Liberal Imagination: An Afterword." In *Transparency and Conspiracy: Ethnographies of Suspicion in the New World Order*. Edited by Harry G. West and Todd Sanders, 287–300. Durham: Duke University Press, 2003.

Cryer, Frederick H., and Marie-Louise Thomsen, eds. *Witchcraft and Magic in Europe: Biblical and Pagan Societies*. Philadelphia: University of Pennsylvania Press, 2001.

Dal', V. I. *Neizvestnyi Vladimir Dal'*. Noginsk: Rossiiskii Osteon-fond, 2006.

———. *Rozyskanie o ubienii evreiami khristianskikh mladentsev i upotreblenii krovi ikh. Napechatano po prikazaniiu g. ministra vnutrennikh del, L. A. Perovskii*. St. Petersburg: [n. p.], 1844.

Daly, Jonathan W. "Criminal Punishment and Europeanization in Late Imperial Russia." *Jahrbücher für Geschichte Osteuropas* 47, no. 3 (2000): 341–362.

Darnton, Robert. *The Great Cat Massacre and Other Episodes in French Cultural History*. New York: Penguin, 1984.

Demos, John Putnam. *Entertaining Satan: Witchcraft and the Culture of Early New England*. Updated edition. New York: Oxford University Press, 2004.

Derzhavin, Gavriil R. "Mnenie ob otvrashchenii v Belorussii goloda i ustroistva byta evreev." In *Sochineniia Derzhavina*. Edited by Ia. Grota, 261–331. St. Petersburg: Tipografiia Imperatorskoi akademii nauk, 1872.

DeVries, Jan. *The Economy of Europe in an Age of Crisis, 1600–1750*. Cambridge: Cambridge University Press, 1976.

Dixon, Simon. "Superstition in Imperial Russia." *Past and Present*, supplement 3 (2008): 207–228.

Dolbilov, Mikhail. *Russkii krai, chuzhaia vera: Etnokonfessional'naia politika v Litve i Belorussii pri Aleksandre II*. Moscow: Novoe literanurnoe obozrenie, 2010.

Dolbilov, Mikhail, and Alexei Miller, eds. *Zapadnye okrainy Rossiiskoi imperii*. Moscow: Novoe literaturnoe obozrenie, 2007.

Dubnov, Simon. *History of the Jews in Russia and Poland: From the Earliest Times until the Present Day*. Translated by I. Friedlander. 3 volumes. Philadelphia: Jewish Publication Society of America, 1916–1920.

———. *Kniga zhizni: Vospominaniia i razmyshleniia*. Edited by Viktor E. Kel'ner. St. Petersburg: Peterburgskoe vostokovedenie, 1998.

Dubnov, Simon, and Grigorii Ia. Krasnyi-Admoni, eds. *Materialy dlia istorii anti-evreiskikh pogromov v Rossii*. Volume 1. Petrograd: Istoriko-Etnograficheskoe obshchestvo, 1919.

Dunbabin, Jean. *Captivity and Imprisonment in Medieval Europe, 1000–1300*. New York: Palgrave Macmillan, 2002.

Dundes, Alan, ed. *The Blood Libel Legend: A Casebook in Anti-Semitic Folklore*. Madison: University of Wisconsin Press, 1991.

Duplessis, Robert S. *Transitions to Capitalism in Early Modern Europe*. Cambridge: Cambridge University Press, 1997.

Dynner, Glenn. "Jewish Quarters: The Economics of Segregation in the Kingdom of Poland." In *Purchasing Power: The Economics of Modern Jewish History*. Edited by Rebecca Kobrin and Adam Teller, 91–111. Philadelphia: University of Pennsylvania Press, 2015.

———. *Yankel's Tavern: Jews, Liquor, and Life in the Kingdom of Poland*. Oxford: Oxford University Press, 2014.

Engel, Barbara Alpern. *Breaking the Ties That Bound: The Politics of Marital Strife in Late Imperial Russia*. Ithaca: Cornell University Press, 2011.

Engelstein, Laura. *Castration and the Heavenly Kingdom: A Russian Folktale*. Ithaca: Cornell University Press, 1999.

Esmein, Adhémar. *A History of Continental Criminal Procedure: With Special Reference to France*. Translated by John Simson. Boston: Little, Brown, 1913.

Etkes, Immanuel. *Rabbi Shneur Zalman of Liady: The Origins of Chabad Hasidism*. Translated by Jeffrey M. Green. Waltham, MA: Brandeis University Press, 2015.

Etkind, Alexander. "Whirling with the Other: Russian Populism and Religious Sects." *Russian Review* 62, no. 4 (2003): 565–568.

Evreiskaia entsiklopediia: Svod znanii o evreistve i ego kul'ture v proshlom i nastoiash-chem. 16 volumes. Moscow: Terra, 1991.

Evtukhov, Catherine. *Portrait of a Russian Province: Economy, Society, and Civilization in Nineteenth-Century Nizhnii Novgorod*. Pittsburgh: University of Pittsburgh Press, 2011.

Farge, Arlette, and Jacques Revel. *The Vanishing Children of Paris: Rumor and Politics before the French Revolution*. Translated by Claudia Mieville. Cambridge, MA: Harvard University Press, 1993.

Foyster, Elizabeth. "Prisoners Writing Home: The Functions of Their Letters c. 1680–1800." *Journal of Social History* 47, no. 4 (2014): 943–967.

Fram, David. *Ideals Face Reality: Jewish Law and Life in Poland, 1550–1655*. Cincinnati: Hebrew Union College Press, 1997.

Frankel, Jonathan. *The Damascus Affair: "Ritual Murder," Politics, and the Jews in 1840*. Cambridge: Cambridge University Press, 1997.

Frederickson, Anne J. "The Dual Faces of Modernity: The Russian Intelligentsia's Pursuit of Knowledge and the Publication History of 'Note on Ritual Murder.'" MA thesis, Arizona State University, 2004.

Freeze, ChaeRan Y., and Jay M. Harris, eds. *Everyday Jewish Life in Imperial Russia: Select Documents.* Waltham, MA: Brandeis University Press, 2013.

Frevert, Ute. *Emotions in History: Lost and Found.* Budapest: Central European University Press, 2011.

Frick, David. "Jews and Others in Seventeenth-Century Wilno: Life in the Neighborhood." *Jewish Studies Quarterly* 12, no. 1 (2005): 8–42.

———. *Kith, Kin, and Neighbors: Communities and Confessions in Seventeenth-Century Wilno.* Ithaca: Cornell University Press, 2013.

Geltner, Guy. *The Medieval Prison: A Social History.* Princeton: Princeton University Press, 2008.

Gentes, Andrew A. *Exile, Murder, and Madness in Siberia, 1823–1861.* New York: Palgrave Macmillan, 2010.

———. *Exile to Siberia, 1590–1822.* New York: Palgrave Macmillan, 2008.

Gessen, Iulii. "'Deputaty evreiskogo naroda' pri Aleksandre I." *Evreiskaia starina,* nos. 3–4 (1909): 17–28, 196–206.

———. "Iz sorokovykh godov: Graf P. Kiselev i Moisei Montefiore." *Perezhitoe* 4 (1913): 149–180.

———. *Velizhskaia drama: Iz istorii obvineniia evreev v ritual'nykh prestupleniiakh.* St. Petersburg: Tipografiia A. G. Rozena, 1904.

Ginzburg, S. M. *Otechestvennaia voina 1812 goda i russkie evrei.* St. Petersburg: Razum, 1912.

Given, James B. *Inquisition and Medieval Society: Power, Discipline, and Resistance in Languedoc.* Ithaca: Cornell University Press, 1997.

Godbear, Richard. *The Devil's Dominion: Magic and Religion in Early New England.* Cambridge: Cambridge University Press, 1992.

Goldish, Matt, ed. *Spirit Possession in Judaism: Cases and Contexts from the Middle Ages to the Present.* Detroit: Wayne State University Press, 2003.

Gramsci, Antonio. *Letters from Prison: Antonio Gramsci.* Volume 1. Edited by Frank Rosengarten. Translated by Raymond Rosenthal. New York: Columbia University Press, 1994.

Green, Abigail. "Intervening in the Jewish Question, 1840–1878." In *Humanitarian Intervention: A History.* Edited by Brendan Simms and D. J. B. Trim, 139–158. Cambridge: Cambridge University Press, 2011.

———. *Moses Montefiore: Jewish Liberator, Imperial Hero.* Cambridge, MA: Harvard University Press, 2010.

———. "Nationalism and the 'Jewish International': Religious Internationalism in Europe and the Middle East c. 1840–c. 1880." *Comparative Studies in Society and History* 50, no. 2 (2008): 535–558.

———. "Old Networks, New Connections: The Emergence of the Jewish International." In *Religious Internationals in the Modern World: Globalization and Faith Communities since 1750.* Edited by Abigail Green and Vincent Viaene, 53–81. New York: Palgrave Macmillan, 2012.

Greenbaum, Alfred. *Jewish Scholarship and Scholarly Institutions in Soviet Russia, 1918–1953.* Jerusalem: Centre for Research and Documentation of East European Jewry, 1978.

Greene, Robert H. *Bodies like Bright Stars: Saints and Relics in Orthodox Russia*. DeKalb: Northern Illinois Press, 2010.

Grigor'ev, Vasilii Vasil'evich. *Evreiskie religioznye sekty v Rossii*. St. Petersburg: Tipografiia Ministerstva vnutrennikh del, 1847.

Guldon, Zenon, and Jacek Wijacka. "The Accusation of Ritual Murder in Poland, 1500–1800." *Polin* 10 (1997): 99–140.

Halbertal, Moshe. *Maimonides: Life and Thought*. Translated by Joel Linsider. Princeton: Princeton University Press, 2014.

Holquist, Peter. "To Count, to Extract, to Exterminate: Population Statistics and Population Politics in Late Imperial and Soviet Russia." In *A State of Nations: Empire and Nation-Making in the Age of Lenin and Stalin*. Edited by Ronald Grigor Suny and Terry Martin, 111–144. New York: Oxford University Press, 2001.

Horecky, Paul L. "The Slavic and East European Resources and Facilities of the Library of Congress." *Slavic Review* 23, no. 2 (1964): 309–327.

Hsia, R. Po-chia. *The Myth of Ritual Murder: Jews and Magic in Reformation Germany*. New Haven: Yale University Press, 1988.

———. *Trent 1475: Stories of a Ritual Murder Trial*. New Haven: Yale University Press, 1992.

Hughes, Langston. *The Ways of White Folks*. New York: Vintage, 1990.

Hundert, Gershon D. "The Importance of Demography and Patterns of Settlement for an Understanding of the Jewish Experience in East-Central Europe." In *The Shtetl: New Evaluations*. Edited by Steven T. Katz, 29–38. New York: New York University Press, 2007.

———. *The Jews in a Polish Private Town: The Case of Opatów in the Eighteenth Century*. Baltimore: Johns Hopkins University Press, 1992.

———. *Jews in Poland-Lithuania in the Eighteenth Century: A Genealogy of Modernity*. Berkeley: University of California Press, 2004.

Hundert, Gershon D., ed. *The YIVO Encyclopedia of Jews in Eastern Europe*. 2 volumes. New Haven: Yale University Press, 2008.

Iz istorii Velizha i raiona. Smolensk: Smolenskaia gorodskaia tipografiia, 2002.

Jackson, Mark, ed. *Infanticide: Historical Perspectives on Child Murder and Concealment, 1550–2000*. Aldershot: Ashgate, 2002.

Johnson, Hannah. *Blood Libel: The Ritual Murder Accusation at the Limit of Jewish History*. Ann Arbor: University of Michigan Press, 2012.

Johnson, Robert. *Travels through Parts of the Russian Empire and the Country of Poland, along the Southern Shores of the Baltic*. London: J. J. Stockdale, 1815.

Jütte, Daniel. *The Age of Secrecy: Jews, Christians, and the Economy of Secrets, 1400–1800*. Translated by Jeremiah Riemer. New Haven: Yale University Press, 2015.

———. "Interfaith Encounters between Jews and Christians in the Early Modern Period and Beyond: Toward a Framework." *American Historical Review* 118, no. 2 (2013): 378–400.

———. "'They Shall Not Keep Their Doors or Windows Open': Urban Space and the Dynamics of Conflict and Contact in Premodern Jewish-Christian Relations." *European History Quarterly* 46, no. 2 (2016): 209–237.

Kaganovitch, Albert. *The Long Life and Swift Death of Jewish Rechitsa: A Community in Belarus, 1625–2000*. Madison: University of Wisconsin Press, 2013.

Kahan, Arcadius. *Essays in Jewish Social and Economic History*. Edited by Roger Weiss. Chicago: University of Chicago Press, 1986.

Kalik, Judith. "Christian Servants Employed by Jews in the Polish-Lithuanian Commonwealth in the Seventeenth and Eighteenth Centuries." *Polin* 14 (2001): 259–270.

———. "Fusion versus Alienation—Erotic Attraction, Sex, and Love between Jews and Christians in the Polish-Lithuanian Commonwealth." In *Kommunikation durch symbolische Akte: Religiöse Heterogenität und politische Herrschaft in Polen-Litauen*. Edited by Yvonne Kleinmann, 157–169. Stuttgart: Steiner, 2010.

Kan, Sergei. *Lev Shternberg: Anthropologist, Russian Socialist, Jewish Activist*. Lincoln: University of Nebraska Press, 2009.

Kaplan, Benjamin J. *Divided by Faith: Religious Conflict and the Practice of Toleration in Early Modern Europe*. Cambridge, MA: Harvard University Press, 2007.

Katz, Jacob. *Exclusiveness and Tolerance: Studies in Jewish-Gentile Relations in Medieval and Modern Times*. Springfield, NJ: Behrman House, 1961.

———. *The "Shabbes" Goy: A Study in Halakhic Flexibility*. Translated by Yoel Lerner. Philadelphia: Jewish Publication Society, 1989.

Kel'ner, Viktor E. *Missioner istorii: Zhizn' i trudy Semena Markovicha Dubnova*. St. Petersburg: Mir, 2008.

Khiterer, Victoria. "The Social and Economic History of Jews in Kiev before 1917." PhD diss., Brandeis University, 2008.

Khvol'son, Daniil A. *O nekotorykh srednevekovykh obvineniiakh protiv evreev: Istoricheskoe izsledovanie po istochnikam*. St. Petersburg: Tipografiia Tsederbauma i Goldenbliuma, 1880.

Kieval, Hillel J. *Languages of Community: The Jewish Experience in the Czech Lands*. Berkeley: University of California Press, 2000.

———. "The Rules of the Game: Forensic Medicine and the Language of Science in the Structuring of Modern Ritual Murder Trials." *Jewish History* 26, no. 3–4 (2012): 287–307.

Kiselev, O. M., comp. *Velizh*. Vitebsk: Gubernskaia tipografiia, 1895.

Kivelson, Valerie. *Cartographies of Tsardom: The Land and Its Meanings in Seventeenth-Century Russia*. Ithaca: Cornell University Press, 2006.

———. *Desperate Magic: The Moral Economy of Witchcraft in Seventeenth-Century Russia*. Ithaca: Cornell University Press, 2013.

———. "Muscovite 'Citizenship': Rights without Freedom." *The Journal of Modern History* 74, no. 3 (2002): 465–489.

Klier, John D. *Imperial Russia's Jewish Question, 1855–1881*. Cambridge: Cambridge University Press, 1995.

———. "Krovavyi navet v russkoi pravoslavnyi traditsii." In *Evrei i khristiane v pravoslavnykh obshchestvakh Vostochnoi Evropy*. Edited by M. V. Dmitrieva, 181–205. Moscow: Indrik, 2011.

———. "The Origins of the 'Blood Libel' in Russia." *Newsletter of the Study Group on Eighteenth Century Russia* 14 (1986): 12–22.

————. *Rossiia sobiraet svoikh evreev: Proiskhozhdenie evreiskogo voprosa v Rossii, 1772–1825*. Expanded edition. Moscow: Mosty kul'tury, 2000.

————. *Russia Gathers Her Jews: The Origins of the "Jewish Question" in Russia, 1772–1825*. DeKalb: Northern Illinois University Press, 1986.

Knight, Nathaniel. "Science, Empire, and Nationality: Ethnography in the Russian Geographical Society, 1845–1855." In *Imperial Russia: New Histories for the Empire*. Edited by Jane Burbank and David L. Ransel, 108–141. Bloomington: Indiana University Press, 1998.

Kollmann, Nancy Shields. *Crime and Punishment in Early Modern Russia*. Cambridge: Cambridge University Press, 2012.

Kotik, Yekhezkel. *Journey to a Nineteenth-Century Shtetl: The Memoirs of Yekhezkel Kotik*. Edited by David Assaf. Detroit: Wayne State University Press, 2002.

Kraemer, Joel L. *Maimonides: The Life and World of One of Civilization's Greatest Minds*. New York: Doubleday, 2008.

Kuromiya, Hiroaki. *Conscience on Trial: The Fate of Fourteen Pacifists in Stalin's Ukraine, 1952–1953*. Toronto: University of Toronto Press, 2012.

Langbein, John H. *Torture and the Law of Proof: Europe and England in the Ancien Regime*. Chicago: University of Chicago Press, 2006.

Langmuir, Gavin I. *Toward a Definition of Antisemitism*. Berkeley: University of California Press, 1990.

Lederhendler, Eli. *The Road to Modern Jewish Politics: Political Tradition and Political Reconstruction in the Jewish Community of Tsarist Russia*. New York: Oxford University Press, 1989.

LeDonne, John P. "The Administration of Military Justice under Nicholas I." *Cahiers du monde russe et soviétique* 13, no. 2 (1972): 180–191.

————. "Administrative Regionalization in the Russian Empire, 1802–1826." *Cahiers du monde russe* 43, no. 1 (2002): 5–34.

————. "Criminal Investigations before the Great Reforms." *Russian History* 1, no. 2 (1974): 101–118.

————. "Russian Governors General, 1775–1825." *Cahiers du monde russe* 42, no. 1 (2001): 5–30.

Lempertiene, Lara. "Sir Moses Montefiore's 1846 visit to Vilna and Its Reflection in Local Maskilic Literature." *East European Jewish Affairs* 41, no. 3 (2011): 181–188.

Leo, Richard A. *Police Interrogation and American Justice*. Cambridge, MA: Harvard University Press, 2008.

Leshtinski, Yakov. "Yidn in Vitebsk un Vitebsker gubernye." In *Vitebsk amol: geshichte, zikhroynes, khurbn*. Edited by Grigori Aronson, Yakov Leshtinski, and Avraham Kihn, 57–92. New York: Waldon Press, 1956.

Levack, Brian P. "The Decline and End of Witchcraft Prosecutions." In *Witchcraft and Magic in Europe: The Eighteenth and Nineteenth Centuries*. Edited by Bengt Ankarloo and Stuart Clark, 7–93. Philadelphia: University of Pennsylvania Press, 1999.

————. "Witchcraft and the Law." In *The Oxford Handbook of Witchcraft in Early Modern Europe and Colonial America*. Edited by Brian P. Levack, 468–484. Oxford: Oxford University Press, 2013.

———. *The Witch-Hunt in Early Modern Europe*. 2nd edition. London: Longman, 1995.

Lieven, Dominic. *Russia Against Napoleon: The True Story of the Campaigns of War and Peace*. London: Penguin, 2009.

Lincoln, W. Bruce. *In the Vanguard of Reform: Russia's Enlightened Bureaucrats 1825–1861*. DeKalb: Northern Illinois University Press, 1982.

———. *Nicholas I: Emperor and Autocrat of All the Russias*. DeKalb: Northern Illinois Press, 1989.

Lindemann, Mary. *Medicine and Society in Early Modern Europe*. 2nd edition. Cambridge: Cambridge University Press, 2010.

Lindenberg, Viktor. "Materialy k voprosu detoubiistve i plodoizgnanii v Vitebskoi gubernii." Ph.D. diss., Iur'ev University, 1910.

Lindenmeyr, Adele. *Poverty Is Not a Vice: Charity, Society, and the State in Imperial Russia*. Princeton: Princeton University Press, 1996.

Lippert, Robert. *Anklagen der Juden in Russland wegen Kindermords, Gebrauchs von Christenblut und Gotteslästerung: Ein Beitrag zur Geschichte der Juden in Russland im letzten Jahrzehend und früherer Zeit*. Leipzig: W. Engelmann, 1846.

Loewe, Louis, ed. *Diaries of Sir Moses and Lady Montefiore*. 2 volumes. London: Jewish Historical Society of England, 1983.

Lowenthal, Naftali. *Communicating the Infinite: The Emergence of the Habad School*. Chicago: University of Chicago Press, 1990.

Lurie, Ilia. *The Habad Movement in Tsarist Russia, 1828–1882* [Hebrew]. Jerusalem: Magnes Press, 2006.

L'vov, Aleksandr. "Mezhetnicheskie otnoshenie ugoshchenie i 'krovavyi navet.'" In *Shtetl XXI vek: Polevye issledovaniia*. Edited by V. A. Dymshits, A. L. L'vov, and A. V. Sokolova, 65–81. St. Petersburg: Evropeiskii universitet v Sankt-Peterburge, 2008.

Maciejko, Pawel. *The Mixed Multitude: Jacob Frank and the Frankist Movement, 1755–1816*. Philadelphia: University of Pennsylvania Press, 2011.

Mann, Bruce H. *Neighbors and Strangers: Law and Community in Early Connecticut*. Chapel Hill: University of North Carolina Press, 1987.

Maza, Sarah. *Private Lives and Public Affairs: The Causes Célèbres of Prerevolutionary France*. Berkeley: University of California Press, 1993.

———. *Violette Nozière: A Story of Murder in 1930s Paris*. Berkeley: University of California Press, 2011.

McAuley, Mary. *Bread and Justice: State and Society in Petrograd, 1917–1922*. Oxford: Clarendon Press, 1991.

McGowen, Randall. "The Well-Ordered Prison: England, 1780–1865." In *The Oxford History of the Prison: The Practice of Punishment in Western Society*. Edited by Norval Morris and David J. Rothman, 71–99. New York: Oxford University Press, 1995.

McReynolds, Louise. *Murder Most Russian: True Crime and Punishment in Late Imperial Russia*. Ithaca: Cornell University Press, 2013.

Mikhailovich, Nikolai. *Imperator Aleksandr I: Opyt istoricheskago izsledovaniia*. 2nd edition. Petrograd: Ekspeditsiia zagotovleniia gosudarstvennykh bumag, 1914.

Minkina, Ol'ga. "Rumors in Early 19th Century Jewish Society and Their Perception in Administrative Documents." *Pinkas: Annual of the Culture and History of East European Jewry* 1 (2006): 41–56.

———. *"Syny Rakhili": Evreiskie deputaty v Rossiiskoi imperii, 1772–1825.* Moscow: Novoe literaturnoe obozrenie, 2011.

Min'ko, L. I. *Narodnaia meditsina Belorussii: Kratkii istoricheskii ocherk.* Minsk: Izdatel'stvo "Nauka i tekhnika," 1969.

Mironov, Boris. *A Social History of Imperial Russia, 1700–1917.* Boulder: Westview, 2000.

Mogilner, Marina. "Human Sacrifice in the Name of a Nation: The Religion of Common Blood." In *Ritual Murder in Russia, Eastern Europe, and Beyond: New Histories of an Old Accusation.* Edited by Eugene M. Avrutin, Jonathan Dekel-Chen, and Robert Weinberg, 130–150. Bloomington: Indiana University Press, 2017.

Monas, Sidney. *The Third Section: Police and Society in Russia under Nicholas I.* Cambridge, MA: Harvard University Press, 1961.

Mordvinov, Nikolai S. "Delo o velizhskikh evreev." In *Arkhiv grafov Mordvinovykh.* Volume 8. Edited by V. A. Bil'basova, 117–144. St. Petersburg: Tipografiia Skorohodovykh, 1903.

Morton, Edward. *Travels in Russia, and a Residence in St. Petersburg and Odessa in the Years 1827–1829.* London: Longman, Rees, Orme, Brown, and Green, 1830.

Moss, Kenneth B. *Jewish Renaissance in the Russian Revolution.* Cambridge, MA: Harvard University Press, 2009.

Moyn, Samuel. *The Last Utopia: Human Rights in History.* Cambridge, MA: Harvard University Press, 2010.

Muir, Edward. *Ritual in Early Modern Europe.* Second edition. Cambridge: Cambridge University Press, 2005.

Muir, Edward, and Guido Ruggiero, eds. *History from Crime.* Baltimore: Johns Hopkins University Press, 1994.

Nathans, Benjamin. *Beyond the Pale: The Jewish Encounter with Late Imperial Russia.* Berkeley: University of California Press, 2002.

Nigal, Gedalyah. *The Hasidic Tale.* Translated by Edward Levin. Oxford: Littman Library of Jewish Civilization, 2008.

O'Brien, Patricia. *The Promise of Punishment: Prisons in Nineteenth-Century France.* Princeton: Princeton University Press, 1982.

Ojeda, Almerindo E., ed. *The Trauma of Psychological Torture.* Westport, CT: Praeger, 2008.

Ostling, Michael. *Between the Devil and the Host: Imagining Witchcraft in Early Modern Poland.* Oxford: Oxford University Press, 2011.

———. "Imagined Crimes, Real Victims: Hermeneutical Witches and Jews in Early Modern Poland." In *Ritual Murder in Russia, Eastern Europe, and Beyond: New Histories of an Old Accusation.* Edited by Eugene M. Avrutin, Jonathan Dekel-Chen, and Robert Weinberg, 18–38. Bloomington: Indiana University Press, 2017.

Palmer, Alan. *Alexander I: Tsar of War and Peace.* New York: Harper & Row, 1974.

Peters, Edward. *Torture.* Expanded edition. Philadelphia: University of Pennsylvania Press, 1999.

Petrovsky-Shtern, Yohanan. *The Golden Age Shtetl: A New History of Jewish Life in East Europe.* Princeton: Princeton University Press, 2014.

———. *Jews in the Russian Army: Drafted into Modernity.* Cambridge: Cambridge University Press, 2009.

———. "'You Will Find It in the Pharmacy': Practical Kabbalah and Natural Medicine in the Polish-Lithuanian Commonwealth, 1690–1750." In *Holy Dissent: Jewish and Christian Mystics in Eastern Europe.* Edited by Glenn Dynner, 13–54. Detroit: Wayne State University Press, 2011.

Polonsky, Antony. *The Jews in Poland and Russia.* 3 volumes. Oxford: Littman Library of Jewish Civilization, 2010–12.

Porter, Roy. *The Greatest Benefit to Mankind: A Medical History of Humanity.* New York: W. W. Norton, 1997.

Pravilova, Ekaterina. *A Public Empire: Property and the Quest for the Common Good in Imperial Russia.* Princeton: Princeton University Press, 2014.

Priestley, Philip. *Victorian Prison Lives: English Prison Biography, 1830–1914.* London: Methuen, 1985.

Ransel, David L. "Mothering, Medicine, and Infant Mortality in Russia: Some Comparisons." *Occasional Paper, Kennan Institute for Advanced Russian Studies,* no. 236 (1990): 1–47.

———. *Mothers of Misery: Child Abandonment in Russia.* Princeton: Princeton University Press, 1998.

———. *Village Mothers: Three Generations of Change in Russia and Tataria.* Bloomington: Indiana University Press, 2000.

Repczuk, Helma. "Nicholas Mordvinov (1754–1845): Russia's Would-Be Reformer." PhD diss., Columbia University, 1962.

Reznik, Semen. *Zapiatnannyi Dal': Mog li sozdatel' "Tolkovogo slovaria zhivogo velikorusskogo iazyka" byt' avtorom "Zapiski o ritual'nykh ubiistvakh"?* St. Petersburg: Filologicheskii fakul'tet Sankt-Peterburgskogo gosudarstvennogo universiteta, 2010.

Robisheaux, Thomas. *The Last Witch of Langenburg: Murder in a German Village.* New York: W. W. Norton, 2009.

Rogger, Hans. *Jewish Policies and Right-Wing Politics in Imperial Russia.* Berkeley: University of California Press, 1986.

Romanov, E. R. *Materialy po istoricheskoi topografii Vitebskoi gubernii, uezd Velizhskii.* Mogilev: [n. p.], 1898.

Roper, Lyndal. *Witch Craze: Terror and Fantasy in Baroque Germany.* New Haven: Yale University Press, 2004.

Rose, E. M. *The Murder of William of Norwich: The Origins of the Blood Libel in Medieval Europe.* New York: Oxford University Press, 2015.

Rosenwein, Barbara H. *Emotional Communities in the Early Middle Ages.* Ithaca: Cornell University Press, 2006.

Rosman, Moshe. *Founder of Hasidism: A Quest for the Historical Ba'al Shem Tov.* 2nd edition. Oxford: Littman Library of Jewish Civilization, 2013.

Roth, Cecil, ed. *The Ritual Murder Libel and the Jew: The Report by Cardinal Lorenzo Ganganelli (Pope Clement XIV).* London: Woburn, 1934.

Rowlands, Alison. "Witchcraft and Gender in Early Modern Europe." In *The Oxford Handbook of Witchcraft in Early Modern Europe and Colonial America.* Edited by Brian P. Levack, 449–467. Oxford: Oxford University Press, 2013.

Rubin, Miri. *Gentile Tales: The Narrative Assault on Late Medieval Jews.* Philadelphia: University of Pennsylvania Press, 2005.

———. "Making of a Martyr: William of Norwich and the Jews." *History Today* 60 (2010): 48–54.

Ryan, W. F. *The Bathhouse at Midnight: Magic in Russia.* University Park: Pennsylvania State University Press, 1999.

Ryvkin, M. D. *Iz istorii ritual'nykh del.* Smolensk: Tipografiia gazeta Smolenskii vestnik, 1914.

———. *Navet: Roman iz epokhi Aleksandra I–Nikolaia I.* St. Petersburg: Dvigatel', 1912.

———. "Velizhskoe delo v osveshchenii mestnykh predanii i pamiatnikov." *Perezhitoe* 3 (1911): 60–102.

Schainker, Ellie R. *Confessions of the Shtetl: Converts from Judaism in Imperial Russia, 1817–1906.* Stanford: Stanford University Press, 2016.

Schedrin, Vassili. *Jewish Souls, Bureaucratic Minds: Jewish Bureaucracy and Policymaking in Late Imperial Russia, 1850–1917.* Detroit: Wayne State University Press, 2016.

Schrader, Abby M. "Containing the Spectacle of Punishment: The Russian Autocracy and the Abolition of the Knout, 1817–1845." *Slavic Review* 56, no. 4 (1997): 613–644.

———. *Languages of the Lash: Corporal Punishment and Identity in Imperial Russia.* DeKalb: Northern Illinois University Press, 2002.

Schulz, William, ed. *The Phenomenon of Torture: Readings and Commentary.* Philadelphia: University of Pennsylvania Press, 2007.

Schybeka, Sachar. "Die Nordwestprovinzen im Russischen Reich (1795–1917)." In *Handbuch der Geschichte Weissrusslands.* Edited by Dietrich Beyrau and Rainer Lindau, 119–134. Göttingen: Vandenhoeck & Ruprecht, 2001.

Scribner, Robert W. "Elements of Popular Belief." In *Handbook of European History, 1400–1600: Late Middle Ages, Renaissance, and Reformation.* Volume 1. Edited by Thomas A. Brady Jr., Heiko A. Oberman, and James D. Tracy, 231–262. Grand Rapids, MI: William B. Eerdsmans, 1994.

Sementovskii, A. M., ed. *Pamiatnaia knizhka Vitebskoi gubernii na 1864 god.* St. Petersburg: Tipografiia K. Vul'fa, 1864.

Shatskikh, Aleksandra. *Vitebsk: The Life of Art.* Translated by Katherine Foshko. New Haven: Yale University Press, 2007.

Shkliazh, I. M. *Velizhskoe delo: Iz istorii antisemitizma v Rossii.* Odessa: [n.p.], 1998.

Šiaučiunaitė-Verbickienė, Jurgita. "Blood Libel in a Multi-Confessional Society: The Case of the Grand Duchy of Lithuania." *East European Jewish Affairs* 38, no. 2 (2008): 201–209.

Silverman, Lisa. *Tortured Subjects: Pain, Truth, and the Body in Early Modern France*. Chicago: University of Chicago Press, 2001.

Skinner, Barbara. *The Western Front of the Eastern Church: Uniate and Orthodox Conflict in 18th-Century Poland, Ukraine, Belarus, and Russia*. DeKalb: Northern Illinois University Press, 2009.

Smail, Daniel Lord. *The Consumption of Justice: Emotions, Publicity, and Legal Culture in Marseille, 1264–1423*. Ithaca: Cornell University Press, 2003.

Smith, Helmut Walser. *The Butcher's Tale: Murder and Anti-Semitism in a German Town*. New York: W. W. Norton, 2002.

Sokolova, Alla. "In Search of the Exotic: 'Jewish Houses' and Synagogues in Russian Travel Notes." In *Writing Jewish Culture: Paradoxes in Ethnography*. Edited by Andreas Kilchner and Gabriella Safran, 291–321. Bloomington: Indiana University Press, 2016.

Sorkina, Ina. *Miastechki Belarusi w kantsy XVIII-pershai palove XIX st.* Vilnius: Evropeiskii gumanitarnyi universitet, 2010.

Spector, Scott. *Violent Sensations: Sex, Crime, and Utopia in Vienna and Berlin, 1860–1914*. Chicago: University of Chicago Press, 2016.

Spravka k dokladu po evreiskomu voprosu. Part 5. St. Petersburg: Kantseliariia Soveta ob"edinennykh dvorianskikh obshchestv, 1912.

Staliunas, Darius. *Enemies for a Day: Antisemitism and Anti-Jewish Violence in Lithuania under the Tsars*. Budapest: Central European University Press, 2015.

Stampfer, Shaul. *Families, Rabbis, and Education: Traditional Jewish Society in Nineteenth-Century Eastern Europe*. Oxford: Littman Library of Jewish Civilization, 2010.

———. "Violence and the Migration of Ashkenazi Jews to Eastern Europe." In *Jews in the East European Borderlands: Essays in Honor of John D. Klier*. Edited by Eugene M. Avrutin and Harriet Murav, 127–146. Boston: Academic Studies Press, 2012.

Stanislawski, Michael. *Tsar Nicholas I and the Jews: The Transformation of Jewish Society in Russia, 1825–1855*. Philadelphia: Jewish Publication Society of America, 1983.

Stan'ko, A. I. *Russkie gazety pervoi poloviny XIX veka*. Rostov-on-Don: Izdatel'stvo Rostovskogo universiteta, 1969.

Strack, Hermann L. *The Jew and Human Sacrifice*. Translated by Henry Blanchamp. New York: Bloch, 1909.

Teller, Adam. "The Shtetl as an Arena for Polish-Jewish Integration in the Eighteenth Century." *Polin* 17 (2004): 25–40.

Teller, Adam, and Magda Teter. "Introduction: Borders and Boundaries in the Historiography of the Jews in the Polish-Lithuanian Commonwealth." *Polin* 22 (2010): 3–46.

Teter, Magda. *Jews and Heretics in Catholic Poland: A Beleaguered Church in the Post-Reformation Era.* Cambridge: Cambridge University Press, 2006.

———. *Sinners on Trial: Jews and Sacrilege after the Reformation.* Cambridge, MA: Harvard University Press, 2011.

Thomas, Keith. *Religion and the Decline of Magic.* London: Penguin, 1971.

Thomas of Monmouth. *The Life and Miracles of St. William of Norwich.* Translated and edited by Augustus Jessopp and Montague Rhodes James. Cambridge: Cambridge University Press, 1896.

Trachtenberg, Joshua. *The Devil and the Jews: The Medieval Conception of the Jew and Its Relation to Modern Anti-Semitism.* Philadelphia: Jewish Publication Society, 1983.

———. *Jewish Magic and Superstition: A Study in Folk Religion.* New York: Atheneum, 1970.

Trim, D. J. B. "'If a prince use tyrannie towards his people': Interventions in Early Modern Europe." In *Humanitarian Intervention: A History.* Edited by Brendan Simms and D. J. B. Trim, 29–66. Cambridge: Cambridge University Press, 2011.

Troinitskii, N. A., ed. *Pervaia vseobshchaia perepis' naseleniia Rossiiskoi imperii, 1897 g.* 120 volumes. St. Petersburg: Izdatel'stva Tsentral'nago statisticheskago komiteta Ministerstva vnutrennikh del, 1899–1905.

Tuna, Mustafa. *Imperial Russia's Muslims: Islam, Empire, and European Modernity, 1788–1914.* Cambridge: Cambridge University Press, 2015.

Velizhskoe delo: Dokumenty. Orange, CT: Antiquary, 1988.

Vengzhinek, Khanna. "Meditsinskie znaniia i istochniki 'krovavykh navetov' v staroi Pol'she." In *Narodnaia meditsina i magiia v slavianskoi i evreiskoi kul'turnoi traditsii.* Edited by O. V. Belova, 81–88. Moscow: Sefer, 2007.

Verhoeven, Claudia. *The Odd Man Karakozov: Imperial Russia, Modernity, and the Birth of Terrorism.* Ithaca: Cornell University Press, 2009.

Voenno-statisticheskoe obozrenie Rossiiskoi imperii: Vitebskaia guberniia. Volume 8. St. Petersburg: Tipografiia departmenta general'nago shtaba, 1852.

Vorodinov, Nikolai, ed. *Istoriia Ministerstva vnutrennikh del.* Part 8. St. Petersburg: Tipografiia vtorogo otdeleniia sobstvennoi E. I. V. kantseliarii, 1861.

Walsh, Robert. *Narrative of a Journey from Constantinople to England.* London: Frederick Westley and A. H. Davis, 1828.

Walter, Jakob. *The Diary of a Napoleonic Foot Soldier.* Edited by Marc Raeff. New York: Doubleday, 1991.

Weinberg, Robert. *Blood Libel in Late Imperial Russia: The Ritual Murder Trial of Mendel Beilis.* Bloomington: Indiana University Press, 2014.

Wengeroff, Pauline. *Memoirs of a Grandmother: Scenes from the Cultural History of the Jews of Russia in the Nineteenth Century.* Volume 1. Translated by Shulamit S. Magnus. Stanford: Stanford University Press, 2010.

Werth, Paul. *The Tsar's Foreign Faiths: Toleration and the Fate of Religious Freedom in Imperial Russia.* New York: Oxford University Press, 2014.

White, Luise. *Speaking with Vampires: Rumor and History in Colonial Africa*. Berkeley: University of California Press, 2000.

Williams, Gerhild Scholz. "Demonologies." In *The Oxford Handbook of Witchcraft in Early Modern Europe and Colonial America*, ed. Brian P. Levack, 69–83. Oxford: Oxford University Press, 2013.

Wiltenburg, Joy. *Crime and Culture in Early Modern Germany*. Charlottesville: University Press of Virginia, 2012.

Wodzinski, Marcin. "Blood and the Hasidim: On the History of Ritual Murder Accusations in Nineteenth-Century Poland." *Polin* 22 (2010): 273–290.

Worobec, Christine D. "Decriminalizing Witchcraft in Pre-Emancipation Russia." In *Späte Hexenprozesse: Der Umgang der Aufklärung mit dem Irrationalen*. Edited by Wolfgang Behringer, Sönke Lorenz, and Dieter R. Bauer, 281–307. Gütersloh: Verlag für Regionalgeschichte, 2016.

———. *Possessed: Women, Witches, and Demons in Imperial Russia*. DeKalb: Northern Illinois University Press, 2003.

Wortman, Richard S. *The Development of a Russian Legal Consciousness*. Chicago: University of Chicago Press, 1976.

———. *Scenarios of Power: Myth and Ceremony in Russian Monarchy*. Volume 1. Princeton: Princeton University Press, 1995.

Yaney, George L. *The Systematization of Russian Government: Social Evolution in the Domestic Administration of Imperial Russia, 1711–1905*. Urbana: University of Illinois Press, 1973.

Zarudnii, Sergii. *Bekkariia o prestupleniiakh i nakazaniiakh i russkoe zakonodatel'stvo*. St. Petersburg: Tipografiia E. I. V. Kantseliariia, 1879.

Zel'tser, Arkadii. *Evrei sovetskoi provintsii: Vitebsk i mestechki, 1917–1941*. Moscow: ROSSPEN, 2006.

Zhuk, Sergei I. *Russia's Lost Reformation: Peasants, Millennialism, and Radical Sects in Southern Russia and Ukraine, 1830–1917*. Baltimore: Johns Hopkins University Press, 2004.

Żyndul, Jolanta. *Kłamstwo krwi: Legenda mordu rytualnego na ziemiach polskich w XIX i XX wieku*. Warsaw: Wydawnictwo Cyklady, 2011.

INDEX

Note: Page numbers in *italics* refer to illustrations.

Kurin, Abram, 25
Kutaisi (Georgia), ritual murder trial
    in, 158–59

laws, on ritual murder accusations: in
    imperial Russia, 28, 29; in
    Western Europe, 4
legal system, of imperial Russia,
    112–13, 133–34
leg irons, use of: to extract
    confessions, 134; in Velizh ritual
    murder investigation, 113
Levin (Velizh doctor), 18, 104
literature: and Jewish political
    activities, 102; and ritual murder
    libel, 5–6, 137–42, 157–58,
    192nn25–26, 192n31; use in Velizh
    ritual murder investigation, 137–
    38, 141, 191n17
Liubavachi, branch of Judaism in, 46
Liutostanskii, Ippolit, 157–58, 192n26
Livenson, Rokhlia, 161
Lukashevich (Inspector), 18, 19, 25
Lutsk, ritual murder case in, 6

magic, belief in: gradual repudiation
    of, 4; persistence in Russia, 11; role
    in everyday life, 4, 11; and search
    for Fedor, 16–17; in small towns
    of western borderlands, 54–56;
    and treatment of diseases, 54–55
Maimonides, Moses, 139–41, 192n26
Maksimova, Avdot'ia: arrest of, 70; on
    church robbery, 129; confession
    of, 72, 105; confrontations
    with accused, 82, 86, 89, 126,
    128, 130; exile to Siberia, 152;
    forced conversion to Judaism,
    testimony regarding, 75–76, 85;
    on host desecration, 126, 127; as
    housekeeper in Tsetlin family,
    24, 67; initial testimony of, 24, 86;
    interrogation by Strakhov, 67–68;
    later testimonies of, 67–68, 69,

71, 72, 73; new revelations by,
    120, 125, 126, 127; questioning of
    testimonies of, 149–50; role in
    Velizh ritual murder, confession
    regarding, 72–74, 76, 77; and
    Terenteeva, 61, 64, 125, 127
material evidence: inquisitorial
    procedure and, 9; in Velizh ritual
    murder case, 69–70, 99, 185n71
medical services, in East European
    borderlands, 53
medical testimony: and decline in
    witchcraft prosecutions, 156; in
    Jewish ritual murder trials, 159; in
    Russian justice system, 149, 151
medical testimony, in Velizh ritual
    murder case, 18–19; questioning
    of, 104; Strakhov on, 105, 137; vs.
    witness testimonies, 150, 151
Mel'nikova, Risa, 162
Middle Ages, Jewish ritual murder
    libel in, 2–3
Mikhailovskii, K. G., 145
Military Statute of 1716 (Russia), 9
Ministry of Justice (Russia), on Velizh
    ritual murder case, 112, 113
Minsk, ritual murder cases in, 6
Mirlas, Iosel': arrest of, 161;
    interrogation of, 125–26;
    testimony against, 129
Modebadze, Sara Iosifova, 158
Mogilev: Jews in, 46; during
    Napoleon's invasion, 44; province
    of, origins of, 34; ritual murder
    cases in, 6, 8
Montefiore, Sir Moses, 111, 112
Mordvinov, Nicholai S., 147–52
Morton, Edward, 8–9, 33, 43
museum, in Velizh, 38, *39*

Nadezhdin, Nikolai, 157
Nafonova, Bliuma, 162
Nakhimovskii, Berka, petitions by,
    103–4, 113, 114